How Dell Does It

Steven Holzner

McGraw-Hill

New York Chicago San Francisco Lisbon
London Madrid Mexico City Milan New Delhi
San Juan Seoul Singapore Sydney Toronto

The McGraw·Hill Companies

Library of Congress Cataloging-in-Publication Data is on file.

1 2 3 4 5 6 7 8 9 0 FGR/FGR 0 1 9 8 7 6 5

ISBN 0-07-226254-0

Editorial and production services provided by TypeWriting, Acworth, GA.

This publication is designed to provide accurate and authoritative information in regard to the subject matter covered. It is sold with the understanding that neither the author nor the publisher is engaged in rendering legal, accounting, or other professional service. If legal advice or other expert assistance is required, the services of a competent professional person should be sought.
—From a Declaration of Principles jointly adopted by a Committee of the American Bar Association and a Committee of Publishers

McGraw-Hill books are available at special quantity discounts to use as premiums and sales promotions, or for use in corporate training programs. For more information, please write to the Director of Special Sales, McGraw-Hill, Two Penn Plaza, New York, NY 10121-2298. Or contact your local bookstore.

How Dell Does It is in no way authorized or endorsed by or affiliated with Dell Inc. or Michael Dell.

Contents

About the Author

Steven Holzner is the award-winning author of 95 books. He got his PhD from Cornell University, and he's been on the faculty of both Cornell and MIT. He's been an avid Dell-watcher for years, and runs his own consulting firm, teaching programming classes for Fortune 500 clients worldwide. You can find more about his teaching and consulting at www.onsiteglobal.com.

Introduction

Computer maker Dell is showing the world how to run a business in the Cyber Age.

—Business Week[1]

Welcome to the Dell story, the corporate success story that's been taking the tech world by storm for more than two decades. When Dell Computer Corporation was formed in 1984, by Michael Dell, it was nothing more than an upstart among dozens of upstarts. Even in the beginning of the 1990s, Dell was still 25th in the list of computer manufacturers.[2] The list included companies you probably can no longer remember, even if you had known their names, companies such as Mitac or Tandon.

In fact, nearly all the other 24 in that list of 25 are gone. But Dell has prospered. In 1992, *Fortune* magazine added Dell Computer Corporation to its list of the world's 500 largest companies.[3]

This is one driven organization. In 1999, Dell surpassed Compaq, acquiring the largest market share in the U.S. personal computer market. The market responded by consolidating in 2002—Hewlett-Packard bought Compaq and, by merging market share, the combined company regained the lead.

In 2003, Dell got the lead back.[4]

In 2001, Michael Dell was the 15th richest man in America, according to the Forbes 400 list.[5] In 2002, he was the 11th. In 2003, the 10th. And in 2004 (the most recent that figures are available), he was 9th.

It's All about Business

Dell is in the high-tech field, but this is primarily a business story. You don't steadily move past dozens of competitors over more than two decades without incredible business smarts. The personal computer field started as one with very high margins, because the pioneers in the market were able to set their prices. But, as the market matured, Dell found it could invade established markets by being true to its own business model. In other words, Dell has been teaching business to the high-tech boys for 21 years now.

This book is the story of that business model and how it works. It's an amazing story, but one that's not difficult to understand. In fact, many of Dell's competitors understand Dell's business model very well; they just can't execute it as well as Dell does. One of Dell's hallmarks is the ability to execute: the corporate will to *do*.

Nor is that business model tied to personal computers; lessons can be learned here for nearly every corporation in any business. Dell has long been expanding past personal computers and, in recognition of that, the stockholders of Dell Computer Corporation approved changing that name to Dell Inc. at the annual meeting in 2003.[6]

Dell Inc. is going to continue to grow by applying the business model you're going to read about in this book. The current target? $80 billion in sales by the end of 2009.[7] Will Dell make it? You should be surprised if it doesn't.

Chapter 1

Go Direct

The direct model has become the backbone of our company, and the greatest tool in its growth.

—Michael Dell[1]

The man you see in Figure 1.1 is Michael Dell, and the book you're reading is about the corporation he founded. From his very early days, Michael Dell enjoyed working with computers—he bugged his parents to buy him an Apple II, and when they did, he promptly infuriated them by taking it apart to see what made it tick. And, at the age of 19, he started customizing and selling computers from his University of Texas dorm room, also much to his parents' dismay, and to the detriment of his grades (he quit at the end of his freshman year).

It's pretty obvious that Michael Dell was a superb techie, and he knows his computers inside out. But this is not a techie story, and anyone reading this book to learn about the hottest new developments in the personal computer (PC) industry is going to be disappointed because this is a business story, and the man you see in Figure 1.1 is first and foremost a consummate businessman. You can see the Round Rock, Texas, headquarters of the company he founded in Figure 1.2.

This book is about the business methods of the man and his corporation. Many people started corporations during the early days of PCs (Dell was founded in 1984, just 3 years after the introduction of the IBM PC), with the same technological gifts and assets, but take a look at the field today: Dell Inc. is the undisputed leader in U.S. PC sales, with a 33.1 percent market share (the next is Hewlett-Packard at 19.5 percent).

Figure 1.1 Michael Dell.

Recently, Dell became number one in the world, with a 17.6 percent worldwide market share. Dell is also number 1 in Britain, Canada, and Ireland—all top-ten markets. Company revenue for the past year totaled $49 billion. The company has about 57,600 employees (or as Dell calls them, team members) around the world.

As the PC market has flattened, Dell also has moved into other arenas, like services, handhelds, printers, and liquid crystal display (LCD) TVs. Dell's 2005 annual report[2] is the very picture of success—look at these growth rates (dollar amounts in millions):

Fiscal Year Ended	Jan. 28, 2005	Jan. 30, 2004	Growth Rates
Net revenue	$49,205	$41,444	18.7 percent
Gross margin	$ 9,015	$ 7,552	19.4 percent
Operating income	$ 4,254	$ 3,544	20.0 percent
Total assets	$23,215	$19,311	20.2 percent

Figure 1.2 Welcome to Dell Inc.

All this from a corporation only 21 years old. Yes, the tech part was and is essential, but in essence, tech was simply the foundation. There's an amazing business story here, of finding niches like no other, of knowing how to grow, of limiting inventory liability, of lightning responses to opportunity, acrobatic escapes from mistakes, and, finally, teaching the tech world what business is all about.

In its March 7, 2005 issue, *Fortune* magazine named Dell Inc. the Most Admired company in the United States. And you don't get there unless you know what the heck you're doing.

So, what has Dell been doing? That's what you're going to find out in this book. In this case, it's richly rewarding to start at the beginning.

The Dell Story

Perhaps the best word to describe Michael Dell is *drive* (another, by his own admission, is *paranoia*[3]). Even *Fortune* magazine calls his smile that "I can eat nails" grin.[4] That drive was evident at an early age, when Dell went after the computer business in his typical, no-holds-barred way at the age of 19, selling customized PCs from his dorm room. So much for his studies.

His father said, "You've got to stop with this computer stuff and concentrate on school. Get your priorities straight. What do you want to do with your life?" Dell's answer was typical: "I want to compete with IBM!" Watch out, Big Blue.

The Dell legend has been embellished considerably over the years, even though it's substantial enough to stand on its own. For example, you'll often see company releases talking about how Dell started Dell Computer Corporation with only $1,000 in assets.

The fact is that, at that time (1984), Dell was already selling between $50,000 and $80,000 a month of customized PCs and upgrade kits to the people of Austin.[5] He had moved out of the dorm room to a condo with more room. That iconic $1,000 was actually the money required to capitalize a company in Texas at the time, and that's what he used to incorporate Dell Computer Corporation (dba PCs Unlimited).

Shortly after, the fledgling corporation moved to a 1,000-square-foot office in North Austin, with some people to take phone orders and three others sitting at 6-foot tables upgrading and customizing PCs. It was a good time to get into the market; not only were PCs being sold uncustomized at that time, but IBM couldn't cover the demand for its machines.

The demand was so great that dealers were routinely getting only 10 percent of their orders from IBM fulfilled, and everyone was screaming for more. So, dealers overordered and sometimes ended up, temporarily, with excess inventory. That inventory was sometimes sold at a discount on what was then called the "IBM gray market," and the new Dell Computer Corporation became one of the biggest customers in that market.

But Dell wasn't about to be satisfied with buying IBM PCs and customizing them. Michael Dell did his research and found an engineer, Jay Bell, who could build him a PC from scratch for $2,000. Dell gave him a week to do it, and at the end of that week, Michael Dell had his first pure-Dell PC.

Dell Computer Corporation was on its way. In fact, it stayed in the 1,000-square-foot facility only a single month, then moved into another office of about 2,350 square feet. Four or five months later, it was out of that and into a 7,200-square-foot facility. Six months later, it had to move again. Business was booming, and the demand for PCs was enormous; the next year, 1985, Dell Computer Corporation moved into a 30,000-square-foot location, which must have seemed limitless at the time. But in 1987, it had to move again.

Imagine how different this story would have been if IBM had been able to handle all the demand for PCs. The competing market that grew up around their ears, and in which Dell Computer was as yet a micro-scopic player, was loud, raucous, and disconcerting. IBM had always been a rather staid, monolithic corporation, and to have literally millions of techno-kids jumping in with screwdrivers and wire-wrap tools must have been unsettling.

One of the important drivers behind this tumultuous flood was the fact that IBM made its machine and its software open-source. Just about everything was published and copyable. The hardware could be taken apart and probed easily enough. As IBM saw its market share diminish, it came to regret that openness, and over and over sought to go propri-etary again. Its supreme effort in this field was the introduction years later (1987) of the PS/2 with its technically advanced (and unpublished) OS/2 operating system. The PS/2 was supposed to confer untold benefits on the user, but users weren't impressed. The market could no longer be captured; it belonged to young upstarts like Dell—particularly like Dell, who knew how to compete vigorously and how to grow intelligently, something Big Blue never managed in this arena, especially when it came to pricing. It has recently sold its PC business to Chinese manufacturer Lenovo.

The market was hot, but so was the competition. Dell was tiny, and it needed all the advantages it could get. Its solution was to go *direct*.

Going Direct

In those early days of the PC marketplace, PCs were still sold largely through retailers; in this case, specialty retailers like ComputerLand and others. Dell's major inspiration in those days was to go direct and elimi-nate the middle man.

Accordingly, Dell started taking phone orders, going direct to the cus-tomer. Michael Dell has said that Dell was the first PC manufacturer that went direct this way. Going direct has become the great hallmark of Dell Computer Corporation, now Dell Inc., and it has served it well.

It was an inspired move in the days of big-box computer stores, and it let Dell sell computers at lower cost; if it cost IBM or Compaq $500 to build and bring a computer to market, it only cost Dell $450.

This simple move changed everything in the years to come. That kind of $50 advantage proved ultimately decisive, because it was insurmount-able by Dell's competitors. If there's one thing Dell's been good at, it's keeping down costs: Dell's rock-bottom construction process was the same or even better, than its competitors and to get the PC to market, the competitors had to add an additional $50.

In fact, that $50 is on the low end—Michael Dell has estimated that going direct has saved his company 25 percent to 45 percent of mark-up on every machine. That's a heck of an advantage, and in the early PC market, it proved decisive.

Giving the Tech World the Business

This is a basic business practice—eliminating the middleman—but like so much else that Dell has done, he did it exceedingly well. As we're going to see over and over again in this book, the PC industry's reliance on fat profits proved to be the downfall of many of Dell's competitors.

Dell has specialized in finding areas in which major profits are going on, and then moving in, using simple business techniques like eliminating the middleman or waiting for component standardization (commoditization figures large in Dell's business practices and in the coming chapters) to puncture balloons and capture the market. These are relatively standard business practices being applied in markets unused to them.

Michael Dell himself highlights Dell's strategy to look for profit pockets and go after them. As he's said about Dell's move into the server field, "In the mid-1990s, it became clear to us that some of our competitors were earning more than half their profits in servers. Furthermore, their servers, while good products, were onerously and unjustifiably priced to subsidize other less profitable parts of their business. By pricing servers so astronomically high, they were practically exposing their vulnerability, while passing extra costs on to some of their best customers. What emerged was an incredible opportunity to disable our competitor's ability to gouge the market, while at the same time to grow our business in servers."[6]

This strategy was first evident when Dell took a look at all the PC retailers out there and decided to avoid them (possibly a result of them avoiding upstart Dell at that time). As far as most PC manufacturers were concerned, you couldn't keep PCs on the shelves then, and it must have seemed that there was a lot of wealth to go around. Adding retailers like ComputerLand—now no longer in much evidence—to the supply chain seemed no problem at all in this world of riches.

But the middleman always takes a cut, and in time, that cut was their downfall as tough competitors like Dell forced prices down. It was a major change in the PC industry, and Dell was squarely in the center of the movement. It used to be that if you wanted a PC, you went to a specialty PC retailer. Now, if you want a PC, you pick up a phone or get on the Internet. (As you're going to see in this book, Dell did try the retail route as an experiment—and it turned out just as bad as it thought it would.)

It also was true that, in those days, the bigger PC makers *couldn't* go direct, because they'd be undercutting the very retailers who carried their products, which violated the distribution channel contracts those PC makers had signed.

Dell was in a sweet spot. The computer industry had gotten fat and, in their riches, had become careless. Dell stepped in to take advantage, as it has so many times since then. In its younger days, going direct meant advertising and taking phone or even fax orders, but it's worth noting that, as much as possible, Dell turns to the Internet these days to go direct, as discussed in Chapter 7. Dell is one company for which the Internet has proven a real boon, and it's maximized its presence there. That's been a tricky thing for many corporations, especially PC manufacturers, who deal with customers who want to customize their machine, but Dell has done it.

As an interesting side note, the relentless emphasis on going direct to the customer using the Internet sometimes left Dell's sales staff feeling a little like threatened middlemen themselves. On the Internet, customers have access to the same information that sales staff do, and can purchase computers as easily. As Dell emphasizes the Internet more and more, sales staff wanted to know if they were being phased out. Dell headed this problem off by explaining to the sales staff that customers often customized their PCs online, but then usually call to actually order—in other words, the Internet was not a threat, but a source of highly qualified leads. (More on this in Chapter 3.)

The middleman allergy at Dell is deep. In the last few years, PC manufacturers have made a move to sell through established retailers like Best Buy and Wal-Mart. Dell even tried it, surprising those of us who watch Dell. In the mid-1990s, Dell started selling PCs through CompUSA (called Soft Warehouse at the time) and Circuit City, as well as at superstores like Price Club and Sam's Club.

But Dell wasn't in this party for long. After some years, it did some internal checking (today, no one keeps track of the internal metrics—data collection and comparison—like Dell, a topic discussed in detail in Chapter 7) and found that, although it was moving a lot of inventory, it wasn't making money. The gross was there, but not the profit.

Dell pulled out. It was the old middleman problem again, and presumably, burnt fingers were licked inside Dell; the commitment to going direct was redoubled. It's remarkable that it took Dell 4 years to realize that it wasn't actually making money in the retail channels—and that realization turned out to be one of the seminal events in Dell's history, prompting it to improve its internal data flow. It was embarrassing to it to discover that no profit came from a large part of its operation (or, for that matter, in the similar operations of its competitors).

At the time Dell pulled out, it was selling through five mass-market chains. Loathe to just pull out and cause hard feelings, it spent some time working on the product mix, seeing if it could find a profit core. Dell also worked on lowering costs for a while, but the profit just wasn't there. Minimal profits appeared, but not enough to justify doing anything but selling direct, following the route that Dell had already had so much success with.

Around 1994, the retail group at Dell was asked to justify itself, and that's become one of the defining characteristics of Dell—asking each group to justify itself. In this case, the retail group came up short, through no real fault of its own—the middleman was the real problem, as it had been in the past. The Dell retail group worked to expand to stores where it thought it could get better margins, including Wal-Mart and Best Buy. But, in the end, not even that helped.

Dell learned five things from this debacle: go direct, go direct, go direct, go direct, and increase the use of metrics. There are few companies in which information flow is as important and as central to business practices as Dell. Management watches every unit within Dell using a set of instantaneously updated metrics, so that performance is tracked practically in real time. Each unit's return on investment capital (ROIC) is narrowly watched at all times, and there's relatively little room for anything but lean operation.

Workers on the assembly floor can see instantly how they're doing by watching televised scorecards on monitors that tell them how well their unit is doing, and how well they should be doing. It makes for more efficient operation, but also, of course, for more pressure.

Going direct relies on data flow, and there's an obsession with data flow in Dell. Despite Dell's size, this is one nimble company, and the data flow—largely on the Internet and Dell's own internal intranet—is an absolutely central part of that. It's no mean trick to make a corporation of 57,600 employees turn on a dime, but that's the kind of thing that Dell excels in. As Dell was growing up, the established companies in the PC world, like IBM (admittedly much larger—today, IBM has 329,000 employees), were not set up with anything remotely like the internal data flow that Dell developed. More on this is coming up in Chapter 7.

It's hard to overestimate the importance of going direct for the Dell business model. In established industries in which the only option is to go direct, this is less of a factor, but in the early days of PCs, this was a revolution. And "Dell Direct" has become a pervading philosophy at Dell. Anyone making a study of Dell comes across this philosophy over and over.

For example, from Dell's web site[7]: "Dell's climb to market leadership is the result of a persistent focus on delivering the best possible customer experience by directly selling standards-based computing products and services." For the careful reader, three clues to Dell's business model are included in this quotation and all are discussed in this book—the direct model, as discussed in this chapter; the emphasis on "the best possible customer experience" (see Chapter 3); and the all-important mention of "standards-based" computing products: that is, Dell's ability to jump into a market when that market reaches standardization and components are available off-the-shelf (see Chapter 4).

Dell has a creed called the "Soul of Dell" on its web site; the direct model holds prominence there as well:

- **Customers:** We believe in creating loyal customers by providing a superior experience at a great value. We are committed to direct relationships, providing the best products and services based on standards-based technology, and outperforming the competition with value and a superior customer experience.
- **The Dell Team:** We believe our continued success lies in teamwork and the opportunity each team member has to learn, develop, and grow. We are committed to being a meritocracy, and to developing, retaining, and attracting the best people, reflective of our worldwide marketplace.
- **Direct Relationships:** We believe in being direct in all we do. We are committed to behaving ethically; responding to customer needs in a timely and reasonable manner; fostering open communications and building effective relationships with customers, partners, suppliers, and each other; and operating without inefficient hierarchy and bureaucracy.
- **Global Citizenship:** We believe in participating responsibly in the global marketplace. We are committed to understanding and respecting the laws, values, and cultures wherever we do business; profitably growing in all markets; promoting a healthy business climate globally; and contributing positively in every community we call home, both personally and organizationally.
- **Winning:** We have a passion for winning in everything we do. We are committed to operational excellence, superior customer expe-

rience, leading in the global markets we serve, being known as a great company and great place to work, and providing superior shareholder value over time.

"Dell Direct" was all-important to the young company, giving it a cost-cutting edge. And that's one of the two ways in which Dell competed with IBM in the early days: in cost and in computing power (which we discuss later).

But there was more to the story.

Staying in Touch with Customers

The direct relationship was important to Dell for cost savings, but it ultimately became as important in another area as well—staying in touch with customers (discussed in depth in Chapter 3). Its direct relationship with customers ultimately led to its industry-beating ability to keep on-hand inventory nearly nonexistent (discussed in depth in Chapter 5) because it allowed Dell to track what customers were ordering in ways that no one else could match.

From Dell's web site[8]: "Dell was founded in 1984 by Michael Dell, the computer industry's longest-tenured chief executive officer, on a simple concept: that by selling computer systems directly to customers, Dell could best understand their needs and efficiently provide the most effective computing solutions to meet those needs. This direct business model eliminates retailers that add unnecessary time and cost, or can diminish Dell's understanding of customer expectations. The direct model allows the company to build every system to order and offer customers powerful, richly configured systems at competitive prices."

Michael Dell himself says,[9] "Our company was founded on the simple premise that by selling personal computer systems directly to customers, Dell could quickly understand their needs and provide the most effective computing solutions to meet those needs."

In other words, going direct to customers keeps you in touch with what customers want. The big PC manufacturers were selling to sales forecasts; Dell was selling to what customers were actually ordering. That knowledge has become crucial in Dell's never-ending quest to lower inventory, something that has saved it untold billions, because less and less money is tied up with that inventory.

"Going direct" is also applied to other areas, such as staying in touch with suppliers, as discussed in Chapter 8. Dell's suppliers are continually given information over the Internet on what Dell's customers are doing—

and on what Dell needs. Dell also provides instantaneous report cards to all its suppliers that tell the suppliers how well they're doing. (One can only imagine how well these suppliers look forward to getting their daily report card from an aggressive and brash young company.)

In Dell, this kind of direct model of contact has culminated in a philosophy of "virtual integration," in which the customer and supplier become, to some degree, part of the company. More on that in Chapter 8 as well.

Get the Word Out

Simply "going direct" didn't win Dell a lot of customers. Even if it was the first to go direct, as Michael Dell says, it still had to get the word out. And that meant advertising. Dell has always been a big one for advertising ("Dude, you're getting a Dell!"); business methods alone won't get you far unless people know about you.

The early PC days were a heady time, and plenty of young corporations were screaming for presence. Magazines like *Byte*, *PC Magazine*, *PC Week*, and *PC World*, among others, were crammed with double-page four-color ads.

The industry was overflowing with money in those days; I was a graduate student working on my Ph.D., and a contributing editor for *PC Magazine*. It was the perfect vantage point from which to watch the industry develop.

PC Magazine was filled with energy and excitement in those days, as was the entire PC industry. The magazine's offices were packed with the latest and greatest machines and peripherals. Someone was always grabbing you and saying, "You gotta see this!" as they pulled you off to witness the newest miracle in some room where it was hard to talk over the whirring of dozens of cooling fans.

The energy and hype of those days was reflected in the magazine's ads. Any subtle advantage over competitors was blasted out in 120-point type. Claims and counterclaims ran at hurricane speeds. Every slight increase in CPU speed, every slight reduction in memory access time, every new monitor was big news. A new CPU chip, like the 386 or 486, threw everyone into paroxysms for weeks at a time.

Figuring large in the pages were the Dell ads. Dell was as vigorous as anyone in getting the word out, because it knew that half of going direct is having an audience to go direct to. The environment was supercompetitive from the first, as it is now, and Dell's ads were as big as it could make them.

In those days, what counted was the tech aspect first; that's what you pumped in your ads to make yourself known. You had put your machines first—speed was the most important. Next was price. Dell was no exception.

Becoming a National Presence

Like other PC manufacturers during the early days, to become known, Dell focused a great deal on the tech aspect, because that's how you did it. The second consideration was price, and Dell, with its direct model firmly in place, already had a leg up on the big boys there.

Because Dell was designing and building its own machines, it could compete in the area of computing speed. Many other companies were practically resellers and couldn't. And some large corporations, such as IBM, were still living in a different market where hypercompetition had no part, which meant that they didn't feel the need for PC speed as much as the upstarts did. IBM liked to sail serenely along on the strength of its name, as it did in other markets; don't forget that, in those days, it was the "IBM PC," after all. You either bought an IBM PC or a "compatible." And IBM had 70 percent of the market then. But that kind of complacency and the resulting loss of trajectory proved fatal.

Michael Dell[10] says of this period, "At the time, performance was the name of the game, and if you could make an IBM-compatible PC that was faster than the IBM PC, it would obviously give you a distinct edge over the competition." That's what Dell worked on doing.

Dell decided to make its move when the premiere machine was an IBM computer based on an 80286 CPU having a speed of 6 megahertz (seems kind of pokey now that everyone's up in the gigahertz range, but that was the big machine then).

To make a splash, Dell decided to come out with an 8-megahertz PC based on the 286. But then, being the hypercompetitor it was, it realized that others would be trying the same thing, so it tried for a 12-megahertz CPU speed instead. (In fact, it got up a 286 up to no less than 16 megahertz in the lab, but there were issues. Dell decided to stick with 12 megahertz, because it was something it could come out with reliably and in volume.)

So there they were, the whiz kids out of Texas, suddenly running double-page ads in *PC Magazine* and others, talking about their 12-megahertz machine and comparing it to what IBM had to offer. Twelve megahertz, it will be noted, is twice as fast as 6 megahertz.

And, in typical Dell fashion, more followed. Dell sold its 12-megahertz machine—the fastest in the industry—at $1,995. That might seem like a high price for a PC during these days of large volume and small margins, but PCs used to be priced much higher than they are today. This price was sensational because the IBM PC it was competing against, the early 6-megahertz 286, was priced at $3,995.

So here was Dell, selling a machine twice as fast for half the price in double-page four-color ads.

That was a breakthrough moment for Dell, because it brought it to people's attention. Even in the days when everyone was trying to compete on CPU speed and price, a full factor of two in both directions was very far from normal. The price brought the new machine in line with a typical compatible 8086-based PC (a predecessor to the 286). But it was the speed that got everyone, because it set a new high-water mark. Some industry watchers even wondered publically why anyone would need such a fast machine (12 megahertz? What would you *need* all that speed for?).

But people loved it. Not the majority of the PC-buying public yet, because Dell was such an upstart and had yet to gain trust (most people were sticking with IBM PCs), but the bleeding-edge guys who would buy any screamer, as fast PCs were called then. And there's always a trickle-down effect from the advance buyers to the middle-of-the-road customer as the envy effect sets in.

The big industry show then was Comdex, and the November 1986 Comdex was coming up in Las Vegas. Dell put together a wall of Styrofoam bricks showing its 12-megahertz 286 machine breaking through it. The display looked amateurish compared to the slick IBM and Compaq booths, but the 12-megahertz barrier had been breached. By Dell.

Speed sold in those days and, at Comdex, the space in front of the Dell booth was packed. The number of orders Dell got taught them another lesson—not only was CPU speed important, but also speed to market. It had to get those machines out there to fill the orders.

To many people, this play made Dell's name. Dell was a good competitor, but there were hundreds of good competitors around. This brought it to people's attention. Dell's previous mention in *PC Week* had been on page 87. Now it was on the cover for all to see.

The tech media, like *PC Magazine*, also started seeing it on the radar, and Dell became one of the six or so brands, such as IBM, routinely reviewed and compared to each other.

It was hard to break into that ring of six, but Dell had done it, largely on the strength of what counted then—CPU speed. Dell has always been committed to high quality and, to the surprise of many, once it was in the top ring and given a chance, it started winning performance awards, not just for speed, but also for support and service. And support and service were just as important to people as those 12 megahertz.

Gaining Trust

With the field full of dozens of upstarts, trust was the big issue in the mid-1980s. The PC market was only a few years old, and all kinds of hotshots were out there. So, were you going to plunk down $3,000 on an unknown brand PC that was going to have issues right out of the box? How could you tell which of these upstarts could be trusted?

The reviews in *PC Magazine* often talked about overheating, for example; it was a routine problem then, and everyone expected it to happen in the hotshot machines. People even bought PCs with mild overheating problems and worked around it. The problem was rife because so many manufacturers wanted to hype speed so badly that they drove their machines at speeds beyond capacity. When a CPU overheated, the machine either just halted or gave erroneous results.

Other problems included screens blacked out, math coprocessors that gave faulty results when certain instructions were executed, and PCs that were simply DOA out of the box.

Software issues were just as big a problem as hardware issues were, which is why the IBM-compatible label was so important. But compatibility came on many different levels, and you never really knew if your expensive word-processing or spreadsheet program was going to run on one of the wildcat machines. I even remember manufacturers that listed their machines as "99 percent compatible" (would you buy that machine?). Some machines, ostensibly PC-like, even from major manufacturers, made no real attempt at compatibility. Others were mostly compatible, but not fully; for example, the Radio Shack–based Tandy 1000, was described by the online encyclopedia *Wikipedia* as "more or less IBM PC compatible." Who could you trust? Were you going to buy software that might not run?

That's one of the reasons why IBM was able to hang on as long as it did. No one was more IBM-compatible than IBM. It had *invented* the PC, for Pete's sake. As far as business customers went, no one was more business-like than IBM. Business customers would still willingly pay $2,000 more for a machine half as fast just to avoid compatibility problems.

Dell, as an upstart apparently going for speed, was definitely in the hotshot category for many customers, and it had a long way to go to gain customers' trust.

Dell recognized this issue. At a time when you're only one among many, one of the best ways to stand out is to come across as safe. And that's what Dell's been working on for years in three areas: quality, service, and support. These topics are discussed in the next chapter, but they also bear looking at here, as part of Dell's growth story.

In fact, by 1986, Dell already had been establishing a name for itself in terms of quality, service, and support. Dell has always worked hard on quality, because it knows that design mistakes stay with you a long time in this game. Dell had been one of the first PC manufacturers to offer a full guarantee, which went a long way toward allaying fears.

In Dell's early days, that guarantee was only a 30-day money-back guarantee, but it reassured many customers (today Dell's standard guarantee is 90 days for desktops, and you can buy 1-, 2-, 3-, and 4-year guarantees). I remember hearing around that time that 10 percent of PCs weren't working or had serious issues out of the box.

In addition to an emphasis on quality and its guarantee, Dell also came up with an innovation of the kind that's gotten the company where it is today. Going direct is great for selling computers but, as you can imagine, customers might have some qualms about servicing those computers. After all, in the mid-1980s, you usually bought computers from a retailer with a built-in service department. If your PC had problems, you took it back to ComputerLand or wherever and turned it over to a greasy-looking crew in the back room. It might take days or weeks, but you knew your PC would get some attention.

But what about ordering a PC over the phone? Were you going to have to package up your PC and send it off to some anonymous plant somewhere? Would you ever get it back? Who would pay if it was destroyed in the mail?

These and similar questions made Dell's competitors sure that the direct model wasn't a winner. After all, what were you going to do, fax your computer back to Dell if it needed service?

But, in that watershed year of 1986, Dell surprised everyone by offering *on-site* servicing. You could talk to a technician on the phone and, if that didn't solve your problem, you'd get some on-site help. Dell would either overnight you a part if it was easy enough to install, or actually send you a third-party technician. The full story is coming up in the next chapter.

As you can imagine, this blew people away. On-site servicing? That was better than anything Dell's competitors had to offer. And it was a smart move: The great majority of problems were handled on the phone or by overnighting parts, but you really could get a technician on-site if the problem was bad enough, and that gained a lot of trust among customers. And because trust had given IBM its edge, it helped Dell chip into its territory all the more.

Go Direct to Business Too: B2B

Another early aspect of Dell's direct campaign was to focus on selling direct to business customers and to treat them in a serious way. It was important that Dell do so, because business purchases of PCs made up a huge slice of the market.

Many business contracts went to IBM because, obviously, it was a very solid business providing those computers that were coming to be more and more essential. Businesses felt comfortable buying from IBM.

Dell had to overcome the impression it gave as an upstart, and it was one of the early compatible manufacturers to do so. It started treating business customers differently, started segmenting its call center and adding specialists to handle business customers.

From its relatively early days, Dell has been very sensitive to the needs of business customers. It found that, by dividing its sales force into business and home sections, it could provide well-trained specialists who could handle the needs of business customers. Knowing your customer base is a Dell speciality and part of its direct philosophy. It has served Dell well in the B2B arena.

Today, Dell offers a totally different line of computers for corporate and institutional customers—the OptiPlex line (corporations often prefer machines easily maintained over networks, something that's not so important for home use). The following is from Dell's web site—note the emphasis on business customers:

> *"Desktop Computers: Dell customers can select from two lines of desktop computer systems. The OptiPlex line is designed for corporate, institutional, and small-business customers who demand highly reliable, stable, manageable, and easily serviced systems within networked environments. The Dimension line is designed for small businesses and home users requiring fast technology turns and high-performance computing."*

Despite the long way it had to go to build its image, Dell has become the favorite among business and institutional customer market segments. That was a particularly crucial move, because those segments are massive.

Another manufacturer I've watched over the years is Gateway and, at one point, it was my favorite. But in my opinion, it never came anywhere close to mastering the crucial business sector as Dell has, especially with its focus on goofy cow-centered ads and boxes with cowhide spots all over them. These ads were playful, but not about to gain Gateway many business customers.

Gateway made another misstep by introducing and investing heavily in its retail stores. In many cities, they introduced Gateway stores—even after the death of so many computer retailers—where you could walk in and buy Gateway products directly. This reintroduction of the middleman, at a time when most manufacturers were hastily phasing out anything like it, made little sense. The Gateway stores became a heavy drag on Gateway's business. If the motto had been "Gateway Direct" instead, you might be seeing a different story today, at least in terms of market share.

Dell's focus on professionalism and service won business customers, and the direct B2B way of life can yield many rich rewards. A single contract could be worth millions of dollars. Dell has worked hard to keep those business customers: At Boeing these days, for example, Dell maintains a staff of 30 or so, just to make sure things keep running.

Dell is persistently on the lookout for new markets, and it responds as agilely as possible. In this case, its early move to provide support for the lucrative business market was an important one.

Execution Is Vital

The direct model was the original Dell keystone. Selling direct to customers is a relatively simple idea, like many of Dell business model keystones, but it permeates all that Dell does. Another point is also worth making, and it's one that's often omitted in discussions on Dell: Dell emphasizes execution.

Plenty of companies jumped on the direct bandwagon, and many companies mimic what Dell does to some extent. What separates them from Dell? Primarily execution—putting your ideas into practice from top to bottom. That's a central point, and one that even many experienced Dell watchers miss.

You don't just need a good idea, you need to do it, and do it, and do it, from the top to the bottom of your organization. As Michael Dell said,[11] "The key is not so much one great idea or patent as it is the execution and implementation of a great strategy."

USA Today[12] says, "Dell's power can be missed because what it does—superefficient manufacturing and direct sales that bypass retailers—seems so simple. Yet McDonald's took a simple concept and built an institution on repeating it."

Many of Dells' competitors have tried to copy Dell's ideas and some aspects of its business model, but they've fallen by the wayside. In many ways, understanding Dell's strategy isn't all that difficult. What divides the quick from the dead here is execution—the ability to put strategies, like going direct, into practice.

From a CNET News.com article entitled "New Reality Forcing Direct Pressure"[13]: "Selling over the Internet directly to customers is appealing to PC makers looking to cut costs and boost profit margins. Just look at Dell's phenomenal success, they'll tell you. But there's a lot more to online sales than simply putting up a web site, PC makers are learning. Companies have to change their manufacturing lines, and not alienate their current dealer base. NEC, in fact, retreated from its direct plunge after sales dropped."

The article ends with an NEC spokesperson saying: "The 'be like Dell' model is not working for us. It did not do as well as we expected."

From a *USA Today* article[14]: 'People have tried to duplicate what Dell does, and they can't,' says Dell board member Alex Mandl, CEO of Gemplus. 'It sounds like a simple model, but getting all this going and perfectly executing it is difficult, if not impossible. Many have tried, all have failed.'"

Too often, entrenched corporate structure is the biggest enemy of business strategy. A business strategy is introduced at top levels, and it filters down only dimly to the strata below. Little, if any, real execution, follows. Mid-level managers note the distant thunder and lightning display above and wait until it's over, knowing that, as always, this too shall pass.

Dell, having grown up as the biggest small corporation around, is different, and its ability to really execute is the single most important meta-lesson about the way it does business. You can learn all the words and ideas about what it does, but it still won't matter unless you can infuse those ideas into your organization with the same kind of penetration that Dell can.

From the same CNET News.com article[13]: "Companies have to change their manufacturing lines, and not alienate their current dealer base. NEC, in fact, retreated from its direct plunge after sales dropped.... 'Unit growth as a priority forces vendors to be more efficient,' said Bruce Stephen, another IDC analyst. But unlike traditional PC makers, Dell was built for direct sales from the bottom up, he said. It is much more difficult for established companies like Compaq Computer, Hewlett-Packard, and IBM to shift strategies mid-game."

The meta-lesson here is not about business strategy, but how Dell itself works in a way that is so different from other corporations. Briefly put, Dell is a tight ship. It's agile and well-controlled and, when the top wants to flex an arm of the corporate body, that arm flexes. It's a well-toned body, fed by fluent information flow and segmented carefully to tune the balance between centralization and decentralization. More on this topic in Chapter 6.

By comparison, so many corporate bodies have nothing like the tone and cohesion that Dell has. The head is only distantly connected, through many fiefdoms and bulwarks, to the arms and legs. The head strains, but the arms don't move.

If you want to know how Dell does what it does, understanding this point is central. You can learn all the words by heart, but you also have to appreciate that the corporate structure at Dell is supple and responsive, not ossified and obstructed. And that's the key, that's the reason that so many competitors haven't been able to do what Dell does. They know the notes, they just can't play the tune—see Chapter 6 for the details.

In large measure, Dell Inc. is the product of one man's vision and, as his corporation grew, Michael Dell molded it. The same can't be said about huge multigenerational corporations like IBM, which are filled with their own internecine battles and fiefdoms.

Having a clear picture of what's going on in all parts of the company—and just as importantly, being able to do something about issues as they arise—has been invaluable to Dell. As a result, a *control* and *cohesion* exist in Dell that you virtually never see in corporations this size. Those two topics—control and cohesion—are important to understand if you want to know what sets Dell apart. You'll see more on them in the chapters to come.

As the entrepreneur, Michael Dell knew what made his company work and what made it agile. He had no formal business training and only limited informal business education in the academic sense—but he had an almost genetic predisposition to sales. So, he fell back on what he knew best—making a big corporation work like the small one he knew so well. (That's not something that someone who inherits a big corporation can do so easily, because the power structures are already in place.) Seeing how Michael Dell did this—how he created a giant company with the agility of a small one—is the topic of Chapter 9.

In corporate terms, Dell is an athlete. Too many corporations have lost the ability to tone themselves in the same way, and one of the points I'll be stressing throughout the book is what Dell does to keep itself in athletic trim. Many corporations—especially high-tech corporations used to large profits and easy days—don't even look at themselves in the mirror at all, let alone trim the fat where it should be trimmed. Dell has excelled in finding that corporate fat and taking advantage of it by undercutting and outperforming the competition.

As you read this book, bear in mind that reading the musical score of Dell's business strategy is not enough. It's not a kind of magical incantation simply to be repeated aloud. What's just as important, and what few Dell watchers understand, is execution, and having a corporate body capable of execution. Dell's business strategy, such as going direct, infuses the company at all levels; it's not just distant lightning.

Here's a quote from Summit Strategies' Dynamic Computing Industry Report Card, March 2005[15]: "Dell has established itself as a veritable execution machine, and IBM seems to be doing better and better in aligning its entire organization around on-demand. While Sun can generally execute, it faces big challenges during the current period of market skepticism, big product transitions, and shifting business models. Although HP's execution is very mixed, we believe it needs a much clearer, better communicated strategy on which to execute."

For example, one of the corporations Michael Dell admires is FedEx, which excels in execution. (If FedEx just delivered 99 percent of its packages on time each day, how long would it be in business?) And, like FedEx, Dell Inc. has a sense of itself as a winner, as a chosen one, and that attitude helps tone the corporate body. Dell has been successful in infusing its business strategies throughout the corporation with this sense of being, collectively, a winner. Everyone wants to be part of a winning team, but it takes more than slogans and the propaganda posters you find on the walls of all major corporations to achieve it (that's not to say that Dell doesn't have its share of goofy propaganda, by the way—Michael Dell running into a rented stadium filled with Dell employees carrying an olympic torch; Michael Dell dressed up as Uncle Sam in posters on the walls, and so on; but that's not what drives the point home).

If you talk to Dell employees, more often than not, you'll find an undercurrent of Dell chauvinism, even if it's not conscious. Not on top, maybe, but it's there. "We're Dell," it says. "We're the winning team." As the "Soul of Dell" says, "We have a passion for winning in everything we do." Even when it's not overt, there's still a feeling of unstoppability, of drive, in the background.

Part of that, inarguably, is the fact that Dell is number one by many measures, both nationally and internationally. There's no arguing with success. But there's also a feeling of toughness, of competitiveness. Dell *knows* it can go into a new market sector and unseat the current champ—see Chapter 6 for examples.

So, this winning culture is not just about being number one—plenty of areas exist where Dell isn't number one—it's the feeling of being on the team that's going to win. In fact, Dell almost seems to revel in being the underdog, which can be a very energizing role. *Fortune* magazine, discussing how Dell Inc. had been chosen as their most admired corporation (*Fortune* March 7, 2005), was talking to Kevin Rollins, Dell's CEO and president (Michael Dell is currently chairman) and said, "You're not an underdog anymore."

Rollins, whose photo appears in Figure 1.3, answered, "Well, we think we are." He went on to list the areas in which Dell is relatively new, such as services and printers, and Dell's plans to migrate from being a PC company to a diversified IT company (see Chapter 10). The *Fortune* interviewer noted that Rollins was going out of his way to make Dell the underdog and remarked on Dell's "chip-on-the-shoulder" mentality.

Rollins has said as much in other interviews.[16] "People delight in saying what they believe are disparaging things about us. That's great,

Figure 1.3 Kevin Rollins.

because it gives us something to prove. We want to be the underdog. We constantly want to be chasing. We never want to lose our edge."

There's a competitiveness here. Not just being number one, but having the will to win. Having that scrappiness. According to *Fortune* magazine, "HP's purchase of Compaq gave Dell, as one wag said, 'a bigger butt to kick.'"

Going Direct in All Ways

It's fair to say that Dell's original inspiration, as far as its business strategy went, was to go direct with the best value it could offer. Getting rid of the middleman and keeping in close touch with customers spurred its original growth.

But Dell has come far from those days—8 years after Dell was founded, it entered the Fortune 500 and, at 27, Michael Dell became the youngest Fortune 500 CEO ever—again, making it hard to preserve that old underdog feeling (today, he owns about 9.6 percent of the company, making him one of the world's richest men, with a worth of $10 billion, give or take).

Dells' success has left many competitors behind; IBM is out of the PC business. Gateway has seen its stock nearly crash. Compaq sold itself to HP—all while Dell has grown its revenues from $25.2 billion in fiscal 2000 to $41.4 billion in fiscal 2004.

Where is that go-direct feeling today? Despite all that massive growth, Dell stays true to the Dell Direct mantra at all levels. If data needs to reach a supplier, you send it direct. If customers are concerned about the packaging, and complaints come back about that, then you tell the packaging people direct. If you can reach more customers by making changes to your web site, you work on reaching them direct. Extra levels are always being cut out; it's part of keeping the corporate body lean and muscular.

Chapter 2

Provide the Best Value

You have to just say [Michael Dell] has done a hell of a job. No one has pulled the levers of cost, quality, and service better than Dell.
— Jack Welch, former GE CEO[1]

This chapter zeroes in on Dell's products and its support for those products. These products are the focus of what we're going to talk about—this is where Dell builds its reputation.

As hackneyed as it sounds as a business strategy, providing the best value is vital. It's been vital to Dell, and Dell puts an enormous emphasis on doing so—so much so that it deserves to be the second chapter in this book.

Many corporations lose sight of providing the best value. The focus drifts to market penetration, blocking competitors, and other issues at the expense of providing the best value. But, in an open and freewheeling market that is heavily reviewed by the media, like the market Dell Inc. was born into, providing the best value is essential. When Dell was just an upstart among so many others, it focused on value to differentiate itself. The strategy succeeded.

In June 2004, Technology Business Research, Inc. (TBR, www.tbri.com) released a report entitled Setting the Standard for Customer Satisfaction: An Analysis of Dell Customer Satisfaction Track Record and Approach.[2] The results, which will be discussed in more depth in Chapter 3, gave Dell an outstanding evaluation in terms of delivering value: "In addition to the fact that Dell remains the value leader, TBR notes that additional factors influence the customer decision to work with Dell. The perception of value permeates throughout a customer's perception of the company overall. Value is the glue that binds, integrating the customer's experience with Dell products and services." Dell's always emphasized giving the best value (although customer satisfaction is slipping these days).

"Value" doesn't just mean cost, either. Michael Dell,[3] for example, says, "We've found that pricing is only one-third of our customer's decision-making process. The other two-thirds represent service and support."

That's an interesting thing to say for the head of what's still largely a low-cost supplier to say—pricing is only one-third of the customer's decision to buy? People often assume that Dell is only interested in keeping cost low, but it's clear that it looks to building customer trust as well.

In Dell Inc.'s early life, IBM dominated the market because people trusted IBM. With dozens of PC manufacturers clamoring for customers' attention, Dell knew that trust was a major issue.

So, service and support, as well as cost, is a big part of providing the best value for Dell. What else? As Jack Welch said in the quote at the beginning of the chapter, "No one has pulled the levers of cost, quality, and service better than Dell." These are the three primary components I'll look at in this chapter—cost, quality, and service.

Cost

Cost is one of the primary components of the Dell mix, and it's built its reputation on providing high-quality, low-cost machines. There's little question that the foundation of Dell's ability to undercut competitors was the direct-selling model that eliminated the middleman.

Dell is known for low cost throughout the industry. Dell products win many awards, and when they do, you'll often see an accompanying commentary on price. For example, in *PC World*'s "Best of 2004," the Dell Dimension 4600 was the best "General-Purpose PC." From the article[4]: "The 4600 line continues Dell's tradition of building strong-performing systems that can be configured to your liking. Dell's range of processors, optical drives, sound systems, and other components let you get a basic or decked-out PC for a reasonable price: $749 to $1500."

Or this, from an Editor's Choice *PC Magazine* award[5]: "Dell rebuilt its Latitude corporate line from the ground up when moving to the Pentium M. The resulting Dell Latitude D600 merits Editors' Choice in the roundup, thanks to its outstanding value-for-the-dollar proposition."

Selling good products at low costs wins you many friends. Dell has always stressed low-cost offerings and vigorously pursued keeping those costs low (although not at the expense of profits—if the sales prices in any sector are so low that profits are in peril, Dell ultimately considers getting out of that sector).

Fortune magazine[6] (June 6, 2005) says, "In the computer business, it's known as the Dell Effect. The Round Rock, Texas, computer maker spots a market where others are making fat profits, figures out how to deliver the same stuff for less, and then drains the profits right out of the pool."

Dell is a supercompetitor on price, and whether you agree with its aggressiveness or not, it makes competitors shake in their boots. Jim Schneider, Dell's chief financial officer, said in an April 08, 2005 *InfoWorld* article[7]: "I can't believe there's another company that makes a dime selling a desktop PC. We are better positioned financially now than at any other point in the company's life." A dime is a pretty thin margin.

Dell specializes in cutting costs everywhere it can, and that'll be a continuing theme in this book. Because its elimination of the middleman (Chapter 1) has become a common strategy, it's less of an edge than it used to be. Dell also cuts its inventory radically (Chapter 5), works with standard components (Chapter 4), is perpetually streamlining (Chapter 6), and puts enormous pressure on suppliers (Chapter 8). Cutting costs at Dell is an obsession, and the customer, for the most part, is the winner.

All this invites comparisons with another major cost-cutting company, Wal-Mart. Many similarities exist, particularly in cost-cutting, supply-chain strategy, and market opportunism.

Is Dell the High-Tech Wal-Mart?

USA Today[8] says, "For inspiration, Michael Dell often looks to Wal-Mart founder Sam Walton. If Dell stays on that path, the implications are profound. Southwest and Wal-Mart reordered their industries, devastating some competitors and forcing others to do business a new way. For tech buyers, a Dell reign would mean lower prices on a broadening array of products, much as Southwest has deflated prices in markets it serves."

Fortune magazine (March 7, 2005) says, "Any cost that can be 'shared with' (read 'transferred to') those suppliers, is. (Does that remind anyone of a certain large retailer headquartered in Bentonville, Arkansas?) Pay a visit to a Dell plant and you can watch workers unload a supplier's components almost right onto the assembly line."

The comparison to Wal-Mart is sometimes taken as an insult, but Dell doesn't see it that way, as in this *Fast Company* magazine interview[9] (the article is entitled "The Wal-Mart of High Tech?") with Kevin Rollins, Dell's CEO. The interviewer says, "Some of your competitors call you the Wal-

Mart of high-tech—you're a highly efficient distributor that delivers bland products."

Rollins replied: "They're trying to damn us with faint praise. We think of it as high praise, when you look at Wal-Mart's success." (He adds, "So beat me with that noodle.")

Likening Dell to Wal-Mart does give you many insights into its operation. Much of Dell's success is predicated on entering established markets with lower-cost offerings. Dell puts significant pressure on suppliers for faster and cheaper delivery and, because of its size, few suppliers can resist. Dell is a relentless competitor, and exploits weakness where it finds it. Dell is rarely a product pioneer in the sense of striking out into new product categories, and it specializes in providing products built out of standardized, commoditized parts (see Chapter 4). Dell also maintains exceptionally strict control over inventory and, like Wal-Mart, prides itself on moving inventory like almost no one else can. In fact, Wal-Mart and Dell have even traded some personnel, as when Randy Mott, CIO at Wal-Mart, jumped ship to become CIO of Dell in 2000 (a position he still holds).

But the similarity should not be overstated. As a manufacturer, Dell is also an aggressive innovator in ways that Wal-Mart, a retailer, could never be. In large measure, Dell still builds the products it sells, and those products are often of significantly higher quality that the competition's. Characterizing Dell as "a highly efficient distributor that delivers bland products" is not a workable generalization; its products are not bland, and they frequently win awards (and Dell relies on those awards as marketing tools).

Dell combines low cost with substantial quality: You'll frequently see reviews like this one in *InfoWorld*[10] (November 12, 2004) on the Dell 5100cn printer: "Considering its modest price, Dell's 5100cn delivers surprisingly good print quality at speeds that can satisfy an ordinary workgroup of as many as 20 people."

Or this one,[11] from *PC World* (January 12, 2005) about the 3000cn printer: "Dell's 3000cn steals the show with top-quality color printing at a rock-bottom price. The $449 Dell Laser Printer 3000cn blew away the competition in every tested category of quality, while printing at respectable speeds and achieving high marks for paper handling and usability. All of this from the cheapest color laser in our current test group, no less."

So, is Dell the Wal-Mart of the computer industry? To an interesting extent, the answer is yes—although that answer is not completely cut and dried. Dell excels at entering markets where high-tech pioneers were making fat profits and, through low-margin competitiveness, taking over. It excels at getting concessions from suppliers. In that sense, Dell has been teaching the high-tech world what business practices are all about.

That's an important nugget to keep in mind if you want to understand Dell's success; it was able to find and exploit a rich field (the computer industry) through the application of standard business practices. Those companies that were exploited, from IBM to HP, had gotten used to fat days and very high margins. Dell moved in and relentlessly taught them how business—not high-tech—works. You can see the result in today's market-share graphs.

In other words, Dell's success story in many ways is a business success story, and it's crucial to remember that. As *BusinessWeek*[12] says, "Computer-maker Dell is showing the world how to run a business in the Cyber Age."

Sustaining versus Disruptive Innovation

Harvard professor Clayton Christensen makes the distinction between "sustaining innovation," which pioneers markets at high margins and "disruptive innovation," which impacts the market through low-margin business techniques. The following is from a June 2005 article at the Motley Fool financial web site[13]:

"Sustaining innovation is when, say, a computer company introduces a faster chip in its product. As a result of the improved product, margins should increase, thereby strengthening the company. Disruptive innovation takes root at the low end of the market." According to Christensen, disruptive innovation is the mechanism by which industries are transformed and prior market leaders (such as Toys 'R' Us) are toppled. Christensen described disruptive innovation as follows:

"A disruptive innovation is a new product or service or a new business model that doesn't attack the core market by bringing a better product to established users in direct competition with the leaders in an industry, but rather it comes into the low end of the market, either through a business model that can compete at much lower costs, can compete profitably at lower costs, or brings to the market a product or service that is so much more convenient and simple to use and affordable that a whole new population of people who previously couldn't afford or didn't have the skill to own and use a product can now own one.

"There are countless examples of this business principle. Target and Wal-Mart rose to dominance in discount retailing as former leaders tried to concentrate on higher-margin items. Dell (Nasdaq: DELL) captured the computer market in much the same way, thereby undermining former leaders such as IBM (NYSE: IBM) and Hewlett-Packard."

When the market leaders concentrate on the high-margin items without cutting costs and monitoring the parts of their operations running in the red, lean, low-margin machines like Dell move in and sweep the market.

Customers appear to appreciate this kind of disruptive innovation. The perception is that, if you go to Dell, you're going to get a good deal. Here's from Summit Strategies' Dynamic Computing Industry Report Card, March 2005[14]: "Why do customers consider Dell to be more strategic to their server and storage strategies...than IBM or HP?... After all, Dell ranks seventh, well behind IBM (but not far behind HP) as a business transformation partner and eighth (way behind HP and IBM, who ranked one and two, respectively) as a technology innovator.

"Perhaps these factors are outweighed by the fact that a vendor's ability to provide 'the most aggressive and flexible pricing, discounts and service agreements' is the second most important factor in assessing strategic vendors—a category in which Dell leads all leading hardware and software vendors. This status is supported by Dell's account/sales team's reputation for 'giving great deals.'"

Dell is not Wal-Mart. Among the obvious differences is that Dell is still primarily a manufacturer and service provider, not a retailer. As such, Dell has control over the quality of its products. And that quality is, on the whole, high.

Quality

From the very beginning, Dell felt the need to compete in terms of quality, which, in computer terms means not only reliability but also performance. The company learned early on that you need performance to stand out in the PC industry.

Dell does good technical work, producing products that usually, if not always, have at least some advantages over their competitors. Dell is sometimes dismissed as simply a discount tech manufacturer, but the fact is that its record of technical innovation when it comes to beating the other guy—as opposed to creating whole new product categories—is very impressive. Dell can take standard components and drive them like few others can—like the hyperspeed 80286 it brought out in 1986 (see Chapter 4).

As Michael Dell has said[15]: "I think we were kind of forced into innovating [technically]. We were not the biggest computer company, we were not the most capitalized computer company, we were not the most famous computer company. So, we had to prove that what we had was better. And so that forced us to invent a lot of new ways of doing things that delivered a lot better value. And so we looked all across the supply chain and the demand chain for innovations that would drive success for our customers."

In the same vein he said,[16] "It's a basic struggle of business—who's got something better that's more valuable? If somebody comes up with something better than we have, then we're in serious trouble. So our job is to outthink the other guys, out innovate the other guys. And quite frankly we live in constant fear. And that's what drives us."

Dell works hard to maintain quality. Its technological innovations are not so much in the areas of entirely new products, as you might see coming out of IBM in the realm of, say, the latest blade servers, but rather in the next step up against competitors—higher CPU speeds, more drive space, greater screen resolution, and so on.

Dell wins awards for that high performance. From a *PC Magazine*, October 5, 2004 review[17]: "With its raw performance and unmatched manageability features, the Dell PowerEdge 2850 made our decision quite simple…. Dell's manageability was more than just a neck ahead of the competition, too. Combining an innovative remote-access card, a full LCD status panel, and OpenManage software, the 2850 will likely be praised by any tech or admin who works with it."

From a March 28, 2005 review in *PC World*[18]: "You can see more on the Dell Inspiron 6000's wide screen than on most other 15.4-inch displays thanks to its WUXGA resolution of 1,920 by 1,200 pixels. In fact, you can work with higher-resolution photographs, more spreadsheet columns, and more tiled documents simultaneously on the Inspiron 6000 than you can on some 17-inch wide screens."

Dell has always worked to stay ahead of the pack when it comes to performance. That's not to say it always manages it, or that its line of offerings is as wide as that of some competitors' in some areas. But Dell knows the value of awards, and tries to win them when it can. At the very least, Dell is always a tough top-tier competitor in terms of performance.

What about Reliability?

What about reliability? Dell comes in well in media rankings. From time to time, the major industry magazines run surveys on reliability, and Dell is always near the top. Here's from a *PC Magazine* article[19]: "Call it Dell's dynasty. For the tenth time in 11 years, the direct-PC powerhouse has grabbed the top grade in overall desktop service and reliability."

And from a *PC World* article[20]: "Dell, EMachines, and IBM stand out on most reliability measures, while HP and Compaq often lag their peers."

Actual numbers, such as defects per desktop, are hard to come by. But a recent *PC World* article[21] noted that among its respondents, "Only 12 percent of Dell desktop owners reported having a system with a failed core component (CPU, graphics board, hard drive, motherboard, power supply, or RAM), compared with a mean of 15 percent in this product category." Dell rated average in notebooks.

In general, Dell reliability is high, usually higher than average. That reliability, which centers at least partially on Dell's emphasis on using industry-standard components, is a cornerstone of Dell's image of high quality and value. Dell machines, so the perception is, last longer and are more reliable.

That's not to say there aren't gripes, and quite a few of them.

The Gripes

Interestingly, one of the very things that Dell has worked hard for—broadening the PC market from high-end users to a very general audience—also has led to a much more demanding environment, as people unfamiliar with computers and peripherals come onto the scene.

The following is from a *PC Magazine* survey of computer reliability in July of 2003[22]: "We constantly receive complaints from our readers about major hardware vendors, but over the past several months, there's been an unusual increase. In particular, we've seen a rise in criticism of the products and customer support of Dell, the world's most successful PC manufacturer. We are therefore somewhat surprised to find that service and reliability have actually improved slightly this year. Once again, Dell is a top vendor in the survey's desktop category, tied with Apple in receiving an A+."

In fact, Dell Desktops had received a minimum grade of A in 12 of the previous 13 *PC Magazine* surveys. As a Dell watcher, I can say that it does often seem as though the amount of criticism levelled at Dell has been increasing with its market share. Blogs filled with Dell gripes exist out there, easily found on Google (for example, http://www.buzz machine.com/?tag=dell).

Wikipedia even lists a "criticisms" section in its coverage of Dell[23]: "Dell Inc. has sometimes received criticism for the large amount of software included on its systems: some users regard a great deal of it as spyware. Some customers accuse the company of making computers with cheap and unreliable parts.

"Consumer groups have also criticized Dell Inc. for treating consumers unfairly. For example, they have accused its customer service of helping businesses faster than individual customers. Customer service critics target Dell Inc.'s outsourcing practices, specifically involving India, claiming they contribute to communication problems between the company and its customers. Dell Inc. has also had numerous criticisms from the Internet community for not offering AMD-based systems, having faulty hardware (most common complaints relate to hard-drive failures, with repeated occurrences even after sending the computer/hard drive in for repair), failing to facilitate upgrading hardware (almost all non-Dell-certified/branded hardware), and the generic monopoly complaints from the Internet/Build Your Own communities. Dell also uses proprietary parts, resulting in certain components like the power-supply and motherboard not fitting or not working at all, and sometimes frying the system if users install different, nonproprietary parts. Dell quality can also suffer due to those (sometimes inferior) parts, as well as due to assembly-line deficiencies. Workers have less than 5 seconds generally to insert a PCI card in its slot, and to screw it in. Dell has also been accused of marketing with Bait and switch tactics and conspiring with its Financial unit to offer zero percent financing, only to deny the offer to customers after the return period is over."

It's hard to determine how many of the Dell gripes you see online are company-specific and how many are because computers are increasingly taken for granted. And, of course, there's the increasingly strident tone of general discourse of the Internet. You can find a great many gripes about Dell quality online, but no matter how many you read, you get the feeling that they're mostly anecdotal, concerning an individual person with some seriously bad experiences. More significant are the systematic surveys of customer satisfaction, because these surveys mirror what larger numbers of customers can expect from Dell.

The Accolades

You've already seen a large number of Dell customer satisfaction mentions from the industry magazines. Among other findings, the TBR report asked users if they'd stay with their current desktop or switch to a competitor's machine. The results show what percentage of customers would stay with their current machine (do we know who Competitor A, Competitor B, and so on are? Nope; TBR doesn't list them by name):

- Dell about 75 percent
- Competitor A about 42 percent
- Competitor B about 65 percent
- Competitor C about 62 percent
- Competitor D about 25 percent

According to this study, Dell obviously leads the field in terms of perception of quality, and significantly so. Note that it5s number here, about 75 percent, is not 100 percent. In other words, 25 percent of users indicated they'd switch, and that fraction allows for many users with significant gripes. Dell has some way to go if it wants to make that 75 percent into 100 percent, but it's clearly far ahead of its competitors, which translates into market share.

Where does all this leave us in terms of customer perception of Dell quality? It's apparent room for improvement exists, but Dell also stands above the rest. That's an impressive achievement for a cost-conscious provider. The general perception of Dell, in other words, is that Dell combines low cost with high quality.

Service and Support

Recall the words of Michael Dell from the beginning of this chapter: "We've found that pricing is only one-third of our customer's decision-making process, the other two-thirds represent service and support."

Clearly, service and support are two large components of providing customers with the best value. Dell started strongly by providing a great value; and service, to all reports, is doing well. But support—tech support and customer support—has noticeably faltered in recent years.

That Was Then

Chapter 1 discussed how Dell stunned its competitors in 1986 by offering on-site service. At first, many competitors assumed that was essentially a joke: How could it make sense to dispatch a Dell technician to someone's home or business every time there was a problem? But that's not the way it worked. If a typical home user had a problem, he first spoke with a Dell technician on the phone who tried to determine exactly what the problem is. If that problem was hardware-related, the technician tried to pinpoint the offending hardware.

If the problem was one that the user could address, the technician might tell him to get some needed tools and open the case (leaving some users asking, "What about on-site service?"). If the problem could be resolved this way (which is most of the time), fine.

If a new part was needed, and it could be installed by the user, Dell could often overnight the part and talk the user through installation. If the solution was not so simple, Dell would indeed dispatch a technician, or at least its ad materials promised it would do so. That technician was not usually, as Dell's competitors assumed in the early days, a Dell employee, but rather a third-party technician.

Today, how fast you actually get on-site service if Dell decides you need it typically depends on your service contract, and there are many to choose from. Support can be limited to a 5 × 10 hour period corresponding to business hours during the week, or a more expensive 7 × 24 option.

The time in which you get a "house call," if needed, is no longer limited to the next business day. Depending on where you live (rural Alaska isn't going to get the same service options as downtown Manhattan), you also can sign up for same-day service. You can get 6-hour service, or 4-, or even sign up for 2-hour same-day service. So, if you've got a mission-critical PC or server and have signed up for 2-hour same-day service, you get a call within an hour after Dell determines you need on-site help, and receive either a tech or a delivered part (delivered by local courier) within 2 hours.

You still hear gripes from unsatisfied customers on this, and you can read such complaints posted on the Internet from time to time. On the whole, however, Dell's system of providing support for its products has been a remarkable success. Dell's support system was designed to allay customers' fears about ordering machines over the phone or the Internet, and it's done that to a significant degree.

On-site service (and today, that includes many services, such as setup services, as well as a permanent presence in some installations for business customers) remains such a cornerstone of the Dell offerings that it is quick to extend that support to any new markets it enters, such as in Europe and Asia. As in the United States, Dell outsources the on-site service, but it's still available. This is true even in large countries that present formidable challenges in this area; for example, from the Dell Asia Pacific site[24]: "Dell is also making on-going investments in beefing up service infrastructures in China. So far, Dell has extended its on-site service in China to 2,569 cities; next business day on-site service to 1,642 cities; 24×7 6-hour response service to 288 cities, and the 4-hour response service to 49 cities in China. Now, 78 percent of customers' issues can be solved in the first telephone contact, and 97.4 percent of them can be solved during the first on-site visit, greatly saving time and costs for customers."

You can imagine the consternation of Dell's competitors when Dell introduced on-site service as a way to gain customer's trust as long ago as 1986. No competitor was offering that; you had to bring your sick machine in, or find someone in the phone book to come and take a look. The fact that Dell managed the actual number of on-site visits with first-contact calls, tech support over the phone, and overnighted parts before turning to actual on-site visits made the plan workable. It must have soured a lot of beer.

It was, even competitors had to admit, an insightful move. And it went far to gain customer trust in the area where it was needed most: If you don't have a physical store to buy from, at least you'll have someone stop by if there's a bad enough problem.

Dell has won a number of awards for service and support, such as *Computer Shopper Magazine*'s Shopper's Choice Best Service & Support award in 2004.[25] In a December 2003 *Information Week* article,[26] Dell took top honors for customer service. And *Windows and .NET* magazine[27] said this in September 2003, "No IT department is like another, and thus every IT department's service and support needs are unique. The unparalleled diversity of Dell's support services is what motivated our readers to vote the company to the top spot in this category."

In other words, Dell has had a history of winning top honors for service, such as its on-site service. Unfortunately, Round Rock, we do have a problem.

This Is Now

Dell has been taking a beating in general evaluations of its tech support for some time now (see for example, resellerratings.com at http://www.resellerratings.com/seller1867.html, where Dell's rating is 1.74 out of 10, Dell's lowest rating in any category). Customer satisfaction on support is generally good, but an undercurrent says that this has become Dell's weakest link, and it's a topic you see again and again on the gripe pages.

A significant amount of the griping has to do with long hold times, clueless tech support personnel, and speaking with hard-to-understand outsourced techs. That outsourced support is only supposed to continue, according to a *NetworkWorld.com* article[28] in May 2005, "Dell plans to increase the number of staff at its Indian call center and software development operations to 10,000 by the end of the year, the company's president and chief executive officer said recently. Dell currently employs about 8,000 in India. Dell stopped routing some technical calls from corporate customers to India in late 2003, after receiving complaints about poor quality of service. The problems were not related specifically to outsourcing in India, Dell President and CEO Kevin Rollins said but were more a reflection of the company's failure to effectively manage the rapid growth of its operations in the country. Dell is trying to reshape itself from a purely PC company to a broad based IT supply company, Rollins said."

The problems were also commented on in a *PC World* article,[29] "However, the outsourcing of tech support to foreign countries by companies such as CyberPower, Dell, and HP/Compaq continues to be a hotbutton issue for PC owners. Compaq, Dell, and HP desktop owners gave these companies below-average marks for phone support, with many respondents saying that the techs were difficult to understand and that it was hard to reach someone helpful."

The technical staff's capabilities is something you see mentioned over and over in the gripe pages. From http://computergripes.blogspot.com[30]: "We found it easy to purchase our Dell PC and it arrived as described. Dell's greatest shortcoming is its pathetic telephone support line. Dell appears to hire for the applicant's ability to speak English. Computer knowledge is virtually zero. Each sentence is followed by the command to 'hold on for a moment.' Some moment! What should be a 5-minute call will take 45 minutes, and even at that, the likelihood of the problem being solved is dubious! Our previous PC online purchase was through IBM and their telephone tech support is excellent. We certainly weren't prepared for the 'Dell Experience.'"

Long hold times are often mentioned by dissatisfied customers. From another poster in the same blogspot site: "I have never in my life dealt with such ridiculous customer service. I left the phone in tears after being on hold for two and a half hours. I cannot restate how horrible the customer service was. After two months of purchasing my computer, the video card went bad. Now, I have to pay for it? There is something seriously wrong with this picture."

The outsourcing looks like it's going to continue. This is from *PC World* in a 2004 article[31] entitled "Dell's Workforce Moves Abroad": "Round Rock, Texas–based Dell employs more people abroad than it does in the U.S., it disclosed in a regulatory filing this week.

"As of January 30, the computer systems giant employed 23,800 employees outside of the U.S. and 22,200 domestically, it says in a filing submitted to the U.S. Securities and Exchange Commission this week.

"The disclosure underscores an increasing trend among IT companies to locate jobs overseas, where labor costs are cheaper. Dell recently established customer and technical support centers in India, China, Morocco, Panama, and Slovakia and has set up design centers in Taiwan and China. Furthermore, it not only has manufacturing facilities in Texas and Tennessee, but also in Brazil, Ireland, Malaysia, and China.

"Although Dell has come under fire along with other companies by critics who say that so-called offshoring is robbing U.S. citizens of jobs, the company's newly anointed chief executive officer [Kevin Rollins] has said that Dell will continue to engage in the practice."

The following is from an October 2005 *BusinessWeek* article (http://www.businessweek.com/magazine/content/05_41/b3954102 .htm?chan=tc): "All tech companies have some unhappy customers, of course, but recent surveys suggest the ranks of frustrated Dell Inc. owners are growing. Complaints to the Better Business Bureau rose 23 percent in 2004 from the year before, and they're up another 5 percent this year. And Dell's customer-satisfaction rating fell 6.3 percent, to a score of 74, in a survey by the University of Michigan. Dell's score puts it right at the PC industry's average for the study, in which Apple Computer Inc. (AAPL) led the way with an 81."

All this presents an interesting picture of a groundswell of dissatisfaction going on—take a look at sites like http://www.ihatedell.net/ for example. The gripe pages make that clear—plenty of customers get machines that don't work out of the box or have something wrong with them, and they bemoan "Dell Hell," but that kind of comment is a constant background for every computer manufacturer. What has been increasing are the comments about Dell's support. And this about a corporation whose hallmark has been service and support.

So, what's going on? Are the support issues a result of uncontrolled growth? Dell grows by large rates every year; could it be that it is not keeping up with its own expansion? Is the support audience changing? After all, as the computer market expands to users with no computer experience, you're going to get more calls and more frustrated customers howling into your ear.

Or, is it an attempt by Dell to cut service to save costs? The media has been taking note, but so far has been relatively kind. In 2004, *news.com*[32] published an article entitled "Growing Pains Hit Dell's Customer Service" that's worth taking a look at.

The article starts, "Dell continues to win market share and turn out record quarterly profits, but two recent surveys show that the company has slipped, when it comes to a more subjective measurement: customer service.

"According to two new reports that rate the satisfaction of PC buyers, Dell's scores have declined in recent months. While statistically, the results are not catastrophic for a company that prides itself on offering superior service, it's a potentially troubling trend Dell executives acknowledge and have taken steps to address.

"The March issue of *Consumer Reports*...included a survey of 4,100 consumers, who gave Dell 62 points out of a possible 100 for its support on desktop PCs. Although it still managed to top competing brands Hewlett-Packard and Compaq, which scored 54 and 51, respectively, Dell's rating represented a decline from the magazine's last desktop support survey, published in June 2003, in which it received a 64...."

The issue is clearly not confined to the gripe pages. A substantial decline seems to be occurring. So, why has the Dell score for customer service and support tumbled?

Is It Growth?

The article continues to say, "Dell's score has 'stayed down and hasn't gone back up,' Fox said. 'We can't say why...but they haven't solved whatever problem that brought it down, whether that's increased volume (or) outsourcing. It's probably a number of different factors.'..."

Rollins is quoted in an article by *EnterpriseInnovator.com*[33] on growth in foreign countries as saying, "Hence, the 'biggest risk becomes one of execution as we grow our team' since Dell has to 'find people, and train them in the fastest growth countries where we have not been really that long.' Rollins believes that 'maintaining execution discipline will be a challenge.'"

This is, of course, a possibility—call centers overwhelmed by avalanches of new customers. Dell is a success story that continually brings in new customers, and certainly that means more pressure on support. If you grow by 20 percent to 25 percent annually, more customers will be beating a trail to your call centers.

The article again mentions growth as the issue: "Although Dell still topped rivals HP and IBM in the TBR survey, its score was the lowest seen since the research firm began tracking Dell's satisfaction levels in the first quarter of 2001. Although part of the change could reflect Dell's rapid growth rate during 2003, the company's fourth-quarter score dipped well below its average rating of 82.9, said Julie Perron, manager of primary research at TBR."

In fact, it is true that Dell had grown rapidly in 2003, as it has for all its life. Shipments soared by 25 percent, year after year—in 2003, to 25.8 million units. Dell's worldwide market share grew to 16.9 percent in 2003, up from 15.1 percent in 2002 (HP's shipments, by contrast, grew 14.5 percent).

So, the growth was there. But was that the problem? After all, service marks had declined persistently since 2001. And Dell is a corporation that handles growth, even double-digit growth, better than any other you can name. If you want to bring your call centers up to speed in terms of response and tech skill, it seems an easy enough extrapolation, given that you know your own projected growth rates. But the service marks have been declining persistently for years (note that it's important to bear in mind that Dell still leads most of the competition in overall service and customer satisfaction).

If it's not growth, maybe the problem is the flood of new users.

Is It More Inexperienced Users?

The news.com article goes on to discuss another possible factor: Expanding your market means that you're going to end up with significantly more inexperienced customers. That's going to mean more calls from users less prepared to understand how to fix the problem, even with tech help: "In some ways, Dell is fighting an uphill battle; its focus on growth naturally means that it will attract more consumers who are naturally less skilled in operating PCs and thus need more assistance.

"'As the proportion of the consumers in the mix rises, (Dell) is naturally going to increase in its share of complaints, even if it isn't doing anything differently,' said Roger Kay, an analyst at IDC. That's because increasing market share requires a 'devil's bargain. You have to support inexperienced buyers in order to get their business.'"

All this is true. As you get new and inexperienced customers coming online during a time of rapidly increasing complexity in both software and hardware, it's going to be hard for them to cope. Over the years, you notice how the tone in the gripe boards has become more strident. Issues that were formerly no big deal, such as waiting on hold for 15 minutes, become major problems. And the tone is only getting louder as computer use becomes ubiquitous.

Once again, however, this is essentially a growth issue. Dell excels at handling growth, and you get the feeling that, if it wanted to be on top of the support issue, it could be (in fact, Dell does not often focus on selling the introductory machine in PC market sectors, but the more powerful second or third machine, and so scoops out many new users right there).

Or Is It Something Else?

Dell has worked on its service issues; no doubt about that. It has routed some calls from Bangalore, India, back to the United States. It has opened an Enterprise Command Center to help handle the needs of large server and storage customers.

But, you still hear endless gripes about inexperienced, and incomprehensible, tech support staff who read from scripts that have nothing to do with the issue that's at fault, long hold times, and declining satisfaction. It's clear that Dell, which is the virtual poster boy for quick response, could have fixed a problem that the media has been noting since 2001.

All this seems to be more consistent with a deliberate policy shift. One might easily conjecture that Dell, which excels in making each unit pay for itself, took a long, hard look at its support unit and found it coming up short. Support is, after all, an expensive proposition, relying as it does largely on speaking to someone on the phone, no matter how much Dell has tried to steer customers to online troubleshooting databases. (Accessible as the Dell Solution Network at http://support.dell.com, or by double-clicking the Dell Support icon on any recent Dell PC or notebook—and to its credit, Dell was one of the first to write its tech support site in plain English, which helped upset users find what they were looking for more quickly). The shortfall would only have increased as the years passed, Dell sold more computers, and more inexperienced users came on board.

Dell still leads the support surveys, when compared to its competitors. But internally, very few companies watch each unit's ROIC as carefully as Dell and, at some point, it may have seemed that throwing more money into tech support, an area it already led in, may have been a study in diminishing returns.

One might easily conjecture that some cost-cutting became the order of the day, a fact pointed to by, among other things, the massive outsourcing of tech support to India. And the fact that customer satisfaction with support has slipped in small, nearly identical, amounts from year to year seems to indicate more of a controlled slide rather than an out-of-control problem. Like many other companies, Dell may have simply come to the conclusion that tech support was becoming too expensive.

That's not something new in the industry, of course. Microsoft, for example, sometimes seems to have forgotten what the word "support" means. In earlier days, you actually used to be able to get significant free tech support from Microsoft, as startling a notion as that may seem now. It's nothing new for the industry, but it is a departure for Dell, which built so much of its business on superior customer service and support.

You still can get some free support from Microsoft. If you buy Windows XP Pro, for example, you can send two free support questions by e-mail, phone, or via online chat. After that, each additional support request will cost you $35, as of this writing. Advanced issues require $245. In other words, if you want serious tech support, you pay for it.

Something similar seems to be taking place at Dell. While free tech support continues its slide, you can sign up for various paid support options. Some of them are 7 × 24, and most of them offer special 800 numbers that you, as a paid subscriber, can call. Here are some of the Dell support plan options that have been appearing[34]:

- Gold Technical Support Service Agreement (Latitude, OptiPlex, Precision, Inspiron, Dimension, and Printers)
- Premier Enterprise Support Service Tiers—Gold Level Contract
- Premier Enterprise Support Service Tiers—Silver Level Contract
- 8G PowerEdge SC Support Services
- CompleteCare Agreement (for business customers)
- Express Tech Support

A Platinum support option is now offered as well. When you sign up for one or more of these options, you get a decidedly different level of support. For example, the Personal Systems Gold Technical Support Services agreement proudly tells you that: "Gold Technical Support includes a 7 × 24 dedicated toll-free-number direct into Dell's Personal Systems or Retail POS Gold Queue, each of which is designed to provide 2 minutes or less average speed of answer."

Here's from the Express Tech Support agreement: "Dell will provide a dedicated toll-free 800 number (or some other toll free number) that will route your calls at a priority directly into Dell's Technical Support queue in the event technical support assistance is necessary under the terms and conditions of the standard warranty of the system. You may purchase Express Tech Support as annual contracts for 1, 2, 3, or 4 years."

This level of attention is a far cry from that recorded in the blog entry earlier in this chapter: "I left the phone in tears after being on hold for two and a half hours."

BusinessWeek (http://www.businessweek.com/magazine/content/ 05_41/b3954102.htm?chan=tc) says, "All of this adds up to a quiet attempt to reset customer expectations in the PC industry. While execs won't say so publicly, the message is clear: That new PC you bring home comes with only the most rudimentary support. More hand-holding costs extra."

From the evidence, then, it looks like Dell, without any fanfare or big noise, is making the transition to a new policy: Beyond a certain level, you get what you pay for in tech support. Presumably, the industry as a whole will take this same path sooner or later. And, presumably, Dell's not going to let its customer satisfaction slip too far. There's a tradeoff here: In the attempt to make tech support pay for itself, or pay more for itself, you can't take it to the extreme of alienating your major customer base.

From *BusinessWeek* (http://www.businessweek.com/magazine/content/05_41/b3954102.htm?chan=tc), "Some industry experts think Dell's plans are simply a practical response to plummeting prices. 'Consumers want to have their cake and eat it, too. They want that $300 PC but expect the same support that came with a machine that 10 years ago cost $2,500,' says Stephen Dukker, who founded home PC maker emachines Inc. in 1998. Cutting costs in this department gives Dell a significant leg up on the competition. From a business point of view, Dell is maintaining its leadership in the support sector of the industry. And, also from a business point of view, it's doing that while cutting costs. But will it work in the long run? Dell may be forced to provide the goods here; *BusinessWeek* says, "John Hamlin, senior vice-president of Dell's U.S. consumer business, says the company is hiring a few thousand additional reps this year and striving to reduce call transfers. Already, he says, hold times have been cut in half from earlier this year, and internal weekly surveys of 5,000 customers show a 35 percent increase in customer satisfaction from a year ago." The trouble is that you keep hearing that from Dell, who promises improvement year after year, and yet customer satisfaction (as measured in the media) keeps plummeting. Is this latest Dell promise just more smoke and mirrors?

To sum up then, the lesson from Dell is that ultimately, value speaks loudly, and to win market share, provide the best value. Of the three measures we reviewed—cost, quality (measured in terms of performance and reliability), and service/support—Dell can't be faulted in terms of cost; it's one of the pillars Dell built its name on. The direct model let Dell save a middleman mark-up of 25 percent to 45 percent, and that's a margin hard to beat.

Quality is also high. Dell routinely wins awards for performance, which is an impressive show for a company that's not out to be on the bleeding-edge of tech. Reliability, as shown in media surveys, is also in exceptionally good shape. Combining good price with high quality is a Dell hallmark, and it continues to do well for them.

The story in the service and support area has become an interesting one. Service continues to get high marks, even as the satisfaction with tech support slides. What's going to happen in the coming years with tech support? Stay tuned.

Chapter 3

Focus Fanatically on Customers

The do-it-the-customer's way mantra has created for Dell the tightest—
and most envied—relationship with buyers in the PC business.
*   —BusinessWeek, 1998*

As the quotation from *BusinessWeek* says, Dell maintains a tight relationship with its customers. How close is that relationship? Fanatically close. Michael Dell[1] says, "Know your customer's pulse—beat by beat."

Does it work? The June 2004 Technology Business Research, Inc. (TBR) report "Setting the Standard for Customer Satisfaction: An Analysis of Dell Customer Satisfaction Track Record and Approach"[2] is definitive on Dell's number-one position in customer satisfaction, saying, "Within the first year to 18 months of TBR's independent satisfaction studies, Dell quickly emerged as a No. 1 ranked vendor and has maintained this customer satisfaction leadership position more consistently than any other vendor.

"As of June 2004, Dell Services has held a No. 1 ranking position for 27 consecutive quarters in the Desktop study, 24 consecutive quarters in the Notebook study, 24 of the last 26 consecutive quarters in the Intel-based Server study, and for 14 of the 15 quarters during which TBR has conducted the Service & Support satisfaction study."

Later, the report adds, "Over time, no other vendor TBR covers has approached Dell's long-standing record in terms of customer satisfaction leadership, consistency and resilience. Again and again, Dell has shown resilience in developing distinct customer satisfaction results."

It summarizes its findings by saying, "Dell is the IT satisfaction leader." Little room for misinterpretation there (although Dell's competitors are putting in tremendous efforts now, and the race is becoming very close to neck-and-neck).

Michael Dell[3] has said that he spends 40 percent of his time with customers. There's little arguing with the fact that Dell's direct model has given it a do-it-the-customer's way culture unlike any other. From involving the customers through the online customization process to letting them track their machine *as it's being built* (Figs. 3.1 and 3.2), to making follow-up calls on service issues every time a customer has an issue, Dell really is in there on this. The direct model let Dell be in touch with customers' needs early on and, from the start, Dell has let its customers take the lead in innovation.

Michael Dell has long spoken of "virtually integrating" customers into the corporation's organization: the idea that customers should be invited into the company by giving them the same access to information that Dell Inc. and the Dell staff has. This is in counterpoint to the more standard "vertical integration," wherein you integrate customers, if at all, into an existing corporate structure that they must adapt themselves to.

Figure 3.1 Building to order in Ireland.

Figure 3.2 Building to order in Austin.

In most corporate cultures, an at least informal barrier exists between the corporation and the customer, and it's interesting to see that line blurred by a large company like Dell. The idea of virtual integration is put to work daily at Dell, and customers really do penetrate and infuse the corporate structure at Dell in a remarkable way.

It's All About Execution Again

The idea that you should focus on your customers is in danger of being treated as a nice background idea, one that's often relegated to bumper-sticker status. It is crucial to realize that, although many of Dell's business principles sound simple, even simplistic, the company's devotion to those ideas is not. Dell's entire corporate structure is built around the principles given in this book, not the other way around, as is the case with many companies where corporate structure or a sluggish corporate culture comes first, and simple ideas like customer focus come next.

Execution is something you've got to keep in mind as you read the Dell story. Kevin Rollins[4] says that execution is Dell's "key to winning." Internetnews.com[5] says, "No one has yet to match Dell's execution in the PC business, despite years of trying."

It's important to stress, once again, that simply reading about Dell's business principles is not enough; Dell excels in *execution*. It's always been above the half-hearted attempts of so many of its competitors that have fallen by the side of the road. This is one energetic company.

From a *USA Today* article[6] first quoted in Chapter 1: "'People have tried to duplicate what Dell does, and they can't,' says Dell board member Alex Mandl, CEO of Gemplus. 'It sounds like a simple model, but getting all this going and perfectly executing it is difficult, if not impossible. Many have tried, all have failed.'"

The same article also says, "Companies in a groove like Dell are, at least for a while, 'practically unassailable by competitors—not because they can't emulate the model, but to do so means practically discarding the business and organizational model they have today,' says Paul Wiefels, author of business book *The Chasm Companion*. 'Most companies don't have the stomach for it.'"

As the TBR report says: "Consistent success in customer satisfaction does not happen by accident. It is the result of deep commitment and constancy of purpose, guiding long-term decision-making and day-to-day actions. Dell clearly demonstrates this unique commitment. The company is extremely unified and consistent in its commitment to customer satisfaction."

The concept of Dell's savvy business machine logic at work among technical wizards is important to bring the picture into focus. Dell succeeded in its early days largely because it came into a market where technological companies were making such fat profits that they felt they didn't have to watch margins. In those days, PCs were built to follow technology and whether customers needed or wanted such machines became a secondary issue; because the market was so hot, the machines still sold. Dell's early competitors didn't have much need for customer focus, but in the long run, Dell won out.

Development among Dell's early competitors was product oriented, not customer oriented. The industry was fat, and what they said went. Dell makes a big point about changing that. As the industry grew fuller, with more and more manufacturers, and as PC sales eventually flattened, Dell's superior business techniques and its *execution* of those techniques brought it out in front. It entered a frantic market of high growth with techniques that would let it thrive once that market matured and growth leveled off. Its early competitors, for the most part, weren't able to make the same change, due to their inability to execute, even after they saw what Dell was doing.

Listen to Your Customers

It's obvious that the first step in being customer focused is to actually listen to them. Michael Dell once said that Dell's three golden rules[7] are: "Disdain inventory [see Chapter 5], listen to the customer [this chapter], and never sell indirect [see Chapter 2]." Critical among these is listening to the customer.

Dell, using its direct model, is perfectly positioned to listen to customers. Its competitors, dependent on resellers, weren't able to match that direct model and so lost their direct connection to their customers. Dell is able to reap great amounts of information from this direct customer relationship, while most of its competitors can't.

The Dell Direct model isn't just about cutting out the middleman's cost, but also cutting out their obstruction to information flow. As the TBR report concludes, "Dell's unique direct model enables it to respond in real time to customer needs and wants."

> Michael Kanellos, editor-at-large at CNET News.com says, "Michael Dell himself is a great listener. When you ask him something, he pauses, digests the whole thing for what seems like seconds, tilts his head to one side and then calmly responds. Granted, he will give pat answers often, but he clearly listens. Doesn't interrupt much either. Very calm. It's a big difference from someone like Steve Ballmer. Talking to him you do feel like you are being taken seriously. As part of that, he's not uppity at all. Once, at Comdex, he bumped me by accident from behind. I was in a cab line. He recognized me instantly, remembered my name, and offered me a ride with his bodyguard in his limo. People were looking at me like I was some sort of VIP."

Dell meets with global and large customers meet face-to-face regularly, and it has account teams that work with them in the field. Dell uses various mechanisms to keep in very close contact with these customers and what they want, such as Dell's Platinum Councils.

As far as small business and consumers go, Dell has continual contact with these people through online and phone sales and support. For this market segment, Dell also has online surveys and real-time focus groups, as well as call surveys. If you've had an issue you had to call in about, no matter what size customer you are, you'll get a follow-up call from Dell to see if the problem was solved satisfactorily (other companies, including HP, are doing this now as well). And you can be sure that Dell tracks all that information carefully.

As time goes on, the Dell sales and support force is able to watch what people are ordering and what problems come up. That information is prized by Dell management, which holds frequent meetings with sales and support staff to determine what customers are asking for. At these meetings, sales and support teams assume the role of advocate for customers. Management may outline company direction, and the team members are encouraged to speak up freely, correcting that view as needed.

The fact that every Dell PC is—as they have been from the first—built-to-order is great for feedback on what customers in each market segment want. Because Dell is famous for its focus on feedback and for knowing what its market is doing on a microlevel, it can get away with keeping little inventory on hand. Competitors, on the other hand, have historically built for lagging demand, as reflected by orders from retailers. Losing that direct contact with their market pinches their margins in obvious ways. Dell excels through its emphasis on information handling.

After 21 years of tracking market data on a micro level, Dell now has a good idea what each market segment wants. Larger corporations, for example, prefer stability in PCs; they're not so impressed by the latest and greatest as general consumers are. They want networked machines that can be remotely maintained and updated with various service packs and software. So, Dell split its PC lines into the OptiPlex (business) and Dimension (small business and consumer) to match those needs.

Unblocked data flow from the customer is crucial. Dell Inc. has no room for obstructing middlemen here. As Michael Dell[8] says: "The challenge in any business is finding the perfect match between what your customer wants or needs and what you can provide."

It's something Dell is never finished doing. The TBR report states: "How did Dell recognize, so early on, the critical nature of the customer experience? Dell came into the business with this understanding. Dell conducted trials among early customers in the business environment and noted that these customers discovered a new level of satisfaction that they found had not been there in the PC business prior to Dell's market entry. It was an epiphany for IT managers that Dell was so far above anything they had ever experienced. Part of this was Dell's early implementation of customer-focused services. Dell was the first to offer a toll-free number for tech support and later was the first to offer on-site service for the masses, including for its Latitude notebook products in an industry where depot repair [which meant mailing in your laptop] for notebooks was the norm. Because Dell had ready access to sales and service data, Dell was able to find patterns. For example, Dell found the marketplace to be set up in such a way that customers were paying an arm and a leg for next-day service. Because the direct sales model gave Dell an economic advantage, the company was able to leverage this into providing even better service."

Let Customers Lead

Gathering data from customers is one thing, but putting that information to work is another. As you might expect, at Dell, customers are given the lead in innovation and product development to a significant degree. And they know it. In fact, Dell won the first JD Power survey of the computer industry (1991) for customer satisfaction partly because customers said they felt they had a way to add input to the process.

The focus on the customer might unsettle the tech guys in many companies. But no less a person than Kevin Kettler, Dell's Chief Technology Officer, has said[9]: "At Dell, our approach to innovation focuses on customer requirements. Customers define what is important. Dell innovates internally and through collaboration with others in the industry. Many of Dell's innovations are shared through standards, rather than locking customers into proprietary solutions. Customers gain flexibility and real value. This approach is direct, customer-driven innovation."

That's an interesting thing for the Chief Technology Officer to say because it sounds like something you'd get from a VP of Marketing. Note the emphasis here is *not* on technology, but on following the customer. Dell is known for (and is a little sensitive about) the relatively small amount of money it puts into R&D, and you see one of the reasons here—the customer leads at Dell, not the technology. (Another reason is that Dell deals primarily in standards-based, mass-produced, less expensive technology.)

Dell is savvy about when to get into a field and what fields make sense for it (such as LCD TVs, which allowed it to leverage its flat-monitor know-how). But once it's in a field, it makes a passion out of following the customers' lead. What does the customer want? What speed? What capacity? Through its sales teams, these are all issues that Dell stays in touch with, on a minute-by-minute basis.

For example, at one point, the industry as a whole was very excited about switching to the MIPS CPU chips. Compaq, AST, Microsoft, and others members of what was being called the ACE consortium jumped on the bandwagon. Dell responded as you'd expect Dell to do: It asked customers. Through a series of forums for smaller customers and face-to-face meetings with the larger ones, Dell sought customer feedback on this idea. It learned that no significant added value was apparent for customers. So, it decided it wasn't worth the substantial investment in engineering and production and dropped the project. If a firestorm of demand had existed, it might have been a different story, but because Dell would have had to design whole new machines for the new chips, the lukewarm interest didn't justify the extra expense.

A similar thing happened with PC TVs. After its customer studies, Dell concluded that not much real customer interest existed.

Sometimes, it's a harder call to make, as with light pens. A lot of hype surrounded light pens at one point, and Dell took a look at them, but concluded that they simply didn't work. Many customers were still caught up in the hype, however, and kept asking about them. Accordingly, Dell built light-pen prototypes and was able to demonstrate them to the media and its customers in case light pens ever took off. But it didn't tool up to produce light pens. Dell's hunch was correct; light pens never took off.

Keep Your Customers in the Loop

You can't have a one-way dialog, and as far as Dell is concerned, that goes for working with customers, too. Dell's policy of the virtual integration of customers into the company comes into play here.

Not only can customers customize their machines and order them online, they can also track those machines. In fact, they can track them before they even leave the plant. After you've ordered a machine, you're given an order number, and you can watch the status of your order *inside* Dell manufacturing as it is completed.

After the order has been shipped, you can get the shipper's tracking number from the Dell web site. All you have to do is to click a link to see where your machine is currently, when it's supposed to be delivered, and what to do if it doesn't arrive. If there's going to be an unexpected delay, they send a warning.

After delivery, you're still in touch. Each Dell PC, notebook, and server comes with a Dell service tag stuck on it, giving you your service number (also visible when you double-click the Dell Support icon to open the Dell Support window). You enter that number online or into a phone menu when you call for help, and it lets Dell staff bring up your record.

You're always in the loop. And being able to track the stages your purchase is going through inside the plant is a nice touch.

If you've made a call to tech support and gotten a case number for your issue, you'll get a follow-up call a day or two later from a Dell staffer to make sure the problem was resolved. That personal touch is also impressive, and the caller will ask about the quality of service you've gotten.

If you want to check out a technical problem online, you have the same access to the technical solutions lists and pages as a Dell technician does, using the Dell Solution Network at http://support.dell.com. In other words, you're virtually integrated into the corporation here as well, and you're in the loop.

The Internet is a big part of keeping the customer in the loop. You can always call and track your order, for example, but most customers seem to like the immediate access of the Internet. And data can be supplied from your company's databases direct to the Internet as well.

This idea of virtual integration to keep customers in the loop is an interesting one. Although Michael Dell likes to refer to this idea as though customers and suppliers are brought into the corporation virtually as partners, that's not correct. What's really happening is that customers and suppliers are brought in primarily in terms of information flow. Customers are able to supply information directly to the sales team and track what happens to their order. They're able to get the same troubleshooting information as the tech support team. Suppliers have access to Dell supply-chain information directly through a secure extranet named valuechain.dell.com on the Internet. Logging on is password protected but, as a supplier, once you're in, you've got access to all kinds of Dell info. And that includes your report card, because you're always being graded by Dell.

In other words, virtual integration really refers to information flow, not control flow. And since the Internet is all about information flow, it's a natural here. Allowing customers easy information access relieves the pressure on tech and customer service staff, and doing the same for suppliers not only relieves the need for staff, but gives suppliers 24-hour information on supply issues. Using the Internet for this kind of information supply is excellent, because most of that information can be updated in an automated way.

When you place an order with Dell as a customer, you'll typically get an e-mail that will start this way:

Dear [Customer Name]:

We have received your order and it is being processed. Thank You.

What's next?

You will receive an order confirmation e-mail within 1 day with your order number, customer number, estimated ship date, and updated purchase amount.

This preliminary e-mail will also contain some other information about where to look online for a full order summary.

As you might expect, however, "virtually integrated" customers and suppliers are not deeply integrated into the corporation as far as control structures go. They have access to information, and Dell has access to information from them, but virtually integrated customers and suppliers make very few decisions directly inside Dell's corporate structure.

As a customer, you can learn all about your order and make a few simple changes, but for any serious modification, you are required to go through Dell customer service or the sales staff. As you can imagine, suppliers are at the mercy of Dell for the most part; there's not much they can change, because it's Dell that makes the demands on them.

Nonetheless, as a Dell customer, being able to track your order from the very beginning, as it's being built, is very reassuring. And to be able to check the actual Ship To address and shipping dates is also reassuring, to make sure the sales rep got your order right.

And, of course, letting you handle all that over the Internet lets Dell save a lot of time answering your calls. Dell's concept of virtual integration, which should more properly be called information integration, lets the customer feel in touch at all times. Even before an order is placed, a customer can look at the quotes and system configurations she is considering—and if the automated information provided isn't enough, she knows she can access Dell support in at least three ways: through e-mail, on the phone, or using online chat (when you log into "My Account," you're given the option of joining an online chat with Dell personnel).

As with much of Dell, the idea of keeping the customer in the loop is a simple one, but Dell excels in its execution. To some companies, keeping the customers in the loop means giving them an order number and a tracking number. To Dell, it means holding the customers by the hand from the very start by letting them view quotes online and letting them track the in-house location of their order, step by step, until it's out the door.

Customer Segmentation

With its focus on customers, Dell may have been the first of the PC upstarts to start segmenting its customer response, a policy it began in 1988. Most other companies segment by product, but Dell started segmenting by customer as well; Dell realized that different types of customers exist, with significantly different needs.

For example, a large company is typically more interested in consistency and stability, and will forgo small performance upgrades. Large companies prefer network-based machines that can be centrally updated as needed, instead of having to send a tech out to every machine in every installation to do the work personally. Smaller users are more sensitive to individual machine issues, such as CPU speed, disk capacity, and so on.

There's another difference here as well—Dell's connection with larger customers, which might purchase thousands of PCs and require on-site support, is *relational*, whereas Dell's connection with small business and individual consumers is *transactional.*

Customer segmentation allows Dell to respond to different types of customers in very different ways. Business customers get a different level of response than consumers. When you call as a consumer for tech support, you'll get someone more than willing to work through a long script with you. When large business customers call, however, the call is routed to either customer service for sales information, or a tech person who assumes she is going to be speaking to other tech people.

Michael Dell[10] has said, "When you've got a huge market opportunity facing you, the only way to handle it is to divide and conquer. That's the basis behind our concept of segmentation. It ensures that as we grow, we are able to serve each individual customer more effectively, and it has become the organizing philosophy of our company." There's an unintentional meaning here as well—in Dell's case, serving "each individual customer more effectively" doesn't just mean from the customer's point of view, but from Dell's point of view also (already discussed in Chapter 2).

Dell's customer segmentation actually started in sales, not in service and support. To better target the needs of various customers, the sales organization was split into groups for large and medium companies, educational institutions, government customers, small businesses, and consumers. The segmentation made sense, and soon it was ported to the service and support teams.

Although many different internal divisions exist within this segmentation, you can get a rough idea of its shape.

This segmentation is reflected throughout Dell. You can even customize the Dell support site by which segment you belong to, which means you're going to see pages different from those people in other segments will.

Organizing segmentation around products, as many companies do, is corporation-centric; organizing primarily by customer segment is customer-centric, assuming that you dedicate full support to each segment. Organizing by product means that you can track sales by product, but you don't really know who's buying.

Dell has enforced the idea of customer segmentation throughout its organization—not only in sales, support, and service, but also in finance and manufacturing. In many ways, each segment has become a separate business unit. Segmentation is fed by Dell's direct connection with its customers. Organizing by customer type rather than product lets Dell refine that relationship. Segmenting by business unit allows Dell to monitor the growth rates, profitability, service level performance, and market share of each segment (discussed in Chapter 6).

Segmenting business units in terms of function, not form, partially explains why Dell can grow while balancing centralization and decentralization. More on that is coming up in Chapter 9.

There's another important aspect of this fully implemented customer segmentation: It spreads throughout the corporation the idea of tuning in to the customer, even to the extent of rivalry between segmented business units. This avoids giving mere lip service to the idea of serving the customer; by spreading the connection with the customer throughout the company, Dell manages to keep that link alive.

I worked for a while in one of Dell's competing PC manufacturers (no longer extant, by the way; the PC section died about 10 years after I left), and everything was strictly stratified by product. The emphasis was on the machines, and the corporation was stratified by product lines. That way of thinking distances the customer in a sort of us/them relationship. Organizing by customer type, while not a panacea, would have definitely helped, focusing otherwise-wasted energy toward meeting customer requirements.

Build-to-Order

Another aspect of Dell's customer focus is its build-to-order philosophy. Every Dell PC has been built this way, unlike many other companies who build for sales forecasts. Dell builds its PCs using a process called *cell manufacturing*, in which one group of people is responsible for building a PC (other cells are responsible for putting the necessary parts into a plastic bin, and another cell packs the finished machine). Among other things, cell manufacturing allows you to build to order in an efficient way.

News.com[11] quotes Tony Amico, an analyst from International Data Corporation, on this: "'To offer build-to-order systems, companies must have cell manufacturing.' Amico says—teams of workers who build each PC from start to finish, rather than a typical assembly line production.

"'If you don't have cell manufacturing, don't do it,' Amico advised, citing NEC's ill-fated NECNow direct sales effort as an example."

Building to order using cells allows Dell to stay in touch with customers and supports their "have it your way" philosophy. Customization is no problem, because that's the way things are done naturally. When you build for sales forecasts, customization becomes an issue, because it's an add-on.

Cell manufacturing also gives customers what Dell calls a single point of accountability. The idea is that one person builds your PC and, if something goes wrong, one person can be asked about it—it gives customers a feeling that someone will be accountable. This same person updates a system's status as it's being built, so that the customer can watch what's going on.

I once purchased a souped-up Dimension PC from Dell that had all kinds of powerhouse extras, including far more memory than was standard. I wanted to ask a few questions about the cache memory and system tests. Sure enough, the salesman I had been dealing with was able to contact the exact person who had put the machine together and get answers—and that all happened after the sale. Although not many customers are going to inquire to this depth, some will, and knowing that you can get answers—that one person is accountable for the hardware— gives you a remarkable feeling of dealing with real people, not some giant corporation who's going to stonewall you in the same way that you've been stonewalled dozens of times before. And it makes for repeat customers.

The "single point of accountability" is a by-word in Dell, and you come across it in many places besides manufacturing. The idea is a customer-oriented one, and it works the same as in manufacturing. Rather than giving the customer the runaround, you give him the straight goods, and you handle the problem.

That's the idea, anyway; your mileage may vary.

Treat Big Customers Nicely

Dell sells plenty of computers to plenty of different types of customers. But, from a business point of view, not all customers are created equal. Realistically speaking, a customer that buys 500,000 PCs is going to be treated differently from a customer that buys one PC every four years.

Internally, Dell refers to its largest accounts as *gold* or *platinum*. A gold account has annual Dell sales of $5 to $10 million; a platinum account has Dell sales of over $10 million annually. Dell's gold and platinum accounts get a different level of service than do other levels of accounts.

The gripe boards don't like to think that's inevitable, but it is. Expecting Dell to treat you personally the same way as it treats Boeing doesn't make much sense. That's not an excuse for poor service, but it is a reason for a different kind of service.

Dell doesn't just go after growth for growth's sake, but goes after what it calls "profitable growth." So, it stresses entry-level PCs far less than items like servers (although note that its margin in lower-level PCs is still far higher than its competitors), which means stressing enterprise customers.

EnterpriseInnovator.com[12] quotes Kevin Rollins on this while discussing China: "In China, Rollins said Dell's strategy remains 'pretty clear' and that is 'to focus on the enterprise,' which means the server, storage, and services opportunity. He added that the 'whole printing and imaging arena' can be seen as a 'strategic pinch-point or opportunity for us to go after new opportunities there.' But there still remains a 'very large desktop and notebook business' there and Dell continues to 'sell a lot of consumer products—but our strategic priority is going after the enterprise.' That's where Dell sees a 'lot of our competitors are still having challenges in that space' and Rollins believes this is 'going to be the case for the next several years' in the enterprise arena, 'particularly the server and storage arena where we have low market share' and which presents Dell with a 'great opportunity,' due to its high margins."

Going after enterprises is Dell's method of cracking new markets, like China. From the same article: "Rollins also explained that Dell is following the same trajectory of market penetration in China as it does in other markets around the world—targeting multinationals with a local presence for market entry since 'we have to get off the ground' and knows those players, then targeting SMBs [small- to mid-size businesses], and after that the government and public sector. This is the 'same as every country in the world we moved into.' The 'profitability looks great, but share is still down' at first, but in time, 'scale is going to advantage us and we're going to have good profitability compared to any market in the world—and far superior profitability' than rivals."

Dell has a relational connection with its bigger customers and a transactional one with its smaller customers: Its connection with its larger customers is ongoing, whereas the connection with the smaller customer is item-by-item.

Treating customers by size makes sense, as long as you don't neglect the smaller customers by doing so. Remember: Small customers may be small separately, but in aggregate, they can be a large part of business. At Dell, small customers interact with Dell in two ways: over the phone, and on the Internet.

Big customers interact with Dell in three ways: over the phone, on the Internet, and face-to-face. If you're a big customer contemplating a big order, Dell will send someone out to see you. As a matter of fact, it will send a whole team. And, if you've got thousands and thousands of Dell PCs in your company, Dell will spend time making sure you're happy. You can also buy various levels of large corporation support. Dell will not only support your machines, but will give you an on-site presence if you want it, as it does with its 30 full-time, on-site personnel at Boeing.

One day in the late 1980s, Michael Dell was touring one of Dell's major U.K. customers, British Petroleum (BP). He saw that an entire floor of the BP building in London (read: very expensive real estate) was being used to customize PCs with company-specific software and other company-specific items like network interface cards (NICs). BP's IT guy turned to Dell and asked him if he could do all this stuff for him.

It was an epiphany, and the foundation of the DellPlus program. Michael Dell agreed that Dell could do the work much faster and much cheaper. Dell already loaded all kinds of software on the machines it sold to BP, just not BP's own software. And Dell already customized each machine's hardware, just not with BP's own hardware.

So, Dell agreed to take the parts and software from BP and install them at the plant, saving BP an entire floor of its headquarters. This change, please note, was not free for BP, but still represented a significant discount over its then present cost.

Dell offers the DellPlus program for its larger customers today, and many take advantage of it—who wouldn't, given the advantages? Dell will install your software and hardware at the plant, and test both, for a reasonable fee—saving you both time and money. When you get your machine out of the box, it'll be ready to hit the desk.

The Enterprise Command Center

As of November 2003, another innovation that Dell brings to its enterprise customers in the United States, Canada, China, Japan, Europe, and Latin America is its Enterprise Command Center or ECC (cool name, huh?), which provides 24/7 support for storage and servers. The original idea was that servers, and often storage systems, can be mission-critical for larger customers, and these customers could purchase contracts that give them access to the ECC. Since then, the ECC has been broadened to include client PCs and other Dell solutions as well.

The center is a 2,600-square-foot installation that's always staffed. If you have a Dell 2- or 4-hour response contract, you have access to the personnel here. And, if you permit it, Dell has access to diagnostics on your machine as well. As the TBR report quotes Jan Uhrich, Dell's vice president of Americas Enterprise Support Services as saying, "Customers tell us that they do not want any surprises. The ultimate measure of success in customer service is for us to mitigate risk or service failures before the customer even knows or, better yet, feels the impact."

Michael Kanellos, editor-at-large at CNET News.com says, "The center looks like something out of a Cold War movie. It's a big dark room with a map of the world on it and a bunch of people with headsets sitting at desks. They monitor little lights on the world map to make sure no emergencies are flaring."

The center handles issues by assigning them a red or green value, and nothing moves from the first phase to the second until all issues are green (by default, all aspects of a new issue are set to red). Much of the diagnostics are now automated and, if there's an issue, Dell lets the customers know and tries to walk them through what's going on. The current critical issues are displayed in the command center using a projector and, if there's a serious issue whose resolution is sticky, staff can retire to the center's boardroom for meetings.

In addition to remote support, Dell often maintains staff on-site for its larger customers, and this staff monitors the machines as well, classifying and tracking all issues. They have direct access to the center when issues arise.

Besides contact with the customer, on-site staff, and the machine itself, the ECC also determines how far away replacement parts are from you and can give you an ETA of parts and techs. The center also has real-time access to software manufacturers like Microsoft and Oracle, something Dell's standard customers can only fantasize about. In fact, the center can also track what's going on by region, watching power outages and other regional problems and keeping customers apprised.

As you'd expect at Dell, the most important information is made central and a perpetual watch is kept on the "time-to-resolve" clock. That metric is tied to performance incentives for employees. And that kind of metric is not just in name only; during a hurricane, Dell will actually move parts between depots to get them out of the storm's path.

Platinum Councils

One way that Dell keeps in touch with its largest customers is through *Platinum Councils*. These are meetings for its large customers in regions around the world, such as Asia-Pacific, the United States, Europe, Japan, and so on.

Traditionally, Michael Dell has spent 3 days at each such council, and presumably he does a lot of talking to CIOs. Dell technologists map out Dell's product plans for the next few years, and most senior Dell executives participate in one way or another. The customers get to ask a lot of tough questions—what about XP's Service Pack 2? What about such-and-such a virus?

The idea is that, theoretically, the customers set the agenda as much as possible. There's at least one Dell person at each council for each customer.

Because these councils have become so popular, Dell has extended similar conferences to other entities, like universities (read: tax-free corporations). Some universities buy substantial numbers of Dell machines and servers, so their CIOs are invited to these similar conferences.

Using the Internet

The Internet is always a major tool that Dell uses to keep in touch with its customers, and that goes for its larger customers as well. Those customers can also order online, just as anyone else can. Originally, larger customers were loathe to place orders for thousands of PCs without a face-to-face, but evidence shows they've been getting used to it.

Larger customers get a special secure site, www.premierdell.com, to work with. Each customer gets a set of "premier pages" that act as a virtual site and that they can customize themselves. Premier pages were first offered in 1997, and they've been successful—by late 2000, more than 50,000 Dell premier sites existed.

In general, Dell has had more success with the Internet than other companies, partly because Dell has emphasized the Internet so much over the years that customers are getting used to it, especially to check configuration alternatives.

An amazing fraction of dell.com site visits end up in calls—5 percent, according to Dell. Those calls are semi-trackable back to www.dell.com, because Dell lists a different 800 number (1.800.www.dell) on its web site than in other advertising materials. And about 0.5 percent of site visits end in sales, a huge proportion for any Internet site.

Thanks to the Internet, Dell's salespeople are indeed channeled more qualified leads; the estimates are that the sales staff is about 50 percent more effective in terms of landing sales than in other industries.

It should also be noted that Dell does extremely well with its direct-mail four-color brochures, 10 percent of which result in calls and 2 percent of which result in sales.

Dell's Lead Is Narrowing

Dell's customer satisfaction is moving downward, and that presents a problem for Dell. An article in eWeek.com[13] states: "When it comes to computers, good service is getting harder to define. Dell Inc. and Hewlett-Packard Co. were neck-and-neck in customer satisfaction during the first quarter, shows a new study by TBR (Technology Business Research Inc.), of Hampton, N.H.

"The survey…polled 648 IT managers at 422 companies in North America on their satisfaction with service and support provided by the three largest computer companies—Dell, HP and IBM—as well as by in-house groups.

"The resulting report, which measures services ranging from telephone support to parts availability as well as respondents' overall satisfaction, paints a picture of how those responsible for purchasing the support services from Dell, HP, and IBM feel about what they're getting. These days, they seem to be having a harder time telling the big three apart."

As to the actual scores: "Dell stayed nearly the same in the first quarter, with a score of 82.1 out of 100 possible points. HP scored an 81.7. Because their scores are within 1 percent of each other—TBR considers a difference of 1 percent or greater or a change in score of 1 percent or more to be meaningful—the two remained tied for second place behind in-house support.

"IBM Global Services, meanwhile, came in with a rating of 79.6. As is most often the case, companies' in-house support scored the highest of all, at 85.3 out of 100. As in-house support represents an ideal, TBR uses it as a benchmark."

At issue is that Dell's support no longer seemed to truly stand out. As the article says, "But still, the difference between the big three, as perceived by survey participants, remains fairly small, said Julie Perron, manager of primary research at TBR."

Interestingly, Dell may have been trumped in service because of the very success of its use of third-party on-site techs.

The Commoditization of Service

The problem is that, now, everyone is using the same on-site third-party techs. Discussing the similar scores, eWeek says, "One reason is because certain areas of service and support, such as fixing broken hardware on-site, have become commoditized. At times, the big three all use the same field-service techs to execute repairs. The report, as a result, shows little difference in satisfaction with the three companies' break/fix services."

So, how do you differentiate yourself from the competition if they use the same techs? One obvious way of doing that is price, and Dell is the winner there, so far. But according to *eWeek*, "HP and IBM have responded with new pricing to try to compete with Dell as of late. But there is a 'continuing lack of services differentiation,' Perron said. 'Price is the main differentiator [among the three]—and even that isn't always evident.'"

So, Dell's competitors are hot on Dell's trail in terms of both pricing and the use of the same third-party techs. What can Dell do to differentiate itself from the pack? Recently, Dell has been bringing more experienced techs into the field—and those techs, assigned to the bigger, more complex jobs, are company-employed, not third-party. Dell is also pushing predictability; Dell gives you time and cost estimates for service that are fairly exact; the contracts aren't open-ended, which removes some of the fear factor.

One problem for Dell, and an area for improvement discussed in Chapter 2, has been customer dissatisfaction with telephone support, which is an area it can still improve in. The *eWeek* article notes that, "Phone support was a major factor in a 2004 support ratings slip by Dell. The Round Rock, Texas, company, saw its satisfaction ratings dip dramatically enough to cost it the lead rating to HP for the first time since the study began in 2000." Although HP took over the lead only temporarily, things are now pretty close to neck and neck.

Phone support is an area in which Dell can improve. But there's another area in which you might start looking for new happenings at Dell—automated support tools.

The Move to Automated Tools

If Dell stays true to its established patterns, one area that might see significantly more activity in the coming years is the increased use of automated diagnostic software to handle problems using minimal service personnel connection.

HP has already started making an initiative here, according to the eWeek article, which says, "HP, for its part, has been expanding the use of automated diagnostic software, according to TBR." The article continues later: "The change, which will work to reduce the number of site visits HP has to make, ultimately could lead to satisfaction gains, Perron said."

HP's rating declined somewhat recently, and that may be because of growing pains as it makes the switch to automated support. But the *eWeek* article quotes TBR's Julie Perron as saying, "it may just be that customers are getting used to [automated diagnostics] or they're starting to implement it."

In other words, why not let the computer tell you what's wrong with it and try to fix itself? Not only can the machine perform diagnostics and attempt repairs, but it can also download drivers and patches from Dell directly.

In fact, signs suggest that this is already happening at Dell. When you start a recently ordered Dell PC, you see a Dell Support icon; double-clicking it opens a window where you can access a Solutions tab ("Access customer care articles, technical articles, support information, and tutorials to help answer your questions.") or a Reference tab ("Find detailed system information, user's guides, tutorials and documentation specific to your computer.")

More tellingly, recently Dell rewrote its Support Alerts software (which displays an icon in a PC's system tray) to create Dell Support 3, and automatically downloaded that new version to Dell machines June 1, 2005. This new package describes itself in this way: "Dell Support 3 conducts real-time scans of your computing environment (PC, peripherals, and network devices) for potential technical support and security issues, sends an alert when an issue arises, offering advice and in many cases the option to choose to run an automated fix."

BusinessWeek, in an October 2005 article, notes, "In November the company will launch a slate of new offerings, including remote assistance so technicians can take control of the customer's PC to fix problems. And, early next year, Dell will introduce a series of one-year memberships so customers can opt for various levels of help, at various prices. One of the options will likely include a quarterly PC tune-up, in which a techie would remotely clean up the hard drive and check security settings."

It's a safe bet to assume that there's a lot of work going on inside Dell with these kinds of tools, and that you're going to see more and more of such tools come pre-loaded on Dell machines. These tools are not a panacea by any means: If the machine doesn't boot or the screen is black, they're not going to be of much use—but they could prove decisive in the battle for customer satisfaction. At least until the next round.

Chapter 4

Celebrate Standardization

⟨∞⟩

*Dell has thrived as downward-spiraling prices and commodification
washed over the company's customers and bashing its competitors.*
                                        —*Fortune* magazine[1]

This chapter is all about one of the top reasons that Dell has thrived while others have died—Dell's love of standards-based technology. Dell's original inspiration was to go direct, but that only got it off the ground. Dell has made crucial innovations in its business model as it has grown; these successive innovations have made it prosper—not its adherence to a single, rigid idea. These crucial innovations have happened five or so times during Dell's life, and its celebration of standards-based technology as a point of market entry is one of those crucial points.

This love of standards-based technology is an idea that Dell applies over and over again to its markets, and which allows Dell to take those markets over. Dell watches tech trends carefully to determine where strong interest exists. In those sectors showing strong growth, typically a few players are doing very well, as in the early days of the PC market, and more recently with servers, for example. Big profits are being made, and that attracts Dell's interest.

Typically, the products in that new market are made using proprietary architecture, and each manufacturer creates its own chips for its own machines. That's the early stages of a lucrative industry that Dell loves to see: Customers have no choice but to buy from the proprietary manufacturers, who are charging gouging prices. Yet, demand is still high, and the product is selling well.

This market sector is ripe for the Dell Effect.

In time, standards are established, and secondary vendors come out with competing machines. These competing machines are also built using proprietary silicon, and they start to give the new-technology pioneer a run for its money. If that technology is robust enough, and in demand enough, the market can support other innovators, and chip manufacturers get into the act. That's when standardized chips enter the market, provided by manufacturers that specialize in creating new chips. The technology shifts from proprietary chips made by various vendors to easily acquired standard chips. In time, competition drives the price of those chips down, when compared to the proprietary architecture of the big players.

At this point, the technology—be it a PC, a cell phone, or a printer—has become standardized. But it's not yet at the point of becoming a cheap commodity. The technology has been tested, found reliable, and can be supported with standard components. Yet those components—the internal electronics—are not yet in widespread use; they're becoming available, but they're not yet a serious threat to the main pioneers in the new field.

That's when Dell swoops in, building machines using less-expensive, off-the-shelf, standardized parts instead of developing its own far more expensive proprietary technology. It uses those components, driving them to the edge of their capability, to create standardized machines that typically perform at least a little better than those offered by the pioneers in the field. That leaves Dell paying far less for its development manufacturing costs and selling machines based on proven, reliable parts.

Dell likes to refer to this as using "standards-based technology." The idea is that after a promising industry sector becomes standardized (but before it becomes commoditized), Dell jumps in. For a long time, PCs were only made by IBM. Then other vendors appeared, and competition appeared. For many years, the market was healthy; the components used in PCs were standardized, and Dell used standardized parts to build products and pull the rug out from under its competitors.

That's what competitors refer to as the Dell Effect. Once again, Dell teaches an entire sector what business is all about. It's not out there on the bleeding-edge of tech, because its main focus isn't technology, but business and profitable growth. When a sector it likes gets fat, and when the products become standardized, Dell is in there before the current players know what's going on.

An article in *ZD Net UK*[2] quotes Michael Dell as saying: "I think, as we look across the $800 billion IT market, we see a maturation of the industry which is driving standards much more rapidly into many sectors of the industry, which is putting pressure on the proprietary business model. And Dell's really the only large-scale computer systems company that completely bases its business around standards. Now, we think that provides us enormous opportunity in many fields."

After the Dell Direct model, this was Dell's next major insight: waiting until a new and promising sector became standardized and then moving in.

Where Did All This Come From?

Where did the inspiration for this come from? It's easy enough to conjecture. In its early days, Dell was an upstart, without access to the research labs that the big players such as IBM or Intel had. It just didn't have the money to build its own silicon.

That also meant Dell couldn't buy proprietary chips from the big players—IBM and others weren't about to sell their chips wholesale to some upstart competitor. There wasn't any profit in that.

So, Dell was locked out of profitable sectors and could only watch the players making big profits. No way through that door existed until the technology got so popular that third-party vendors started emulating it, and the picture was standardized enough to make using third-party chips possible. Dell had an entrance into sectors it had been locked out of, and it jumped in with a vengeance.

This is verified by Michael Dell himself, who has said[3]: "As the industry grew, however, more specialized companies developed to produce specific components. As a small start-up, we didn't have the money to build the components ourselves. But we also asked, 'Why should we want to?' Unlike many of our competitors, we actually had an option: to buy components from the specialists, leveraging the investments they had already made and allowing us to focus on what we did best—designing and delivering solutions and systems directly to customers."

The funny thing was, it worked. In the long run, it worked better for Dell than for the original pioneers in those sectors that Dell invaded. The bigger players were saddled with R&D costs that Dell didn't have. The standardized parts were cheaper than the proprietary versions. And, as competition arose between parts vendors, the price of those standardized parts went down even more. Eventually, players who use standardized parts have a way of taking over tech fields and wresting control from those who stick with proprietary parts, something that it took the big players, such as IBM, many years to learn.

Since jumping in after standardization not only worked, but worked better than being a pioneer, it's easy to see how that configured Dell's stance in the industry. Why go in for deep-dish R&D when you could rely on others to do it? Why spend billions on proprietary silicon that would become standardized after a while, and the standard version would win anyway? The answers to these questions influenced the Dell stance on tech R&D ever since.

> It's interesting to note that Dell has become so large that it's direct-ing the tech market whether it wants to or not. Simply by purchasing in high volume, or pushing Intel into 64-bit chips faster, Dell influences what's going on. When Dell talks, tech companies like Microsoft, Intel, and Samsung listen.

Using Standards-Based Technology

Dell is the champion of standards-based technology, and that's given it the edge in sector after sector. It's a lesson that's not peculiar to technol-ogy, but can be applied across the business base: Pioneers do fine for a while, but they're in danger of being undercut as standardization takes over, and they can be significantly undersold.

From *CFO.com*[4]: "'Dell likes to wait until the components that go into a product are standardized and available from a number of suppliers at competitive prices,' explains Richard Gardner, a securities analyst and managing director at the San Francisco office of Smith Barney. 'Then it enters the field with the same kind of manufacturing and fulfillment expertise that it brought to PCs.'"

In fact, Dell has made occasional forays into high-tech pioneering and gotten its fingers burnt at times, which undoubtedly reaffirms its orig-inal stance on waiting for standardization. Early in its life, Dell developed a leading-edge machine it called the Olympic, using standardized chips. This was to be a tech wonder, a "boil the ocean" product that spanned the desktop, workstation, and server markets. But customers weren't interested. The prototypes of the Olympic, shown at Comdex in 1989, didn't really meet customers' needs.

In 2000, Michael Dell[5] says: "We knew that technologically, this prod-uct line made sense. There were ideas within it that made for great inven-tions, like the graphics and disk technology that were later incorporated into highly successful products; that, however, just wasn't enough. We weren't then—and we certainly aren't now—in the business of convincing people to buy something they didn't want, so we canceled Olympic before it ever saw the light of day, and admitted we made a mistake. We had gone ahead and created a product that was, for all intents and purposes, technology for technology's sake, rather than technology for the customer's sake."

Dell Computer was left to recoup its expenditures on this costly mistake. And it learned a lesson: Don't bleed to lead. Michael Dell summed up the Olympic failure[6]: "What we didn't realize was that bleeding edge technology was the last thing we needed." With a few aberrations here and there, it's a lesson Dell Inc. has never forgotten.

Creating Standards-Based PCs

Dell began its love affair with standards-based technology with PCs. In this arena, Dell learned when to step into markets and how to take them over as market sectors moved from innovation to standardization.

As *Forbes* magazine says[7]: "The continued strength in sales of no-name computers is further proof that PCs, largely, are indistinguishable from one another. Computer companies that have spent extra dollars on doing something technologically unique with PCs wind up regretting it. It adds extra costs to a system that won't be recouped, because customers in large part don't want to pay for it. Case in point: many of Dell's patents have nothing to do with technology per se, but with the process of efficient fulfillment. It is this that makes Dell such a fearsome competitor."

The emphasis on standards-based technology has continued since not long after Dell was founded in 1984, and Dell PCs have been crammed with standard components ever since. That applies not just to CPUs, of course, but to video controllers, disk drives, keyboard interfaces, and so on. Dell often is able to drive those standard components better and faster than others, as with the 12 MHz (6 MHz in the lab) 80286 CPU in 1986, so it often still captures the performance edge. But that's using standard components for the most part. The big benefit? Keeping the price low.

Jumping in between standardization and commoditization is not something Dell does only with PCs; it pervades all their technology.

Creating Standards-Based Servers, Too

Dell has brought its standards-based philosophy to servers, too. Ever since its entry into the server market, Dell has stressed standard components, often in multiple grid or stack configurations, to beat the established players in this market. The mantra has become familiar to those in the server market: You can buy a dedicated (and proprietary) power machine from vendor X for $5,000,000 or a stack of 64-blade server modules for a total of one tenth the price. Which would you pick?

Although Dell has done some technological innovation, including packing blade servers tighter so that you can fit more into a rack, the story here is also mostly one of standards-based manufacturing. Summit Strategies says in its 2005 Dynamic Computing Industry Report Card: Systems Vendors[8]: "Dell, meanwhile, has a comparatively narrow, generally technologically 'me-too' line of 1- to 4-way x86 servers. However, it delivers exactly what its rapidly growing customer base wants, and is now preparing for new generations of technology (multicore processors, clusters, grid, etc.) and implementations (distributed, grid-based, and scale-out) to bring the rest of the industry into Dell's own market sweet spot."

An article from techweb.com[9] says: "The commoditization of IT equipment will accelerate in the years ahead with many companies that generate much of their revenue from proprietary products facing an uncertain future as customers opt for similarly efficient but less expensive technologies, according to Michael Dell, chairman and chief executive of Dell Inc.

"Dell, whose $40 billion company has snatched market share from rivals in the PC sector by leveraging its vaunted manufacturing and supply-chain efficiencies to lower prices—a strategy Dell has now trained on the server market—said he foresees stronger demand for IT equipment in 2004."

As servers got more popular, their components became more standard. Dell Inc. is now heavily involved in all server tiers: presentation, application, and database. Michael Kanellos, Editor at Large of CNET News.Com also notes, "Dell also was really aggressive in selling servers. For a while, if you bought 100 PCs, you'd get a complimentary server. It seeded the brand."

Creating Standards-Based TVs

In the last few years, Dell has gotten into the field of flat-screen TVs, basing its entrance on it expertise and supply-chain advantages with flat-screen PC and notebook monitors (there's not much difference between a flat-screen TV and a flat-screen monitor). And it's bringing the same strategy to this field.

BusinessWeek Asia[10] tells us, in an article titled "Your Next TV" that "It will be flat, ultra high-tech, and made in Asia. Now, Americans want a piece of the action.

"Every day, across Asia, thousands of liquid-crystal and plasma displays roll out of factories owned by Samsung, Matsushita (MC), Sharp (SHCAY), Pioneer (PIO), LG, and five Taiwanese companies. These are among the world's top suppliers of the elegant thin televisions that are now streaming into homes everywhere. The Asians have committed $35 billion in flat-panel capacity in 2004 and 2005. And as the TV manufacturers place their bets, legions of suppliers of glass, semiconductors, and other components are revving up their own production lines.

"The surge in investment and proliferation of suppliers have driven panel prices down to levels unthinkable even two or three years ago. That has opened the door to a set of competitors the Asians never expected to face: Dell Inc. (DELL), Hewlett-Packard Co. (HPQ), and others in North America. They are making a concerted push in flat TVs, sourcing the panels from Asia and using the same global supply-chain wizardry they have employed so effectively in PCs, printers, and other products."

Pursuing More Standards-Based Technology

It's part of Dell's strategy to keep branching out in many fields, for reasons discussed at the end of this chapter. *USA Today*[11] notes that Dell is using the same standards-based techniques as it branches out: "For most of Dell's existence, Dell has applied that capability [of entering a market after standardization and before commoditization] to PCs, moving up the chain into higher-priced laptops, workstations and, lately, servers. Now Dell is increasingly moving beyond computers, like when Wal-Mart moved beyond its traditional base of rural stores and applied its model to urban areas. Over the past couple of years, Dell has thrown new kinds of products in the hopper: switches, network storage machines, handheld computers and, most recently, printers. [And] Dell said it will build electronic cash registers for retailers."

According to *BusinessWeek Asia,*[12] this philosophy even applies as Dell enters the services market: "For the past two decades, Dell's hyper-efficient ways have forced its hardware rivals to sacrifice profits or surrender market share—and often both—to compete with the Round Rock (Texas) company. Now, Dell is looking to commoditize parts of the services business in the same way it did hardware. It's aggressively expanding in basic phone support and repair services, and it's promoting a range of newer offerings, from helping businesses load software on employees' machines to helping them recycle and replace old models. It's mundane stuff compared to the big-think consulting provided by IBM (IBM), Electronic Data Systems Corp. (EDS), and others. But if Dell has its typical impact, it could put a sizeable crack in one of the most reliable profit centers of its rivals. 'You have to take Dell seriously,' says Stan Schatt, senior research director at research firm Current Analysis."

Dell knows what it's doing, and it knows when to jump. Because so much of its business model is based on exploiting promising new market sectors, it watches the market and does its research. As *USA Today*[13] put it: "Some of Dell's soul is obvious—namely the much-publicized manufacturing process that allows Dell to hold virtually no inventory of parts and make computers more quickly and cheaply than any other company.

"But a part of Dell's soul is often overlooked. It's the company's ability to know when to enter a new market so it can ride it like a surfer on a perfect wave."

Know What's Going On and When to Jump

Dell is a sharp organization: Even though it has the resources to jump into any market it wants to, it is careful and insightful about picking its battles. And when it jumps, the sector it jumps into suffers the Dell Effect. It's safe to assume that Dell has market analysts watching not only tech markets but other sectors as well, and that plenty of other competitors are going to get an education in the Dell Effect.

The *USA Today* article continues by saying that the key is "Dell's ability to re-apply its superefficient model to the right products at the right time. 'We have to keep throwing stuff in the hopper at the top,' Rollins says. But that's tricky.

"As Michael Dell explains it, Dell operates on a belief that all technologies follow a similar pattern. Soon after a technology product comes to market, it is a high-priced, high-margin item made differently by each company.

"Over time, the technology standardizes, the way PCs standardized around Intel chips and Microsoft operating systems. Then parts makers blossom, manufacturing costs drop and the technology starts becoming a commodity.

"Dell monitors those patterns. At a certain point between standardization and commoditization, a technology is ripe for Dell. The incumbents are making 40 percent or 50 percent profit margins and are vulnerable to Dell storming in and making a profit on far slimmer margins. Yet there's still plenty of room for Dell to drive out costs by perfecting man-ufacturing and using its buying power to get cheaper parts.

"'Our business model excels in that transition [between standardiza-tion and commoditization],' Rollins says."

Dell is famous for doing its research into the patterns of tech growth. In an article in chiefexecutive.net[14] interviewing Michael Dell, note how candid Dell is about the standardization move as part of Dell's "magic formula": "The magic formula in our business is figuring out what stage of the evolution a given technology is at and when it's right for Dell to use its business model and customer relationships to make a product that is much higher in volume and lower in cost. Some would call it commoditization or standardization, but we constantly look at our busi-ness and say, 'Well, where are these new technologies on the continu-um? And when is it the right time for us to start a new activity? When is the right time to go after a new type of customer, a new geography? Should we be focusing more on large businesses vs. small businesses vs. consumers? What about services? What about professional services or financial services?' We have many more choices than we could ever exe-cute on. We're not constrained by capital. We're constrained by, 'How many of these things can you actually achieve with a high degree of suc-cess and profit?'"

In the mid-1990s, the PC industry was entranced with the idea of "network computers," also called NCs. Many believed the NC a revolu-tionary idea. At root, it were a stripped-down PC without storage—no hard drive. All software and user data was intended to stay on a central server; in other words, the NC was essentially a front-end for that server.

The NC appeared with a lot of hype at Comdex 1997, and blipped onto Dell's radar screen. The hype was that the NC, as a very cheap front-end, was going to bring about the demise of the PC. Doing its research, Dell looked into the NC concept and decided that it wasn't fundamental-ly different from the basic idea of terminals connected to a central serv-er; an idea that had been around for two decades at that point. Michael Dell doubted that the NC would ever amount to much; the advantages of a distributed computer and its fast response time were just too great. He came to the conclusion that there was nothing but hype behind the NC.

But a demand for NCs still existed, and Dell couldn't understand why. Customers, particularly business customers, were asking for NCs. What was going on?

So, to probe the issue, Dell turned to its major customers. It found the answer—the autonomous PCs that everyone was using had gotten a little too autonomous. People were messing up their machines, and that demanded site visits all over corporate installations. The massive number of software updates that everyone reluctantly takes for granted today were just starting to appear.

In other words, the problem was one of PC management. Corporations wanted to handle software updates in one centralized location as much as possible, and they also wanted to handle other client software issues, such as Windows problems, in as centralized a way as possible. The NC centralized all that troubleshooting by putting everything on a central machine, while sucking all the power out of the client machines.

Dell was smart about this. It realized that the primary issue for their corporate customers was not the nature of PCs as client machines per se, but their decentralization. To manage those PCs was the real goal, and the marketplace wasn't offering anything at that time besides NCs, which corporate customers were attracted to. Dell's answer was to introduce the *managed PC*. Managed PCs gave users the flexibility and power of a PC, but with a connection to remote support services. These networked PCs let network administrators remotely configure software, patches, and even hardware. And that addressed the real issue in the market.

Today, you don't see NCs around. But you do see managed PCs in nearly every corporation. What corporate user isn't familiar with the dialog boxes that appear regularly (sometimes a little too regularly) explaining that their machine needs to be updated and that the updating would begin as soon as they clicked the OK button? All that can be managed remotely now, a far cry from the days when you continually saw a tech person working from cubicle to cubicle, clutching a set of diskettes or a CD.

Introducing managed PCs was a triumph for Dell, and another case study in how maintaining close customer ties gives it a big leg up. As software updates became almost a weekly experience, it was harder and harder to get away from the need for managed PCs. Dell recognized the need for them very early on. Adieu, NCs.

Dell versus Proprietary Standards

Dell has become known in the industry as an iconoclast when it comes to proprietary standards of any sort. That's hardly surprising, given the way its business model celebrates standardization.

Michael Dell has said,[15] "Promoting industry standards—rather than inventing new proprietary technologies to solve customer needs—has really worked well for us and our suppliers, and has made the market more efficient."

An article in enterpriseinnovator.com quotes Michael Dell as saying[16]: "'We don't invest in stuff that's beneficial just to us that doesn't help our customers,' noting that a lot of innovation is disguised as something good for the customer that is actually good for the manufacturer. As an example, he recalled the early generation of digital camera, which had all sorts of proprietary ports, leading customers to demand a USB port, which 'the camera manufacturers initially resisted,' and 'those aren't the kind of things that benefit the user.' He said all too often, 'there are times you'll pay much more for something because it's available from only one company—that's not innovation.'"

The following is from a *Fortune* magazine[17] interview with Dell's Senior VP of Products and head of R&D Jeff Clarke: "Clarke argues that Dell's R&D effort is focused solely on open-standards-based computing (read Wintel), while the competition spends much of its R&D resources on proprietary systems that often don't cut it in the marketplace."

And, from Kevin Kettler, Dell's Chief Technology Officer, being interviewed in *ComputerWorld*,[18] after being asked where he sees technology moving in the next 3 years: "One of the key shifts that is occurring is that with the addition of blades and the need to manage blades, it's produced a razor focus at Dell around the systems management infrastructure and how do we move from a systems management infrastructure that has traditionally been very proprietary, very monolithic in nature to something that is going to provide greater flexibility to manage....

"What I've described has been a desire for customers, but the industry hasn't been rallied around it. That's the key thing that's happening right now. We're doing a lot of work getting people excited about plugging into an open infrastructure like that, and that's going to lead to a ton of innovation. Ultimately, if we do our job well, customers will benefit."

One way that Dell's competitors have tried to fight back is through the continual reintroduction of proprietary standards. HP has tried to go proprietary with its internal architecture, as has IBM. IBM's big move to reintroduce proprietary standards in the PC market was the PS/2 and OS/2 combo, which was a failure. However, reintroducing proprietary standards never works in those markets that Dell is involved in, or never works for long. If a significant market exists for a new technology, it'll be copied and improved upon by competitors.

At this point, the market is too firmly in the hands of standards-based companies like Dell in any case. Customers have become too savvy on price to get themselves into a situation where there's only one option, because they know that, without competition, they're going to pay stiff prices.

From Summit Strategies' 2005 Dynamic Computing Industry Report Card: Systems Vendors[19]: "Although Dell has made somewhat slower progress at the high end of its product line (as in four-way and blade servers), the industry and the market are indeed—as Dell has always claimed they would—migrating toward Dell's approach of using ever more tightly linked clusters of continually higher-performance, industry-standard servers and operating environments to perform jobs that were traditionally reserved to large-scale SMP boxes running 'proprietary' versions of UNIX."

It's true that standards-based marketing has helped cut prices for customers. Dell's entry into a market makes sure that's going to happen; Dell estimates that its entry into the server market made its competitors cut their prices by about 17 percent, for example.

Dell Inc. is aware of what it does to competitors with its standards-based marketing. An article[20] at techweb.com talking about Michael Dell says: "Dell said although many corporations, especially small- and medium-size companies, are finally spending more on IT equipment, they are often opting for hardware not based on proprietary technologies. The tactic is gutting revenues at some vendors, Dell said."

"Gutting revenues at some vendors" sounds like the Dell Effect at work. There's no question it's helped customers' wallets. But what has all this done to innovation in the tech industry? Has innovation become a luxury that tech companies who compete with Dell can no longer afford?

Dell and Innovation

In an interview[21] at enterpriseinnovator.com, "Michael Dell said he believed that 'Innovation comes in many forms,' and at Dell, the key ingredient to innovation was that it 'provide value to customers.' He explained, 'At Dell, if you do something that saves a customer money, you're an innovator,' but 'if you invent something that doesn't save somebody money, we don't care.'"

An Image Issue?

The fact that Dell follows innovators and undercuts them in terms of price has been a sore spot in the media's relations with Dell Inc. As *Fortune* magazine puts it in an article on Dell[22]: "Dell also spends less on research and development than HP, IBM, and the others, a point that makes the folks at Dell a little prickly and defensive."

According to *Fortune*, Dell spends less than $500 million on R&D, which is less than 1 percent of sales. On the other hand, HP and IBM spend about 6 percent. The media has picked up on this; from an article in cfo.com[23]: "Dell is innovative as far as its processes go, but not necessarily with its products. Last year, according to information provided by Dell, the company spent only 1.3 percent of its $35.4 billion in sales on R&D, compared with 5 percent by HP, 6 percent by IBM, and 10.5 percent by the technology industry on average.

"'Dell benefits from others' technological breakthroughs,' says Mark Melenovsky, an analyst at IDC in Framingham, Massachusetts. 'By competing in a standards-driven market, it leverages the R&D of other companies.' Michael Dell rejects the idea that his company is merely a techno-mimic, pointing out that it holds some 750 patents.

"Still, whereas other vendors strive to be the first with a new technology, Dell plays a different game. 'They let others do the innovations, wait until they become standardized, and then move in with their own version of the product,' says Galen Schreck, a Forrester analyst. 'Meanwhile, other vendors are adding fluff to increase market share—little tack-ons to their products that aren't really necessary and add cost. Dell cuts right through that, figuring out what customers must have without the fluff. There are many places where Dell is "good enough," a quality product from a name brand that you don't have to pay a premium for.'"

Newsweek[24] characterizes Dell as having fun at the competitor's expense: "Dell finds it hilarious that companies like IBM, HP, and Sony fund researchers to come up with ideas that break the mold. PCs, says Dell spokesperson T. R. Reid, have reached a period of 'standardization.' They aren't the glamorous gizmos they were in the industry's early days. They are commodities, largely undifferentiated devices loaded with the chips made by Intel, running the software made by Bill Gates's minions. Dell doesn't like the term commoditization—it makes PCs sound cheesy. But the company nonetheless owes its success to it, because commoditization eliminates differences between its products and those of its competitors. That means it competes on cost, service, and business model."

Dell on the Defensive

All this puts Dell on the defensive; obviously, it doesn't want to look like a parasite on the innovations of others. Dell explains its small R&D budget in a variety of ways. From *Newsweek*[25]: "Dell saves money by not spending its shekels to seek major breakthroughs. That path (as opposed to spending R&D money on things like product integration) 'squanders shareholder money,' said Rollins."

Here's more on that from an enterpriseinnovator.com article,[26] where Michael Dell explains that Dell's innovation is targeted at the customer: "Dell noted his company 'ensures there is a return on R&D,' and that Dell enjoys a 'far higher level than any of our competitors' when it comes to its R&D ROI. Dell added that his company has over a thousand patents, and invests more than half a billion dollars a year in R&D. He said, 'We kind of have this model of open innovation and collaboration,' and explained that 'our job is not to reinvent the things that an Intel or a Microsoft are creating,' saying 'that's not innovation, that's waste.' Dell said, 'Our job is to understand what the customers' requirements are,' and that his company is figuring this out adeptly. 'Whether it's through Dell.com or our hundreds of thousands of face-to-face customer visits every year, we have a tremendous pulse on the customer,' and the 'magic comes on the intersection, defining what the right solution is that lines up those fundamental technologies and the customers' requirements.'"

Michael Dell casts some doubt on the innovation of others later in the same article: "With Microsoft investing so much in developing the OS and Intel advancing chip research, Dell can concentrate its R&D efforts on 'system level technologies,' and in finding 'in solutions that are usable, reliable, digestible by customers.' Dell said, 'We have to have a really good understanding of what's inside those at a really deep level.' He noted that Dell 'invests heavily' in manufacturing R&D, 'Whereas a lot of our competitors have outsourced their manufacturing.' He added, 'A lot of companies wave the flag of innovation while really trying to protect their proprietary solutions.'"

It's true that some R&D goes into protecting proprietary solutions, but in this context, the remark comes across as defensive. And although Dell does hold many patents, they're largely for manufacturing processes, another point Dell is defensive about.

From *Fortune* magazine,[27] "I raise this innovation issue with Michael Dell, too, and ask him why he even cares whether people think Dell innovates. 'I don't care as much as I used to,' he says. 'It's complete nonsense though. I mean, come on. Let's see: innovation: Business process, supply chain, change in industry, customer value totally different, change the whole cycle in which technology is brought to market—well, there may be a few innovations in there.'"

From an article in techweb.com[28]: "In remarks aimed at those who have criticized his company for not spending as much as some rivals on

R&D, Dell said the PC maker seeks to leverage existing technologies that can be brought to market more quickly.

"'There's an abundance of great technology available to Dell to bring to market and we don't want to replicate or duplicate them,' he said. 'Anyone who has developed a great technology and wants to get it to market should come down to [Dell's Austin, Texas, headquarters] and talk with us.'"

To be fair, Dell does a fair bit of tech innovation—as with memory and motherboard bus development—but that's usually in the context of existing technology. Will we see Dell break new ground in totally new directions? From an interview in *Fortune* magazine[29]: "Question for Kevin Rollins about innovation: 'Could Dell ever come up with a PlayStation or an iPod on its own?' 'We could. But I don't think that's our strategy,' Rollins insists."

And, on occasion, the innovation doesn't even exist within the context of existing technology. Douglas King of Magnatrax (involved in the design and distribution of building products and materials) explains the reason for their migration away from Dell as "Definitely performance...we had split our business between Dell and Gateway, and the HP performance was far superior in our opinion, and in the last year, we've introduced over 200 Fujitsu machines as well (laptops and desktops) which perform very well—the Fujitsu laptop especially, are the best laptops I have ever worked with."

Dell and Its Business Partners

Given its posture on standards-based marketing, Dell ends up seeking a great many business partners. You're always seeing announcements like this from *PC Magazine*[30]: "Dell Computer announced three new technology partners Thursday morning, a tip-off that the company plans to branch out into other consumer directions. Dell named imaging giant Fuji Xerox, photography maven Kodak, and electronics powerhouse Samsung as the new partners.

"In a keynote address here at the Consumer Electronics Show, founder and CEO Michael Dell said that every time his company enters a new market, prices decrease because of the additional competition and customers benefit. The shift, which Dell called the 'Dell Effect,' accelerates the adoption of the technology in question, he said....

"Some analysts have said the company is better at business processes than products, a charge Michael Dell said is largely true. Dell expects to serve 1.4 billion custom-generated Web pages on Dell.com to more than 60 million visitors, he said. By partnering with Lexmark in printers, for example, Dell has sold roughly 2 million units to date and climbed to third in total market share during the third quarter 2003 with a 13 percent market share, Dell said."

Dell relies on the innovation of its business partners, passing the cost of innovation on. Dell also spends a great deal of time directing the path of the innovation undertaken by its partners; as Michael Dell has said, somewhat euphemistically, when discussing video chips[31]: "We were willing to invest our engineering expertise evaluating the different companies and products, then help our chosen partner by providing input, ideas, specifications, and talent so that we could both succeed."

And, more directly[32]: "We choose deliberately when to influence others to improve their existing technologies, and when to create technologies ourselves."

This process is discussed more in Chapter 8. Largely passing the cost of innovation on to business partners saves Dell Inc. a great deal of money. Bear in mind that Dell does innovate, and that, according to the company, it employs some 4,000 engineers.[33] But Dell does not often strike out into totally new territory, and it often says that its innovation is customer-driven. Much of that engineering talent is taken up by work on manufacturing processes and getting current machines to work better within the context of standards-based technology. When it comes to groundbreaking technology, however, you don't think of Dell. That's not its strategy, as Kevin Rollins would say.

When it comes to tech innovation, Dell outsources a lot of the work, as it does in other areas, and that allows it significant control over its suppliers. *ComputerWorld* interviewed Kevin Kettler, Dell's CTO,[34] and asked: "To what extent does Dell influence the development of the core technologies that go into its products?"

Kettler's answer: "One of the best-kept secrets around is what exactly our influence is in this area, and I consider it very extensive. Dell has core teams that are working [with silicon designers] on where we think customer requirements are and where we think innovation needs to occur in basic silicon design.

"We are down at very low levels with chip set architectures, chip set partitioning, processor interfaces, processor architectures. Right now, we have discussions going on on products we won't see produced until the 2009–2010 time frame. We have a very regimented process and approach. We will typically drive the requirements based on what we are generating from our direct customer touch."

ComputerWorld asked, "To what extent does Dell help design the specifications surrounding the emerging standards it supports?" Kettler said, "There's an amount of the architecture definition around [the] PCI Express [bus] that was created by Dell engineers. Another example is a specification called Disk Data Format [DDF]. One of the people on my team wrote that specification and brought it forward to the Storage Networking Industry Association.

"DDF is in response to customer feedback. A customer would build out a Dell server or external storage array and might have a set of disk drives with their company's data on those drives. [Then] they might migrate to a different machine. What was at issue was that each of the five controller manufacturers was using proprietary formats to lay out the data and tables associated with the formatting on the drive. So [Dell technology strategist] Bill Dawkins heard this and went off and wrote a specification on how that architecture should fit together and has driven it through a standards body. It's been accepted, and we're starting to see silicon from some companies.

"At the end of the day, when customers plug and play drives, they won't run into the potential for that data to be unrecognized and misinterpreted as a blank drive and formatted over. So it's a huge win. It's direct, customer-driven innovation."

In other words, Dell is able to set the standards and will presently start to "see silicon from some companies," an enviable position to be in. Using its immense market presence, Dell is able to influence suppliers, and it uses that ability extensively (bringing Wal-Mart to mind once again). It's an advantage of scale that smaller competitors find hard to struggle against, and it's a strategy that only larger companies can pursue.

Becoming a Dell partner or even supplier is very much sought after in the industry, and that's not likely to change quickly. Despite the heavy requirements Dell puts on its suppliers (see Chapter 8), they make money, usually a lot of money. Suppliers are falling all over themselves to get into the supply chain. Is it any wonder that Dell can outsource so much R&D?

Let It Go If Need Be

In its emphasis on standards-based sector entry, Dell watches the markets extremely carefully. What it does in the market is carefully planned and, if it is doesn't work out, Dell will yank it without fanfare, as it did with the Olympic. Dell isn't in the business of trying to sell a product for which there's no market. Competitors have gotten attached to product lines that they kept pushing for a long time—sometimes years—after it was evident they had missed the niche. Dell, whose marketing—as its management will frequently tell you—is customer-driven, doesn't do that.

One of Michael Dell's internal sayings is "Don't perfume the pig."[35] In other words, when something's a stinker, get rid of it. When it comes to market entry mistakes, Dell is a proponent of cutting losses early. (Has this happened recently in the Chinese, low-end PC market where competition is especially fierce? Some industry-watchers think so and have written about Dell's "retreat" in that market—for more on this, see the discussion at the end of this chapter.)

In other words, Dell doesn't just go after standards-based technology for its own sake, but monitors the market both before and after product entry. Dell often gives you the impression of a company that's been designed by engineers, rather than along traditional business principles. This is particularly evident in the intense amount of information flow that hurtles around the company. It's not restricted to inventory; all business units are evaluated on ROIC on almost a minute-by-minute basis, and sales staff can see how well they're doing second by second. Metrics exist for everything, and they're closely watched. This is in contradistinction to many companies that still have no established metrics whatsoever, depending instead on occasional reports and presentations given at business meetings.

The products and product line ROIC metrics are watched particularly closely and, if something isn't cutting it, it'll be cut.

Dell's Competitors Take Note

Dell's competitors are not dummies, and they've taken note of Dell's standards-based approach for some time. In fact, they've started taking much the same approach in recent years. *BusinessWeek*, in the article "Computer Giants Are Creating Clever New Products by Snapping Together Industry-Standard Building Blocks"[36], asks: "What's the use of innovating? Seemingly none, if you're in the computer business. It has been a joyless, nearly profitless existence of late. Since 2000, the server business has shrunk from $69 billion to $49 billion, says researcher IDC. The only company making enough to brag about is Dell Computer Corp. Analysts expect the Round Rock (Tex.) company to see this year's profits rise 22 percent, to $2.5 billion.

"What really irks rivals is that Dell doesn't even share in the heavy research and development required to create new products. Instead, it rides gleefully on the coattails of industry leaders Intel Corp. and

Microsoft Corp. Last year, Dell spent a wispy 1.3 percent of its $35 billion revenue on R&D. By comparison, Sun Microsystems Inc. spent 14.7 percent of its $12.5 billion in 2002 sales on R&D, yet racked up $587 million in losses trying to sell its powerful servers. 'We've seen this movie before, and at the end of the day, Dell gets the girl'" says former Merrill Lynch & Co. analyst Steven Milunovich.

So, will widespread standards-based technology use be the death of innovation as the industry has known it? The *BusinessWeek* article goes on: "That doesn't mean innovation in the computer business has been left on the cutting-room floor.... The face of computer innovation is changing, however. Today's engineers are creating cutting-edge machines using commodity, industry-standard building blocks. Call it innovation, Lego-style. Chips from Intel and Advanced Micro Devices (AMD) Inc. have cut the performance gap with what computer makers IBM and Sun use. Microsoft's Windows server program is now robust enough to do many of the tasks of pricey Unix systems. And the Linux operating system is free and particularly good at serving up Web pages.

"Snap it all together, and computer makers have a running start at building state-of-the-art machines. That frees them to use their smarts to solve other problems—from developing self-healing computers to packing more power into ever smaller devices. 'The challenge we face is how to do extraordinary things with affordable components,' says William R. Pulleybank, director of IBM's Deep Computing Institute."

In other words, Dell's competitors are catching up in using standards-based technology, much in the same way that they're hot on Dell's trail when it comes to on-site service. Does that mean that innovation is dead in the industry? Hardly. But it does mean two things.

First, competitors have gotten smarter about innovation and, in markets where the technology has been standardized, they'll no longer be so eager to pursue innovation. Instead, they'll follow Dell's path, building products, even advanced products, using Dell's techniques of using standards-based components. Competitors are much less likely to attempt proprietary solutions as a way to maintain market share. They've learned this lesson from Dell, and they're increasingly putting it into practice. You're less likely to see innovation, especially that based on proprietary components, in established tech markets.

Second, innovation will move more rapidly to new markets. Dell's competitors realize that innovation still gives them an edge, but only until a market sector becomes standardized; at that point, it's time to think about moving on. So, innovation will continue. For that matter, note that innovation will also increasingly involve using standardized components to achieve higher returns, as with blade servers.

Is Commoditization a Long-Term Problem for Dell?

Dell likes to step into a market when that market has become standards-based and before commoditization occurs. But commoditization does occur, meaning that items like PCs increasingly become treated like toasters or microwave ovens. Commoditization reduces margins: Prices plummet and low-cost competitors crop up like flies.

A commoditized market sector doesn't grow, or it grows very slowly. A successful tech market sector has three cycles: innovation, standardization, and commoditization. Dell's competitors went after the innovation cycle, and they made big profits—for a while. Dell entered the market as the standardization cycle began and punctured its competitors' balloons. The next step, however, the commoditization cycle, is a different ball of wax. So, will Dell only make big profits for a while, in those markets it penetrates?

While Dell still has market share to capture, this shouldn't be a major problem. As it expands from one-third of the PC market to one-half, for example, it should still do well in that area. However, Dell is smart enough to see the writing on the wall, and when a market sector becomes commoditized, it knows that it has to ultimately think about moving on. Dell has been doing that: entering more and more market sectors, such as servers, printers, LCD TVs, services, and so forth.

An article by online stock watcher Sharewatch[37] states: "But even Dell knows the commoditization of the PC business means that the company needs to branch out into other areas for revenue growth. And like its PC brethren, Dell has locked on to computer services as a source for future expansion."

Dell's nimble response to a commoditized market sector can be the source of confusion in the media. Recently, there's been stir in the press on Dell's operations in China, where competition in the PC market is hot. Dell has repeatedly been accused of "retreating" from low-end PC sales.

A late 2004 article on enterpriseinnovator.com[38] states: "On August 16th, Dell announced that it's shifting focus away from the low-end PC consumer market in China—as aggressive competitive pricing from local rivals has driven down ASPs and margins, giving Dell a bitter taste of its own medicine."

An opinion piece on yeald.com[39] states: "Now Dell seems to be in retreat. Growth estimates for China have been slashed. A new approach is being advocated: Dell is going to 'hang out' in the higher price ranges for a while—the implication being that the company is going to come back into the lower end when conditions are more favourable.

"This is a dangerous strategy to follow. It gives the impression that Dell doesn't have the stomach for a fight. It confirms that Dell is not invincible and can be beaten by its own tactics. It voluntarily cedes market superiority to Lenovo from which the Chinese company can further expand its market reach to Dell's detriment—both inside and outside of China."

As evidence, the article says: "Just as worryingly for Dell is that while individual consumers account for 38 percent of the market in China , they account for less than 10 percent of Dell's sales in the country. This is reflective of a wider problem outside of the U.S. Consumers buy about 40 percent of PCs in the global markets Dell is targeting, yet they account for less than 20 percent of the company's sales. It is a further reflection of Dell's isolation from the people."

Is this a real problem? Is it written that a market must be a simple copy of its demographics? Or, do Dell's moves reflect an understanding of how to handle already commoditized markets? In fact, the very low-end commoditized PC market has not held much interest for Dell for years now.

Some people are starting to realize this. From a later article at enterpriseinnovator.com on Dell and China[40]: "Even in China, where pundits have been abuzz about Dell's retreat, Rollins made the case that it was business as usual, with Dell rejigging its mix to emphasize lucrative profit pools, while reducing its emphasis—but hardly withdrawing—from lower-margin volume markets that offered Dell little real appeal.

"Fresh of its recent bruising in the headline, Rollins argued that Dell was not in retreat in this promising market—and that it was still a 'very simple story on China.' He explained that 'quotes attributed to our Asia-Pacific manager were accurate but misunderstood,' and that 'our strategy is always to go after profitable growth' and in so doing, 'from time to time we will shift our portfolio to maximize profitability.' And so it has done in China. 'We have not exited any sector of the business arena that we participate in,' proclaimed Rollins. Even the 'low-end consumer PC market,' hardly Dell's favorite due to puny margins, is one that is 'still available on our web site at the low-end price point.' As Rollins explained, 'our desire obviously is to go after high-end profitable price points,' and to 'go after high-end mix to maximize profitability,' especially as 'competitors get aggressive and profitability is reduced' on the lower-end. So as for all those doom and gloom headlines on Dell's market withdrawal, 'that story was accurately reported, but misunderstood in terms of our long term strategy.' Dell was thus not exiting from any segment, including the low-end consumer. 'We're there for the long run.'

"According to Rollins, there is thus no 'disruptive threat from below' that Dell is recoiling from. As in every market, Dell 'benchmarks our business against every one of our competitors.' And unlike many of its rivals in the China market, 'we manufacture our Chinese products in China, sell them in China, service and support them in China.' As such, Dell's 'P&L on Chinese business is a superior to the P&L of anyone else in China,' just as this is 'true elsewhere.'"

Critics here have been confused by stereotyping Dell as a low-cost PC manufacturer, and they would be well advised to remember that Dell changed its name from Dell Computer to Dell Inc. years ago; it's not tied to any one market sector. Dell has an excellent understanding of what happens to margins when a sector becomes commoditized, and lowest-cost PCs haven't been a favorite at Dell for a long time (including in the U.S. market). Dell is after profitable growth, not just growth, and it looks as if it knows what it's doing when a market sector moves from standardization to commoditization.

The P&L sheet rules at Dell, not market demographics: That's what's keeping Dell at the top.

Chapter 5

Have Zero Tolerance
for Inventory

The longer you keep [inventory] the faster it deteriorates—you can literally see the stuff rot. Because of their short product life cycles, computer components depreciate anywhere from a half to a full point a week. Cutting inventory is not just a nice thing to do. It's a financial imperative.
—Kevin Rollins[1]

This may be the most crucial chapter in this book for many businesses, because it's about inventory control and reduction, a critical skill for the twenty-first century. Inventory reduction is a coming revolution, and those caught at the tail end will suffer. Dell's manufacturing—which you can see at work in Figures 5.1 and 5.2—is superefficient at needing almost no inventory.

Inventory is a major drag in any business that has to maintain supplies on hand. This is certainly truer in the high-tech industry, which is pioneering zero inventory, than in nearly any other, because that inventory "goes bad" as you watch it. What's zero inventory done for Dell? According to news.com[2]: "In 1994, Dell Computer was a struggling second-tier PC maker. Like other PC makers, Dell ordered its components in advance and carried a large amount of component inventory. If its forecasts were wrong, Dell had major write-downs.

"Then Dell began to implement a new business model. Its operations had always featured a build-to-order process with direct sales to customers, but Dell took a series of ingenious steps to eliminate its inventories. The results were spectacular.

Figure 5.1 Building a PC.

"Over a four-year period, Dell's revenues grew from $2 billion to $16 billion, at a 50 percent annual growth rate. Earnings per share increased by 62 percent per year. Dell's stock price increased by more than 17,000 percent in just more than eight years. In 1998, Dell's return on invested capital was 217 percent, and the company had $1.8 billion in cash.

When it comes to inventory, how little is little? In 2000, Dell had about 6 days' worth of inventory; in 2005, in its Austin factory (the Morton L. Topfer Manufacturing Center, called TMC), it's down to 5 to 7 hours. In some areas, it's 2 hours.

A lead time of 2 hours sounds almost ridiculous: How can Dell be resupplied that quickly? In fact, suppliers now maintain warehouses near Dell and can get the goods over to its assembly lines quickly, a process Dell calls just-in-time delivery of inventory. Does that mean much of the warehousing has been off-loaded onto the suppliers' shoulders? Bingo. But the suppliers are, in turn, using the same zero-inventory lessons back up through their supply chains as well.

Figure 5.2 On their way out the door.

Only 2 hours of inventory? Trucks that must appear at the 100+ docks of TMC every couple of hours? Some observers say that smacks of compulsion, of an obsession to keep the warehouse empty. And, so it does. You may have heard of demand-chain management, but isn't that carrying it a little too far? Dell doesn't think so.

How important is zero inventory to Dell? Michael Dell calls going direct "Dell Direct version 1.0." And he calls tight inventory controls "Dell Direct version 1.1."[3] For that matter, his three golden rules of Dell[4] are: disdain inventory, listen to the customer, never sell indirect. Note that disdaining inventory is number one.

Nearly every corporation that maintains inventory can learn from Dell Inc., and that includes Wal-Mart, the former inventory management champ.

Zero Inventory Is a Critical Advantage

Because of computers and the way they handle information, zero, or near-zero, inventory control is going to be a major business factor in the coming years, and Dell leads the way. Inventory is a drag on any business; one reason that purely Internet-based business has looked so good to entrepreneurs is because these businesses need no inventory on hand.

Inventory means capital investment, and that investment is a formidable challenge to any start-up. In these days of zero-down real estate loans, more and more entrepreneurs are trying to control start-up costs, and destroying inventory is the way to do it. Dell represents the ideal, achievable only with mammoth purchasing power, but still an ideal every inventory-burdened corporation should look to.

Inventory control will be a major trend, and it's an important one to understand. In the short-run, it'll permit more start-ups, because smart companies with tiny inventories come online with minimal capital investment. In the long run, it'll be crucial to help compete with overseas competitors who have the advantage in labor costs. During the Industrial Age, you needed massive investment in both inventory and machinery; now that industries change at light speed; however, overinvestment in either can pull you down.

It's better than simply reducing capital investment. Through the way it manages its billing cycle, Dell actually funds its operations in large part by maintaining zero inventory: It bills customers immediately, but pays suppliers 36 to 45 days later. So, it can float an enormous amount of cash, on which it earns a ton of interest. Besides reducing and reversing capital investment, zero inventory means that stock depreciation and obsolesce—a central concern in high tech—is almost no problem. High-tech components can lose up to 3 percent of their value as they sit in the warehouse, and if they are losing that value in someone else's warehouse, so much the better for you.

Zero inventory also forces a company to keep in close contact with what customers are ordering and what they're likely to order. Dell's made that a focal point from the beginning, but it's a wise policy in general. Maintaining zero inventory naturally keeps a company more agile. In fact, true zero-inventory keeps a company on the knife's edge of responsiveness, which is where Dell likes to be.

Many companies maintain a supply of inventory, and demand comes second; in Dell's model, demand comes first, supply second. In the other companies, massive supply often substitutes for market knowledge. The investment to maintain that supply on hand is fat, and Dell is an expert at trimming fat. It's another place where it's been successful at reducing costs while others were sticking with tradition.

Asset Management Reduces Capital Investment

Reducing inventory is a style of asset management that reduces the capital investment you need, an important gain for any business. From an article in news.com[5]: "The seeds of Dell's success were sewn in its failures of an earlier time. In 1994, Dell created two important products that were deficient due to quality problems. Sales plummeted and Dell faced a serious cash shortfall. At the same time, the company realized that it had to accelerate its growth in order to move from the list of declining second-tier manufacturers (Commodore and Zeos, for example) to the group of prospering top-tier producers (IBM and Compaq Computer, for example), and this required even more cash.

"The executives met to decide how to generate the funds to keep the company alive. The decision was made to dramatically reduce inventories. The heads of manufacturing and marketing were charged with devising a way to run the business without component inventories. At first they resisted. Then they developed a way to meet this goal.

"The new Dell business model developed over a period of time. The first set of objectives focused on lowering inventory by 50 percent, improving lead time by 50 percent, reducing assembly costs by 30 percent, and reducing obsolete inventory by 75 percent."

That's easy enough to understand; to any start-up that takes a good, conscious look at operations, the investment in inventory must appear massive.

As your investment in assets goes down, the ratio of sales per asset climbs, something all businesses want to see. The following is from an analysis at the Motley Fool web site[6]: "Norfolk Southern has $12.4 billion in assets reported in its last quarter, but it only generates a paltry 38 cents in sales for every dollar of assets it has deployed. By way of comparison, Dell Computer generated $8.7 billion in sales on $3.2 billion of assets over the last year, or $2.71 in sales per dollar of assets employed. Generating more sales on less assets means tying up less of the capital the business generates in fixed assets. The term 'capital-intensive' literally refers to the way some businesses require more capital to function than others. Given these two companies and their assets-to-sales ratio, it is clear that Norfolk Southern is more 'capital-intensive' as a business than Dell Computer....

"You cannot argue with the kind of profit margins that a railroad like Norfolk Southern generates. However, because the company has to deploy and maintain billions in assets to get those profit margins, the business is not necessarily as exciting as it would otherwise be for the investor. Because Norfolk has to maintain thousands of miles of track and hundreds of trains, it constantly has put new capital into its assets in order to generate revenues. This means that instead of being able to return the cash generated from operations to investors, Norfolk has to reinvest it in its assets in order to stay in business. In spite of this, Norfolk generates plenty of cash flow. If it could actually improve its sales per dollar of assets employed, it could generate tons of cash.

"Five quarters ago, Dell Computer realized that one of the ways it could improve shareholder return was to notch up its asset management policies. Specifically, Dell realized that if it could more efficiently manage its inventory of computer components, it could increase the return on equity. As inventory and accounts receivable are Dell's two most significant assets, by minimizing these the company could increase the sales per dollar of total assets employed and therefore increase the basic return on equity of the business. The money that went into inventories to generate a dollar of sales decreased, leaving Dell with more cash on the balance sheet to distribute to shareholders in the form of stock repurchases.

"Dell Computer is a clear case of how improved asset management can increase shareholder return. Better asset management eventually shows up in the form of high profit margins, but high profit margins by themselves do not guarantee that shareholders will receive excellent returns. In order to ensure that return on equity is high, investors must look for businesses that have high margins and high asset turnover rates, whether it is sales-to-assets or looking at the inventory turns, the day's sales outstanding (or collection period), the payables period, or the turnover in fixed assets."

As *Fortune* magazine[7] puts it: "Obviously, that low inventory frees up mountains of cash for Dell that is otherwise tied up at IBM and HP."

Finance Your Operations with a Negative Cash-Conversion Cycle

Dell does more than just trim its capital investments by maintaining zero inventory; it also uses creative billing to finance its operations. It bills customers immediately, but pays suppliers later, which lets it float the accounts receivable cash and effectively pay for its operations at the suppliers' expense.

Fast Company magazine[8] has this to say: "The implications of working in this kind of hyperdrive…are profound. It changes the finance model, and it's an enormous competitive weapon. On average, computer makers pay their suppliers 30 days before a PC is shipped to market, bought by a customer, and paid for. But Dell's build-to-order model lets it receive payment from its customers immediately—through credit cards, either online or over the phone. It pulls the parts directly from its suppliers and builds and ships the product within four days. Yet the company doesn't pay those suppliers until 36 days after it receives payment from the customer. So, Dell has achieved a cash-conversion cycle (that's the time between an outlay of cash for parts and the collection of payment for goods made from them) of negative 36 days. That means it operates with negative working capital, eliminating the need to finance its operations. 'By collecting money for products from customers before it owes money to its suppliers, Dell has made it so its suppliers finance the cost of Dell's operations,' says Tom Mentzer, executive director of the integrated-value chain forums at the University of Tennessee at Knoxville."

Does that give Dell an advantage over competitors? You bet. According to the *Fast Company* article, "Hewlett-Packard doesn't disclose its cash-conversion cycle, but with its average of six weeks of inventory, the number is sure to be positive. Meanwhile, with just a few days' worth of parts on hand, Dell turns its inventory 107 times per year—an astounding advantage over HP and IBM, which flip their inventories 8.5 and 17.5 times per year, respectively. It's a fundamental law of manufacturing that the faster you turn inventory, the lower your costs. That's why Rollins will say, with a twinkle in his eye, that Dell has a built-in structural advantage over its competitors. Roger Kay, vice president of client computing at market researcher IDC, says he's right: 'Various industry assessments report that Dell's cost advantage through close-to-zero inventory is as high as eight points, which in a commodity business is huge. HP's net margin on PCs is so tiny—barely 1 percent—that Dell, by forgoing a point or two of margin, can put HP's PC division under water.'"

As always with Dell, fighting competitors is a matter of margins, and nearly no one beats Dell in that department.

The Advantages of Low Inventory in High Tech

Another advantage of zero inventory is peculiar to the high-tech field. Obsolescence is the big problem here: What you buy today might be utterly out-of-date 6 weeks from now. Michael Dell says[9] that "Inventory is the worst thing to own in an industry in which the value of materials or information declines quickly, which today means any industry—from computers to airlines to fashion. In the electronics industry, for example, the rapid pace of technological change can sink the value of inventory you're holding over the course of days."

Dell Computer learned this lesson early on, when buying memory chips in 1989. In those days, Michael Dell believed in inventory as a buffer against the ups and downs of sales,[10] "But instead of buying the right number of memory chips—which we would do today—we bought as many of those suckers as we could get our hands on.... We bought more chips than we needed, at the peak of a cyclical market. And then prices plunged. To make matters worse, we also got caught 'crossing the street' technologically, as memory chip capacity went from 256K to 1 megabyte almost overnight. We were suddenly stuck with too many chips that nobody wanted—not to mention the fact that they had cost us a ton of money. There we were, the company that had been built on dealing direct, trapped by the very same inventory quandary that had been plaguing our indirect competitors."

With component costs declining .5 percent to 3 percent a week, keeping low inventory pays off. And when there's a sea change, as when memory chips went to 1 megabyte from 256K, you're not left holding the bag. Of course, Dell's commitment to standards-based technology helps here as well, because such technology changes slower than the absolute bleeding edge.

To be able to approach true zero inventory, a company has to be able to make its suppliers jump when it wants them to. Dell has that power because of its size and consequent huge purchasing power. As it's gotten bigger, that power has only increased. Few companies have the same power as Dell does over its suppliers. But it's useful to know how Dell does what it does here—how it manages its suppliers—because any movement toward lower and tighter inventory control can help.

Choose Your Suppliers Carefully

Dell chooses its suppliers carefully and, if those suppliers don't keep up, they're out. Usually Dell goes with bigger suppliers because its growth will be less of a problem for those suppliers. Michael Dell has said[11]: "Suppliers need to have a sprint capacity to work with us, and our demand can't represent a disproportionate amount of their total capacity."

There can be no slip-ups. *Fast Company* magazine puts it this way,[12] "To get a slice of its lavish procurement pie, Dell's legions of suppliers must do things its way. They must be flexible enough, cost-competitive enough—and above all, fast enough—to compete on Dell's terms. 'Those suppliers who are the most consistent over time get the lion's share of our business,' says Marty Garvin, Dell's procurement chief. 'The ones that aren't get less and less. And those who can't scale over the long run, well, their business goes away.'"

The message is clear: Dell's way or the highway. It works because, if you get Dell's business, there's a lot of it. (Also note that compliant suppliers, willing to hold a few weeks' worth of inventory for Dell, reduce Dell's risk of running out of supplies, so cutting-edge zero-inventory isn't as risky as it often seems.)

Reduce the Number of Your Suppliers

Dell also makes a point of limiting the number of its suppliers, which at one point numbered over 500. As you can imagine, that number of suppliers makes for a logistics nightmare, because any one of them could become the weak link in the chain. And a supply chain is only as strong as its weakest link.

Here's what Michael Dell has said[13] on limiting the number of suppliers: "Just as you look for a sweet spot in the customer market, try to offer products in the sweet spot of the demand. You might think, 'Okay, to cover 100 percent of the market, we might need eight different varieties of a specific component, but we can cover 98 percent of the market with only three.' That defines the sweet spot."

In limiting the number of suppliers, Dell appears to have gone with larger suppliers. Such suppliers offer multiple products that Dell is interested in, letting Dell collapse the number of suppliers. This also raises the volume of business each such supplier does with Dell, which tuned them better to what Dell wanted and asked for, including volume discounts.

In addition to reducing the number of its suppliers, Dell reduces the number of parts it needs for manufacturing. Michael Dell has this to say[14]: "Inventory velocity has become a passion for us. To achieve maximum velocity, you have to design your products in a way that covers the largest part of the market with the fewest number of parts. For example, you don't need nine different disk drives when you can serve 98 percent of the market with only four."

Replace Inventory with Information

Dell likes to say that it replaces inventory with information. As Michael Dell says[15]: "The key is in providing your suppliers with all the information they need to make an informed decision." This trade-off between inventory and information is an interesting one, and it's taken almost literally at Dell. Dick Hunter is Dell's supply-chain chief for the Americas, and he thinks of inventory as a sort of ignorance, which is revealing[16]: "In his view, companies keep inventory as a hedge against poor demand forecasts and an inability to see into their supply chains. 'Most companies love a big order backlog; when the semiconductor industry has six months' worth of orders, they're happy,' he says. 'If I've got more than three days' backlog, Michael is calling me.'

"Dell has ripped away the psychological safety net that lots of inventory provides. Instead, it lives in a state of constant, self-imposed paranoia: It must meet demand, which is always in flux, with just the right amount of supply. If it fails, its manufacturing operations will crash within a matter of hours. But Hunter sees no other way to go. 'It's a real misconception that more inventory means less shortages,' he says. 'Even if you flood your warehouses with thousands of components, it's almost a given that you won't have that one-cent screw when you need it most. Then you're in the worst of all worlds: You've got a ton of inventory, but you still can't do the build. If you don't have solid processes that monitor demand and supply on a real-time, continuing basis, then I don't care how much inventory you've got. Invariably you'll have a lot of the wrong stuff and none of the right stuff.

"'But when you have basically zero inventory, it's like draining a swamp—all of the stumps start to show,' he says. 'The problems reveal themselves, and you can take immediate corrective action to fix them.'"

Dismissing inventory as ignorance is a powerful idea. Not all companies will want to live on the inventory edge as Dell does, nor should they. Dell is in a tough market, and it invests a lot inventory-trimming effort that wouldn't make sense for many small businesses, at least to that degree. But inventory does act as a buffer against fear of the unknown. It's much easier simply to pile up inventory and feel good about it as an asset when, in fact, it ties up a great deal of capital to do so.

Theoretically, the only inventory worth having is that inventory you use at the point-of-sale, because the inventory in the warehouse is just sitting there. That's what Dell tries to do with its thin inventory model. When inventory gets too high, when there's a great deal of money tied up in it, it's a sign of market ignorance. This is especially evident in cases such as Dell's, where the market changes rapidly. Your mileage may vary significantly—a grocery store whose market is static, for example, might have fewer difficulties with stockpiling a 3-month supply of canned beans, since their customers will always buy them. Even so, that ties up capital that could be put to more productive use.

Living on the inventory edge makes sure you stay in close contact with your market. In Dell's case, here's a comment from news.com[17]: "First, as inventory dropped, lead-time performance improved. This happened because Dell was not simply carrying component inventory against forecasted sales, but rather was aligning inventory and sales, managing profitability on a daily, weekly and monthly basis."

Trading inventory for information means closer contact with suppliers as well. At one point, Dell's order fulfillment and inventory tracking used to be manual, but no more. Working with partners who excel in strategy execution like Accenture, Dell has automated the entire process, and, through the secure extranet valuechain.Dell.com, has connected its suppliers on an almost minute-by-minute basis.

Here's what Accenture says about its work with Dell[18]: "Dell has completely automated its ability to take thousands of orders, translate them into millions of component requirements and work directly with its suppliers to build and deliver products to meet customer requirements. In fact, more than 90 percent of Dell's component purchases now are handled online: Suppliers use an Internet portal to view Dell's requirements and changes to forecasts based on marketplace activity, and to confirm their ability to meet Dell's delivery requirements. Then, as Dell factories receive orders and schedule assemblies, a 'pull' signal to the supplier triggers the shipment of only the materials required to build current orders, and suppliers deliver the materials directly to the appropriate Dell assembly lines.

"Explains Dick Hunter, vice president, supply-chain management: 'We now schedule every line in every factory around the world every two hours, and we only bring into the factory two hours' worth of materials. We typically run a factory with about five or six hours' worth of inventory on hand, including work in progress. This has decreased the cycle time at our factories and reduced warehouse space—space that has been replaced by more manufacturing lines.'

"Not surprisingly, the project has produced more than just enhanced supply chain efficiencies and accelerated, highly reliable order fulfillment. At any given time, there is less than four days of inventory in the entire Dell operation, while many competitors routinely carry 30 days or more. In addition, automation has helped Dell react more quickly to correct potentially out-of-balance situations, made it much easier to prevent components from becoming obsolete and improved response times across the supply chain by providing a global view of supply and demand at any specific Dell location at any time.

"Lastly, the initiative has helped Dell's suppliers communicate more effectively, reduce obsolescence (and resulting supplier returns), improve exception management, increase forward visibility and cut transaction costs."

As Michael Dell[19] has said: "Just as the Internet increases customer intimacy, it can also be used to enhance supplier intimacy." And[20] "The link between the day-to-day demand trend and the incoming material from your suppliers is absolutely critical to your success—so the shorter you make that link, the better off you are."

Nor is that information flow one-way. Dell is always giving feedback on supplier performance and routinely awarding its best suppliers at well-advertised events—and it has a reputation of "challenging" even its top suppliers to do better at those events. Information about defects per thousand, for example, is always flowing back to suppliers. As Michael Dell puts it[21]: "The other thing that the Internet gives us is immediate transmission of quality data. We have data on product quality that come in every minute of the day. We'd like our suppliers to see the information in real time."

You can imagine what fun it is to be a supplier on the receiving end of Dell's continual feedback. Many suppliers are out there competing for Dell's favors, and the you-can-be-replaced feeling among some is strong. Dell has the reputation of being a tough negotiator with suppliers—very tough in some cases—and it has the purchasing accounts to back that up.

It's no secret that Dell puts a lot of pressures on its suppliers. But, as a supplier, it's tough to say no to Dell: Your margin will be low, but the volume will compensate, at least to some degree. But it's tough being told to continually redefine yourself. And now that Dell is holding to its zero-inventory policy, suppliers find that inventory offloaded on them as well.

Let Suppliers Hold the Inventory

Dell is able to work with only 2 hours of inventory because it can order parts that fast from its suppliers. So, guess who ends up holding the inventory bag? Again, from the *Fast Company* article: "But there is a dark side to Dell time: The company is fast in part because it has shifted some of the inventory burden to its suppliers. 'The yin and yang of being a major supplier to Dell is that you get a whole bunch of business,' says [executive director of the integrated-value chain forums at the University of Tennessee at Knoxville Tom] Mentzer, 'but the price of being a supplier is that you carry the inventory. If there is a supply-chain disruption, the supplier is stuck with the inventory, not Dell."

The article goes on to quote Navi Radjou, a vice president at Forrester Research, as saying: "Inventory remains a problem for suppliers; the average supplier is not better off than it used to be."

Suppliers Try for Zero Inventory, Too

Dell's suppliers are no dummies: They try for the zero-inventory model as well. The reasons for them are just as sound as they are for Dell—reducing inventory avoids tying up capital and sticking you with obsolete inventory.

Integrated Solutions Magazine[23] did a study on some of Dell's suppliers, such as National Semiconductor, trying to reduce inventory and had this to say, "'When you look at it from a high level, it's a pretty straightforward process,' claims National Semiconductor Senior VP and CIO Ulrich Seif after quickly running through the semiconductor manufacturer's supply chain. Come down from the 30,000-foot view, and Seif knows that things get real complicated, real fast. National's customers expect JIT (just-in-time) replenishment, while National's accountants want the $2.1 billion company to carry as little inventory as possible. Testing large volumes of the same product at one time reduces National's labor costs, but customers order in smaller quantities with different product mixes. And, while the steps in National's supply chain may be similar to those of any manufacturer, there are differing views on how to optimize those steps—even within National. 'I talk to our planning people, and my head starts spinning. They can talk all day about different optimization issues and conflicts,' adds Seif."

To some extent, National believes it can cut inventory and transfer the burden of that inventory to its own suppliers. The same article states: "National's customers were demanding JIT replenishment, but the company was not holding itself or its suppliers to the same standard when it came to maintenance part inventory and replenishment at its three manufacturing facilities (Maine, Texas, and United Kingdom). National customer Dell Computer, for instance, optimizes its supply chain by requiring its suppliers to manage Dell's inventory. While National was supporting Dell with vendor-managed inventory, the semiconductor manufacturer realized it could also leverage vendor-managed inventory with some of its suppliers. 'We are doing the same thing to our suppliers of spare parts and maintenance materials that Dell is doing to us. We pass some of the inventory burden onto those suppliers,' explains Seif."

But, as Seif says, going for zero inventory isn't that easy to do.

Some Suppliers Find Zero Inventory Hard to Do

It's not easy to be as fanatical as Dell is on this point. The *Fast Company* article says: "Even Maxtor, which has modeled itself on Dell's build-to-order strategy, can suffer from missed forecasts and bloated inventory. Like Dell, Maxtor owns its factories and controls its supply chain; it is built for speed and flexibility. Yet Maxtor recently saw its inventory swell to nearly six weeks because of lower-than-expected shipments. This past July, it reported a second-quarter net loss of $26 million, in part due to lower sales to Dell because of problems with 40-gigabyte drives."

In that same article, note the comment that Dell requires Maxtor to hold at least a week's worth of inventory so that Dell can hold only 2 hours' worth: "A look further up the supply chain at the suppliers of Dell's suppliers reveals that there's only so much inventory they can cut. MMC Technology supplies 65 percent of the disks for Maxtor's hard drives—in all, some 50 million disks a year. MMC, too, has adopted parts of the Dell model. The company's factories, which are based in the United States, run full-out every day of the year, producing the least costly product in the industry. And yet, for all of its relentless focus on making itself more efficient, MMC is stuck with three weeks' worth of inventory, and there's nothing it can do to change that. It takes a week of performance testing before MMC can release its finished disks; it takes a week to ship the disks from California to Maxtor's Singapore factory; and Maxtor requires MMC to warehouse buffer stock for up to one week (just as Dell does with Maxtor). Ultimately, Maxtor carries inventory for Dell, MMC carries inventory for Maxtor, and raw-materials suppliers carry inventory for MMC. Dell, of course, carries next to nothing. 'Dell does business with suppliers who are willing to hold its inventory,' says [vice president of client computing at market researcher IDC] Roger Kay. 'And if they're not willing, Dell will find suppliers who are.'"

What emerges are two points about why Dell's suppliers have a tough time cutting inventory. One is the familiar point that Dell excels at execution, more than any other, similar company. National Semiconductor's Seif says, "I talk to our planning people, and my head starts spinning. They can talk all day about different optimization issues and conflicts." That doesn't sound like fanatical devotion to zero inventory—the will to *do*. The fact that it takes a week to ship disks from California to Maxtor's Singapore factory also doesn't sound like fanatical supply-chain minimalization. Dell makes an effort to keep its manufacturing close to the point of sale, which is one reason why it still maintains plants in the United States when others have long since gone offshore. So, the first impression is that the corporate *will*, the thorough commitment to rebuilding corporate structure as needed, may be lacking.

But there's obviously something else going on here as well, as when Dell requires suppliers to maintain a week's worth of inventory. Many suppliers don't have the buying power that Dell does, and so can't get the same order of compliance from their supply chain that Dell can. The big fish get their way; the little fish do their best.

Get Suppliers to Store Inventory Close by

Part of maintaining close links in your supply chain is keeping your suppliers close by. Dell insists that its suppliers locate nearby. Michael Dell told suppliers exactly that[24]: "We went back to our local suppliers and said, 'We have a global business and we want you to be a global supplier. We want you to service our factories all over the world. But in order to do so, you must develop the capability to serve Dell around the world. And it worked: A vendor who started with us in Ireland knew we were building a manufacturing center in Malaysia, so it set up a plant next to our plant in Panang and then another next to our plant in China. When we recently decided to expand operations in Round Rock, Texas, the same company added a plant there. Next stop: Brazil."

Dell manages its supply chain by continually looking at each section's profitability and ROIC—there's a metric for everything in Dell. One result of those metrics was the discovery that closer suppliers helped the bottom line far better than distant suppliers did. Michael Dell noticed that early on,[25] "We came up with the phrase 'proximity pays' as a result of translating the ROIC metric down to each component and each supplier. Once we could measure the true returns to our shareholders from buying one component versus another, it was very clear that those suppliers that located their factories close to ours helped us to deliver a higher ROIC thank those that were farther away." Once, again, Dell's emphasis on information flow points the way.

As an article in *Fortune* magazine[26] says, "The company [Dell] urges its suppliers—everyone from drive makers to Intel—to warehouse inventory as close to its factory as possible."

It's another cost of doing business with Dell: Not only are you going to have to handle Dell's inventory, but you're going to have to store it right next to the Dell plant, even if that Dell plant is in China or Brazil. Dell gets away with this because it can and, obviously, it's not shy about asking.

Don't Take Delivery Until You Need to

Other companies might have to pay for inventory when it's shipped, but not Dell. Dell often won't purchase inventory until it rolls onto their assembly line—literally. Here's from *Fast Company*[27]: "Dell's clout with its suppliers is epitomized by a set of thin white lines on the floor of the TMC plant. The lines form a rectangle that fronts each of the 110 cargo bays encircling the factory. Tractor-trailers loaded with parts line up at the bays. When an assembly line runs low on disk drives, a signal goes out. A forklift wheels onto a trailer bed, snatches a pallet of disks, and pulls out onto the floor. When the forklift crosses the white line, a scanner records the shipment's bar code and the parts move from the supplier's books to Dell's. Dell doesn't pull the part until it has a customer order; it doesn't take ownership until it pulls the part."

When the part disappears into Dell, Dell accepts ownership. And you'll be paid for it 36 to 45 days later. Actually, one or two suppliers still exist that Dell needs because it has come to rely on them, and with which they have relatively little leverage. Intel comes to mind, because they've got a lot of power over the Wintel PC manufacturers. Interestingly, *BusinessWeek*[28] magazine reports: "Chip maker Advanced Micro Devices Inc. has filed an antitrust lawsuit against Intel Corp., accusing its market-dominating competitor of forcing customers into exclusive deals to keep them from buying AMD microprocessors. The suit, filed late Monday in U.S. District Court in Delaware, alleges Intel has bullied 38 companies, including large-scale computer-makers [the AMD complaint includes a mention of Dell], wholesale distributors and retailers, to secure a monopoly in the highly competitive x86 microprocessor market."

Go for Cross-Docking

Wal-Mart, another inventory wizard, has a money-saving process that's been called "cross-docking." The idea is that inventory comes in on one dock, is offloaded, moved to another dock, and loaded onto a Wal-Mart–bound truck. In other words, what comes in goes out immediately, no warehouse needed.

The Economist magazine explains this process this way[29]: "While superficially mundane, Wal-Mart's pioneering system of 'cross-dock-ing'—shifting goods off trucks from suppliers and straight on to trucks heading for the company's stores, without them ever hitting the ground at a distribution centre—has been fundamental to the company's ability to offer lower prices, the platform for its outstanding success. Is it not over the top, though, to glorify such a common-sense change with the title 'innovation'? For sure, it does not call for a higher degree in one of the obscurer corners of science. But Wal-Mart did something no competitor had ever dreamed was feasible and that was highly innovative."

Cross-docking is good to maintain low inventory; there's no warehouse for cross-docked products; they're ready to roll. As at Dell, Wal-

Mart signs products in electronically, and they're tracked all the way to the shelves.

Does cross-docking work at Dell? Can Dell unload components and sell them directly? Sure can. The manufacturer puts the Dell logo on the component, such as a monitor, and it can be shipped directly. All Dell has to do is to unload boxes from one dock and send them to another for shipment. Once again, zero inventory.

You might think this should be different from the Wal-Mart process—what about quality testing? Shouldn't Dell test equipment before it goes out the door with its name on it? The Dell solution is one you might expect—quality testing is outsourced to the supplier. Michael Dell has said as much[30]: "We have a supplier that makes very good, reliable monitors that we are confident about putting our name on. We worked hard to get them to under 1,000 defects per million, at which point, we decided not even to take them out of the box for testing. At that level of quality, the steps involved in [quality] confirmation—shipping them via truck from the supplier to us, unpacking them, touching them, testing them, repackaging them, and then sending them to the end user—would only risk damaging the goods."

That's the idea—outsource quality testing as well as warehousing to the supplier. In Dell's case, it works. And Dell also keeps its suppliers in touch, minute-by-minute, on how those suppliers are doing as far as quality control goes. Defect data is updated almost continuously on the supplier's extranet. By passing back defect data, Dell can get its suppliers to do better, to handle quality issues and, when the defects per thousand are low enough, Dell can simply cross-dock components like monitors—they don't even come out of the box. When monitors simply move from one dock to another, they don't even get stacked as inventory.

Protect Your Supply Chain

Living on the knife edge of inventory helps Dell save billions of dollars a year, but there's an obvious catch here—when sitting on a knife edge, you're liable to get cut. With zero inventory, Dell is much more open to supply-chain issues than other manufacturers. If a problem occurs, supply dries up immediately (which is one of the reasons suppliers have to hold inventory—once you've held Dell's supply chain up, you're in serious trouble).

Because there's no fat in Dell's supply chain, means it's fault intolerant. It saves a lot of money that way, but the flip side is that Dell must watch that supply chain extremely carefully. If problems arise, Dell must know about them ahead of time. One such episode was during a union dockworkers' strike; Dell had foreseen the strike and had already reserved a number of 747s to fly supplies in. Other manufacturers tried to charter 747s after the strike had begun, but by then, the price had doubled.

Fast Company says[31]: "Two years ago, a 10-day labor lockout idled 10,000 union dockworkers, shut down 29 West Coast ports extending from Los Angeles to Seattle, and blocked hundreds of cargo ships from unloading the raw materials and finished goods that fuel U.S. commerce. The port closings paralyzed global supply chains, bloodied retailers and manufacturers, and ultimately cost U.S. consumers and businesses billions.

"Analysts expected that Dell, with its just-in-time manufacturing model, would be especially hard hit when parts failed to reach its two U.S.-based factories. Without warehouses filled with motherboards and hard drives, they figured, the world's largest PC maker would simply find itself with nothing to sell within a matter of days. And Dell knew all too well that its ultralean, high-speed business model left it vulnerable to just such an intolerable prospect....

"Fortunately, the same ethos of speed and flexibility that seems to put Dell at the mercy of disruptions also helps it deal with them. Dell was in constant, round-the-clock communication with its parts makers in Taiwan, China, and Malaysia, and its U.S.-based shipping partners, who alerted it to the possibility of a lockout some six months before it occurred. Hunter dispatched a 'tiger team' of 10 logistics specialists to Long Beach, California, and other ports; they worked hand in hand with Dell's carrying and freight-forwarding networks to assemble a contingency plan.

"When the tiger team confirmed that the closings were all but certain, Dell moved into high gear. It chartered 18 747s from UPS, Northwest Airlines, China Airlines, and other carriers. A 747 holds the equivalent of 10 tractor-trailers—enough parts to manufacture 10,000 PCs. The bidding for the planes grew fierce, running as high as $1.1 million for a one-way flight from Asia to the West Coast. But because Dell got in early, it kept its costs to about $500,000 per plane....

"Meanwhile, Dell had people on the ground in every major harbor. In Asia, these freight specialists saw to it that Dell's parts were the last to be loaded onto each cargo ship so they'd be unloaded first when the ship hit the West Coast. The biggest test came when the ports reopened and companies scrambled to sort through the mess of thousands of backed-up containers. [Dell's] tiger team had anticipated this logistical nightmare. Even though Dell had PC components in hundreds of containers on 50 ships, it knew the exact moment when each would be cycled through the harbor, and it was among the first to unload its parts and speed them to its factories in Austin and Nashville. In the end, Dell did the impossible: It survived a 10-day supply-chain blackout with roughly 72 hours of inventory, and it never delayed a customer order."

That's very impressive. But it does point out a weakness in Dell's strategy—its supply chain has little slack to absorb faults when they occur. Dell trades inventory for information, and nowhere is that more crucial than here. By monitoring their supply chain—even when it comes to rumors of dock strikes—Dell can head off problems. But it takes a lot of monitoring to do that.

Dell's good at that kind of monitoring, and has multiple systems in place. But Dell's also the extreme when it comes to zero-inventory obsession. Any company that maintains inventory can benefit from keeping strict control and minimizing inventory, but the cost of super savings when it comes to ultra-low inventory is eternal vigilance.

Reduce Inventory by Forecasting Customer Needs

One way that Dell is able to keep its inventory low is by keeping in close touch with suppliers. Another way is by anticipating demand by keeping in close touch with customers[32]: "'Sell what you have' was the phrase that Dell developed for the crucial function of matching incoming demand to predetermined supply. This occurred at several levels.

"At a monthly 'master sales plan/master production plan' meeting led by CEO Michael Dell, top-level managers agreed on a five-quarter rolling forecast with a strong focus on the 'current quarter plus one.' In this meeting, Dell's functional department leaders balanced and agreed on internal product strategies, competitive factors and constraints. At the meeting, the sales commission plan was set to equal the production plan. Through this process, Dell synchronized the company every 30 days.

"At a weekly 'lead-time meeting,' senior executives in sales, marketing and supply chain management collectively interpreted demand trends and supply issues to determine where component surpluses or shortages were likely to develop."

The article goes on to note: "The weekly lead-time meetings had a very strong effect on Dell's culture. Once the sales executives agreed on a set of products to be made, they 'owned' the task of ensuring that these products would be sold. The product lead times were posted daily for all to see, and this drove the daily profitability management process.

"Dell's core philosophy of actively managing demand in real time, or 'selling what you have,' rather than making what you want to sell, was a critical driver of Dell's successful profitability management. Without this critical element, Dell's business model simply would not have been effective."

An interview with Kevin Rollins, in another article in *Fast Company* magazine,[33] discusses Dell's connection with the customer as a link in the supply chain: "One of the untold secrets of the supply chain is the direct connection with the customer, which means taking an order from the customer and not through an intermediary. Most people think of the manufacturing process as the supply chain. When we think of the supply chain, we think from the customer all the way back to the component supplier. Because we don't have any intermediaries, we can see directly into the demand side—we get good information directly from the customer, which enables us to forecast well. That lets us optimize the manufacturing-procurement chain and move very fast.

"Our competitors all try to copy our supply-chain model, but they don't have the front-end! They sell through distributors and resellers and aggregators, so there is no way for them to know what the demand is. They're always out of position. They have bad forecasts on the front-end and they don't know what their suppliers have in inventory....

"Dell also works the other end of the supply chain—the customer—to eliminate the evil of inventory. Essentially, it's replacing inventory with information. The company keeps a massive database that tracks the purchasing patterns and budget cycles of its corporate customers, and predicts upgrade purchases by individual repeat consumers, which enables it to forecast demand with about 75 percent accuracy. Three times a day, Dell updates its demand forecast for key suppliers on its extranet portal. When Dell misses a forecast—which it does from 5 percent to 25 percent of the time—and finds itself running out of, say, 15-inch flat screens, it runs a one-week special for 17-inch screens. Its direct-to-the-customer model allows it to shift demand to match what its suppliers can deliver. Supply-chain experts call this 'demand shaping,' and Dell has mastered this competitive weapon, too. But while such tactics have helped Dell to almost eliminate inventory from its balance sheet, its suppliers cannot claim to have done the same."

In other words, Dell tracks customer demand and tries to predict it. And when they're off, they run a sale—no great wizardry there.

Manage by Profitability

Dell watches everything it does in terms of profit and ROIC, and that helps it when it comes to reducing inventory. When you're metrics-obsessed, you really can replace inventory with information. As news.com says,[34] "In many companies, inventory substitutes for profitability management, tying up valuable capital and preventing the company from focusing on day-to-day business alignment. In most companies, managers face a choice between managing inventory and managing away the need for it. If you manage by profitability over inventory, you can have your cake, and eat it, too."

The article explicitly mentions Dell: "Through its use of profitability management, Dell matched supply and demand on a daily, weekly and monthly basis. As it sharply reduced the variance, the need for inventories simply disappeared." To say "simply disappeared" is overstating the case, because it took an enormous amount of work. The point is that this effort was made possible in large part by handling information flow—specifically by working with the unit-by-unit profitability metric. In other words, Dell trades inventory for information, not just in terms of supply and demand, but in terms of profitability as well.

Dell versus Wal-Mart on Inventory

Low inventory is healthy for a company. In fact, it's one of the signs The Motley Fool says investors should look for[35]: "I would advise that every shareholder in a manufacturing company examine the inventory numbers very, very closely each and every quarter. Many times, your analysis will be able to clue you in on the company's direction before the company does...and that's what investing is all about."

Wal-Mart has been a traditional leader in terms of inventory control, but Dell is doing better. According to David E. Runkle, Research Officer for the Federal Reserve Bank of Minneapolis[36]: "From 1993 to 1998, Wal-Mart's sales, general and administrative expenses stayed roughly the same or rose slightly. Dell, on the other hand, relentlessly cut these expenses as it moved certain tasks, including sales, to the Internet. Because Dell was able to reduce its expenses so drastically meant that its pretax operating margin grew much more rapidly than Wal-Mart's during this time. From 1994 until 1998, Wal-Mart's pretax operating margin (profits before taxes, divided by total sales) was roughly flat at around 3.5 percent. But Dell's pretax operating margin doubled from 4 percent in 1994 to 8 percent in 1998.

"As remarkable as these operating performance results were, an even bigger difference between Dell and Wal-Mart can be seen in inventory management. Since Dell was always a direct retailer that built to order, rather than built to inventory, we would expect that they turned over their inventory much more frequently than Wal-Mart, even before the impact of the Internet. And as we can see in the years 1993 through 1995...Dell turned over its inventory about 10 times a year, whereas Wal-Mart, which had to stock substantial inventory in its stores, turned over its inventory five times a year. However, after 1995 Dell's inventory revolution hit, and from 1995 to 1998 Dell mastered supply-chain management so well that it achieved more than 50 inventory turns a year."

When it comes to inventory management, Dell is the (low-cost) leader.

Chapter 6

Always Adapt, Always Execute

Dell is an execution machine, that's all there is to it. They're an operations company, and they stay incredibly true to their operating model.
—Barry Jaruzelski, management consultant at strategic management and technology consulting Booz Allen Hamilton[1]

This chapter is about Dell's ability to adapt and execute. These are themes you'll see throughout this book, and they're strong suites at Dell. Dell is a world leader in execution, and you can't tell the Dell Story without stressing that. That fact makes it a nimble company, allowing it to adapt to internal and external conditions and streamline itself. All that's coming up in this chapter.

Build a Culture of Execution

Dell is a by-word for execution. From an article[2] from the Wharton School: "Flawless execution of the well-known 'Dell model' has a lot to do with Dell's success."

The following is from The Motley Fool's site[3]—note that the characterization of Dell as selling commodities here isn't strictly true, as discussed in Chapter 4, because when a field gets totally commoditized, Dell, the champion of profitable growth, looks to other fields: "Dell makes its money by delivering commodities faster and cheaper than the next guy. Some of the commodities that Dell makes are better than the next guy's, and some are not. This, of course, stands to reason since both

Dell and the next guy make a whole line of commodities at various prices and the higher-priced ones are better than the lower-priced ones....

"It is very tough for a commodity business to be a high-margin business. Dell's business isn't. When your business doesn't have high margins, then there better be other ways to make money. Fortunately for Dell, there are, and they are often summed up in the word execution.

"Here are some examples of Dell's execution:

- "Dell's commodities work better when they are delivered,
- "When Dell's commodities don't work, they are fixed or replaced faster,
- "Dell keeps less inventory on hand to build its commodities,
- "Dell needs less of a sales force because a large portion of its orders come directly from the Internet."

One half of this book's mission is understanding the elements of the Dell business model; the other half is about putting that business model to work. It's hard to stress that enough. Execution has made the difference between Dell and its competitors for years. Those competitors study Dell's business model but they can't put it into practice, and that's the crucial point. Being able to put into practice—execute—is what it's all about.

The idea of real execution is still largely misunderstood in the business world. Larry Bossidy (named CEO of the year in 1998 by *Chief Executive* magazine), Ram Charan, and Charles Burck wrote a famous book called *Execution*.[4] Among other things, they have good things to say about Dell: "The system works only because Dell executes meticulously at every stage. The electronic linkages among suppliers and manufacturing create a seamless extended enterprise. A manufacturing executive we know who worked at Dell for a time calls its system 'the best manufacturing operation I've ever seen.'"

These authors give talks and routinely find that the audiences they talk to, including high-level management, have no idea what execution really means. The subtitle of the book is "The Discipline of Getting Things Done," and it's still a vastly underappreciated idea, especially when you compare a standard corporation to Dell Inc.

Where has the ability to execute gotten Dell? You already know the answer. As *Internet News* says in a December 2004 article[5]: "In the first nine months of the year, IBM's Personal Systems Group, which includes its PC business, earned $70 million in pre-tax profits on $9.25 billion in sales. That's a razor-thin margin of 0.75 percent. Grocery store chains boast better margins.

"Contrast that with Dell. Like IBM, Dell doesn't break out sales of PCs and notebooks, but they make up 79 percent of Dell's business. With overall margins of 8.6 percent so far this year, it's probably a safe guess that Dell's PC business is pretty profitable."

Commitment to Execution

Michael Dell built Dell Inc., and he has been able to infuse it with his energy. To some measure, Dell Inc. is an extension of Dell the man. The result is that Dell Inc. doesn't have to put up with the rigid structures and hierarchies that other corporations its size have to.

Michael Dell is a big fan of execution[6]: "Some businesses are founded on the idea of the silver bullet—one almighty product or patent that sits in a safe, guarded place twenty-four hours a day. But that's not where growth is coming from in today's—or tomorrow's—economy. The key is not so much one great idea or patent as it is the execution and implementation of a great strategy.

"Look at Disney or Wal-Mart or Coke. You can understand their strategy—it's really not that complicated. But it's genius! It's completely comprehensible, yet few companies can really replicate their success.

"Why? It's all about knowledge and execution."

And he's right. He's been fortunate enough to be able to guide Dell Inc. with that vision from the very start. The book by Bossidy, Charan, and Burck says that execution is really the major job of a business leader and a core element of an organization's culture. At Dell, those two come together.

Being able to execute means maintaining an unyielding commitment to execution and putting it all into practice through effective leadership. An article[7] in thinkingmanager.com comments: "Michael Dell talked of the management flexibility that enabled Dell Corporation to change strategies 'when things were not going right' in its PC business and of 'leadership that was strong enough to change things quickly.'

"That's essentially the Clean Break approach, but Dell added an organisational lesson: 'Companies that learn to manage change are in the best position to continue to take the risks needed to stay out in front.'"

Maintaining that commitment isn't easy. An article in news.com[8] asked Kevin Rollins what worries him most, and his answer was all about exactly that—maintaining that total commitment to execution: "We still have a business model highly dependent upon the execution of our company every day. It's not a model in which we develop a proprietary widget and sell it without worrying, because no one can catch us on the technology.

"We have to do it every single day. So, all customers have to have their needs met, products need to be shipped every day, the quality standards need to be met—just a whole series of to-dos. Therefore, it takes a lot of discipline to pull that off. We have to train a lot of people—because we grew this year between 15 percent and 20 percent in revenue, and we've got 41,000 employees worldwide. We're adding new people every day, and none have ever worked at Dell. So they need to come in and understand how to execute every day. That's really hard. It's hard to keep that execution intensity at the level where you don't ever make a mistake; you don't ever upset a customer. And we do. We fail, but not very much—that's the biggest challenge. It's a very intense execution model."

The news.com interviewer asked Rollins if the important thing was to sweat all the little details. Rollins answered (note that both Kevin Rollins and Michael Dell like to discuss Wal-Mart a lot): "Sam Walton (the founder of retailer Wal-Mart Stores) told a story. When asked, 'What's the secret to the success of Wal-Mart?' Every time reporters would ask him, he'd tell them something different.

"The answers boiled down to the concept of successfully doing 100 things right every day. We're a little bit like that. Wal-Mart just does a lot of things right. While we're not completely similar—because we develop our own products and manufacture our own products as well as sell them—the execution discipline there is very similar. We're not willing to accept defeat or failure. We don't have that in our psyche."

Corporate Will

Rollins says, "We're not willing to accept defeat or failure," and that's exactly the point. Execution is the implementation of corporate will. And most corporations have very little effective corporate will.

The problem is often one of motive integration. Everyone has a different motive; some high-level management exists for power and compensation. Some employees exist to put in their time and that's it. In the worst cases, the corporation is no more than a collection of employees in a formalized but dysfunctional structure. Their motives are like the tiny magnetized domains in a bar of iron—all those mini-domains are magnetized, but they all point in different directions. The net result is zero.

Great corporations get motives integrated. The microscopic domains in that iron bar align with each other, and the result is a powerful magnet. That's the kind of discipline you need to be effective, to become a great corporation.

And that's where most companies fail. From a *USA Today* analysis of Dell mentioned in Chapter 3[9]: "Companies in a groove like Dell are, at least for a while, 'practically unassailable by competitors—not because they can't emulate the model, but to do so means practically discarding the business and organizational model they have today,' says Paul Wiefels, author of business book *The Chasm Companion*. 'Most companies don't have the stomach for it.'"

How do you align all the tiny magnets in your organization? You can't do it through fear or coercion, at least, not in the long run. Making employees fear for their jobs is no long-term solution—not when they can simply jump ship in a relatively free labor market. Compulsion lowers morale and makes employees think of themselves first; the magnet breaks down into tiny domains once again.

So, how do you get people involved and aligned? How do you integrate motives and build a corporate body that works? You have to build something people *want to be a part of.* You have to show them that you have a winner, that your new way of looking at things is also in their interest, that it addresses their point of view, too.

From a Harvard Business School discussion on Dell[10]: "To double its revenues in a five-year period, the company had to adapt its execution-obsessed culture to new demands. In fact, Michael Dell and CEO Kevin Rollins realized they had a crisis on their hands. 'We had a very visible group of employees who'd gotten rich from stock options,' Rollins says. 'You can't build a great company on employees who say, "If you pay me enough, I'll stay."' Dell and Rollins knew they had to reignite the spirit of the company.

"They implemented an employee survey, whose results led to the creation of the Winning Culture initiative, now a top operating priority at Dell. They also defined the Soul of Dell: Focus on the customer, be open and direct in communications, be a good global citizen, have fun in winning. It turned out to be a huge motivator. And they increased the focus on developing people within the company. 'We've changed as individuals and as an organization,' Rollins says. 'We want the world to see not just a great financial record and operational performance but a great company. We want to have leaders that other companies covet. We want a culture that makes people stick around for reasons other than money.'"

Dell's winning culture is an important one—Dell's a winner, and by being here, by being part of Dell, you are too. According to Michael Dell, an important part of integrating motives at Dell was to have employees start thinking like owners. That's a goal at many corporations, and in many large corporations, it usually fails. Stock options have been tried over and over, but they don't connect an employee to the company on a day-by-day basis. The performance of the entire company is wrapped up in those stock options, not just one individual's performance. The coupling is very weak.

Dell went after a stronger coupling of employee to corporation. Michael Dell said this regarding this issue[11]: "To motivate an employee to think like an owner, you have to give [them] metrics [they] can embrace. At Dell, every employee's incentives and compensation are tied to the health of the business. And one of the best ways we've learned to evaluate its health is Return on Invested Capital, or ROIC. ROIC is a measure of how effectively Dell creates shareholder value relative to its cost of capital. In this way, ROIC helps allow you to identify your best-performing businesses and those that aren't delivering the performance they should.

"We became interested in ROIC as a result of our experiences back in 1993. We had to sort through a variety of different businesses selling through retail, selling to large companies, selling to small companies, selling to consumers, selling different types of products, selling in many different geographies, each with different characteristics—and figure out which ones were succeeding and which weren't. We determined successful strategies by measuring return on invested capital and growth for each business. Where we were doing our jobs well, our businesses were delivering a high return on capital and a high level of growth.

"ROIC became a focusing device. We introduced it in 1995, with a company-wide push to educate everyone about the benefits of a positive ROIC, with articles in the company newsletter, posters, talks by managers, and 'Messages from Michael' devoted to the topic.

"We explained specifically how everyone could contribute: by reducing cycle times, eliminating scrap and waste, selling more, forecasting accurately, scaling operating expenses, increasing inventory turns, collecting accounts receivable efficiently, and doing things right the first time. And we make it the core of our incentive compensation program for all employees. We decided to reward employees around a matrix of ROIC and growth; higher performance directly correlated to higher ROIC, which came back in the form of higher compensation."

From an employee's perspective, compared to other companies, Dell comes across as a winner. It's brash, it succeeds. It's got energy, it's got destiny. It's cool. It's motivated by a central mission, and you can feel a part of something bigger than yourself. Through the strong ROIC coupling, you're encouraged to think more like an owner than an employee. ROIC can be determined on the basis of business unit, department, or group; it's as finely divisible as it need be.

From a corporate perspective, this kind of alignment is essential; it integrates the motives of your people with your organization. Corporate structure and its ability to adapt—see the upcoming section—also is vital. But to maintain that all-important corporate will, you have to align motives as Dell does very effectively. A remarkable performance when you consider that we're talking about 57,000 employees.

Adapt

If you can execute, you can adapt. If you can't execute, you can't adapt. It's that simple. Dell's market is one in which you must adapt quickly and decisively, and so many of its competitors haven't been able to do that. They couldn't execute to the same degree, and they couldn't adapt to the same degree.

On that point, Michael Dell has said[12]: "Many companies are justifiably afraid of change. When you assume that things are 'as good as they can be,' the concept of change can only appear negative, threatening the status quo. Companies spend countless precious hours and dollars on crisis management, attempting to contain and/or minimize change, without ever considering that the very thing they fear could be the best thing that ever happened to them....

"Change no longer represents the occasional need to react to far-reaching trends or industry influences. It's more like the Chinese character for crisis, which represents both danger and opportunity. Change is opportunity. It is also constant, direct, and temporary, for once things change, you can bet they'll change again. Learning to thrive on constant change is the next frontier."

An article[13] at themanufacturer.com interviewing Stanford University supply chain analyst Hau Lee makes this point as well: "Success then, it appears, does not stem from a single supply chain model. Instead, Lee suggested, they evolve. Observing the changes a company makes over time points to this type of development. He uses Dell as an example. 'People say they have a direct model. Actually, deep inside the Dell direct model, there are many pieces,' he said. 'The information they use, the relationships they have with suppliers, the kind of combination model they use, the channel, all are evolving. The key to success is that the company doesn't just find one supply chain strategy or one network and say, "this is it." It's the adaptive part of it that makes a difference.'"

For Dell, constantly adapting, or trying to, is part of the process. Michael Dell[14] says, "So while it may seem counterintuitive, a lot of our time is spent planning and preparing for change, projecting and encouraging people to look forward to it and see it for the opportunities it provides."

He sums it up this way[15]: "Expect to live in a flexible, dynamic, fast-moving environment that is the norm, rather than the exception. To thrive on change, you must understand how to give in to it, flow with it, and derive strength from it. There's no other way."

Part of this, Dell says,[16] is a willingness to experiment: "You also need to embrace an experimental attitude in making decisions. Sometimes you can't wait for all the data to present themselves before making a decision. You have to make the best decision you possibly can based on your experience, intuition, available data, and assessment of risk. There's a guaranteed element of risk in any business, so experiment—but experiment wisely."

When you experiment, don't be afraid of failure[17]: "To encourage people to innovate more, you have to make it safe for them to fail."

Adapt to the Market

As you already know, Dell Inc. is a company to watch when it comes to adapting to the market. It monitors what sells and adjusts to match; that's one of the specialties of the Dell Direct model. Dell keeps in close touch with its customers, and it is able to forecast what the market wants with some accuracy.

It also knows when it's time to move on and start looking for other opportunities, as when a market sector becomes commoditized. From the Wharton School piece mentioned earlier in this chapter: "And business services are one major way around the slowdown in the U.S. PC industry. 'Last year Dell, like everybody else, figured out that their products were rapidly becoming more and more commoditized, so they came up with an idea: There's money and margin to be extracted in service,' [Wharton professor Morris] Cohen says." So, Dell made the move to services to flesh out their scope.

Dell's can adapt as needed partly because of its lean inventory model. The Motley Fool[18] notes: "As for keeping up to date with the latest industry trends, Dell can transition product lines easily because it clears out all its old inventory in a matter of days. With no baggage, it can be nimble. If people want set-top boxes or PDAs or Web-surfing cell phones or wristwatches with a pager in them, Dell can stock it. The main consideration Dell has is what areas it wants to do business in." Once again, it's corporate survival of the fittest.

Adapt to the Technology

It goes without saying that, in Dell's business, one of the biggest things to adapt to is the technology, which changes fairly rapidly in most fields Dell has become involved in.

CIO magazine says this[19] about Michael Dell and the swift changes in the tech field: "CIOs struggling with the breakneck pace of change in information technology shouldn't look to Michael Dell for sympathy. 'If you're waiting for things to settle down and never change, you're in the wrong business,' he says.

"'You may find yourself in a business where the pace at which technology is used defines whether a company succeeds or fails.'"

Dell's ability to respond to changing technology is based on its own zero-inventory model, as well as its own considerable tech know-how—and the ability to outsource the need for that know-how to suppliers. Dell says that[20] leveraging the know-how of others has let Dell Inc. respond quickly to tech changes in a now-familiar pattern: "Leveraging our suppliers' expertise has allowed us to scale our business very quickly without having to become an expert in surface-mount technology, semiconductor manufacturing, or building motherboards and other electrical assemblies, all of which would require an enormous commitment of intellectual and mentary capital."

Dell also invests in the education of its employees, using the Dell Learning center to keep them up to speed on the technology and changing market place. An article at centerdigitaled.com[21] comments: "In order to survive the transition and growing pains that accompany such growth as Dell has had, the company had to continually adapt in order to keep pace with the changing marketplace. Dell recognized employee education would be critical to the company's future growth. They recognized a fundamental need to integrate training into the corporate culture not only to achieve greater employee productivity, but also greater company-wide growth as reflected in earning, revenue and stock price. In 1993, Dell established Dell University, today known as Dell Learning.

"Dell Learning is the vehicle through which Dell' employees acquire training and learn new skills immediately applicable in the workplace. With Dell Learning's establishment, the company made a commitment to employee training. They knew that learning must not only be made easy, but also synchronous with work. Keeping this in mind, the goal for Dell Learning was to be both innovative and capable of delivering custom-configured education directly to employees."

Dell now offers courses to customers as well.

Adapt to Your Environment

Any company as big as Dell is going to make waves wherever it goes. For example, Dell is investing roughly $100 million in a new manufacturing plant in Forsyth County North Carolina (because of its fast delivery promises, it's difficult for Dell to locate out of the country)—after having bargained for about $242 million in state incentives—but it is running into problems. Dell Inc. is headquartered in Texas, which has no corporate tax, a nice perk for Dell. However, North Carolina is thinking about changing the way corporate tax is calculated.

From journalnow.com, an online partner of the *Winston-Salem Journal*[22]: "An attempt to change how corporate income taxes are calculated in North Carolina could raise taxes significantly more than first projected for such multistate companies as Dell Inc., the state's chamber of commerce said yesterday.

"The budget plan that the state Senate passed last month would change the way multistate companies apportion income for tax purposes in North Carolina.

"Though fiscal analysts for the General Assembly estimated at first that the change would amount to $10 million a year in additional corporate taxes, they have since raised their estimate to at least $45 million a year."

Dell has responded by lobbying strongly against the change, although they say they're still going ahead with the new plant. From the same article: "[Rolf Blizzard, the vice president for governmental affairs at N.C. Citizens for Business and Industry] said that several companies, including Dell, are lobbying against the change, and that one sampling found that just 18 companies would pay a total of $4.2 million more in corporate taxes to the state under the proposal." Dell can be expected to adapt to its environment vigorously.

Another challenge for Dell in North Carolina is coming down the road. The *Los Angeles Times* reports[23]: "A group of taxpayers asked a North Carolina court Thursday to declare that tax incentives worth $279 million [including local incentives] granted to Dell Inc. for building a factory in the state are unconstitutional and should be rescinded.

"The incentives, approved by the North Carolina Legislature in 2004, discriminate in favor of in-state economic activity in violation of the state constitution's commerce clause, according to a lawsuit filed Thursday in state Superior Court in Raleigh. The plant in Winston-Salem will be Dell's largest when it opens in September.

"North Carolina, which outbid Virginia for the $100-million plant, competes with other states for investments by offering companies tax breaks and other incentives. Such grants amount to 'corporate welfare' and discriminate against smaller companies that can't get them, according to the North Carolina Institute for Constitutional Law, which is representing the seven plaintiffs.

"'What we're seeing in this competition to attract investment is the economic Balkanization of the states,' said Robert Orr, director of the institute. 'Businesses know they can play one state off another to get the best deal.'

"The state of North Carolina, Forsyth County, the city of Winston-Salem and state and local officials also are named as defendants." It's going to be interesting to see how Dell adapts to this one.

Adapt through Segmentation

Dell segments by customer type, but it also segments its business structure. This segmentation, which is covered in more depth in Chapter 9, is important to understand because it's Dell's way of growing its organization while balancing centralization and decentralization naturally.

Dell has a flexible corporate structure that allows it to grow in flexible ways. Dell Inc. has become a master at handling growth and, internally, it uses segmentation to divide its business units as that growth happens.

Being able to adapt its organization flexibly is essential for Dell. Many companies, unaccustomed to such massive growth, have ossified their corporate structures. Michael Dell has said[24]: "An overly rigid hierarchical structure restricts information flow, which can't be good for anyone. The same can be said for overly rigid business processes. In many organizations, management processes become etched in stone and create a permanent bureaucracy. At Dell, we realize processes serve the business, not the other way around. We tell our people that if they can come up with a better process or solution for improving our business—and all the parties concerned agree—then they're free to change it."

Problems with Rigid Structures

He explains the organizational problems Dell faced[25]: "Like many companies, we had organized our business around functions, such as product development, finance, sales and marketing, and manufacturing. But what happened was that, as a functional organization, we had grown beyond those self-imposed boundaries to the point that the functions had begun to take on a life of their own. As we grew larger, it became increasingly more difficult to work as an integrated team. Instead of moving coherently forward in a unified way, the functional divisions had given way to a loosely linked collection of fiefdoms—or 'silos' as we called them.

"Without a clear vision of how each division contributed to the company's overall well-being, the managers of the different functional groups had begun barricading themselves in their own silos and had begun to think primarily of promoting and protecting their own group's interests. In the thick of our growth, our team had lost sight of our fundamental values: serving the interests of the customer, the shareholder, and the company as a whole. The information systems group, for example, would say, 'We're the information systems group and our job is to create information systems,' rather than, 'We're the information systems group and our job is to facilitate the flow of information to our employees, customers, and shareholders.' This kind of compartmentalization makes it nearly impossible to for the necessary links among people so that they will talk to one another and work together towards a common set of goals. Instead of having a company where everyone takes responsibility for their actions and contemplates and understands how those actions affect other parts of the company, you have an environment in which people are saying, 'That's not *my* job. That's his job.'"

That's a fair statement of how so many corporations are organized these days—which is to say, they're not organized. The division into self-serving fiefdoms is all too familiar to anyone working in most major corporations and is the despair of organizational consultants. The corporate structure is rigidly built around corporate functions, and there's no built-in way to change, none whatsoever. No thought has been given to providing a way to change that structure or to let it adapt. What person who has worked in management at a major corporation hasn't been seriously frustrated at the politics, the feudalism, the power lust you encounter in all directions?

That frustration turns quickly into resignation, and people just stop fighting "the system." When that happens, they turn to their own fiefdoms, maintaining a defensive posture against an apparently antagonistic corporate structure and culture. The corporate structure ends up not only having problems, but also having no way of dealing with those problems.

Michael Dell says[26]: "I believe that much of the confusion that occurs in corporations today stems from stymied communication and complex hierarchies. We're allergic to hierarchy. Hierarchical structure to me fundamentally implies a loss of speed. It implies that there's congestion in the flow of information. It implies the need for layers of approval and command and control, and signoffs here, there, and everywhere. That's inconsistent with the speed with which we all need to make decisions, both as leaders and as a company, in this fast-paced marketplace."

Segmenting

What was Dell's solution? He says[27]: "When you've got a huge market opportunity facing you, the only way to handle it is to divide and conquer. That's the basis behind our concept of segmentation. It ensures that as we grow, we are able to serve each individual customer more effectively, and it has become the organizing philosophy of our company."

Dell segments in response to the market—in other words, to match the engine that drives the company. Originally, segments were developed to target the customer better, in other words, as a sales adaptation. But as time went on, it made sense to let that organization penetrate the entire corporate structure.

Dell says, "What started as a sales concept to maximize opportunities soon evolved into a series of complete business units, each with its own sales, service, finance, IT, technical support, and manufacturing arms. It really makes sense for our business. Our direct connection to our customers enables us to understand the different needs of different customers. Segmentation takes the closed feedback loop and makes it even smaller and more intimate."

In other words, Dell selected the market as the inspiration for its corporate structure. By following the market, it's been able to grow organically, in a natural way. That inspiration has been essential in allowing it to maintain its hypergrowth. That makes sense—you model your business after the market is serves and, when that market changes or expands, so does your business.

So, instead of organizing the business around traditional business structures, Dell is organized to follow the market. When a market segment gets too big for its business unit, that unit is segmented into smaller ones. In this way, an organic growth occurs that lets Dell balance centralization and decentralization. How does Dell manage growth? By making its corporate structure into a mirror of the markets it serves. More on this in Chapter 9.

As Michael Dell says[28]: "Segmentation offers a solution to the fundamental issue that has challenged Dell since the very beginning: how to sustain our growth as we got bigger. You can grow small companies quickly, but it becomes increasingly more difficult to sustain a high rate of growth in a large corporation. Segmentation allows us to scale our business very rapidly, because every time we determine that there is sufficient momentum to segment a unique customer group, we'll break it off, give it its own organization team, and let it act as a small company."

In other words, segmenting along market sector lines lets Dell act, to a remarkable degree, as a conglomerate of small businesses. That's a wise thing to do in Dell's case, because small businesses can grow at rates far exceeding those of large businesses, which have to carry tremendous amounts of baggage around with them. And what better model to segment around than the market itself?

Once again, it's a matter of information coupling, which Dell is very good at. The internal structure of many corporations was set up following traditional principles and ad hoc additions and, over time, it calcifies. It's not about to change, even as its market does. Dell watches the market as a guide that its internal structure should follow. That helps everyone involved think as owners would, in natural market terms. No special organizational wizardry is needed; just follow the market.

As Michael Dell said, it's easy to lose sight of overall objectives with the wrong corporate structure and to devolve into defensive fiefdoms. Following the market, and making sure everyone knows you're following the market, gives your corporation the kind of control and cohesion first discussed in Chapter 1. The overall objective is there, right in front of everyone's eyes, all the time.

So, how do you make sure you're following the market? If you're Dell, the answer is one word: metrics.

Using Metrics

Dell is obsessive about using metrics to track what's going on. It uses metrics to watch the market by monitoring sales, unit by unit. When sales dip, Dell knows it immediately. When they pick up in another area, Dell knows all about it.

Watching sales that closely lets Dell track its market and, because of its scale, it's aware of changes in that market before almost anyone else is. When the change is significant enough, Dell reorganizes its internal units to match, and it knows when to do that by following the metrics on each of those units.

Dell says[29]: "One of the great things about segmentation is that it has allowed us to see growth rates, profitability, service level performance, and market share in each unique segment, and adjust our activities accordingly. We found that we had some businesses that were earning a very high profit but not growing very fast. We found other businesses that were growing very fast but not earning much of a profit. We didn't want either. We wanted businesses that were growing quickly *and* earning a reasonable profit."

In other words, segmentation lets you track not only the market, but also the performance of each of your business units. As you can gather, he's talking about the ROIC of each unit and, at Dell, each business unit is constantly challenged to justify itself on the basis of its ROIC.

Dell goes on to say: "Segmentation also enabled us to measure the efficiency of these businesses in terms of their asset use. This meant we could evaluate our return on invested capital in each segment, compare it with other segments, and target what the performance of each should be. It became a great way to identify what needed to happen for us to reach our full potential in each business."

Dell also makes sure that information flows in other ways throughout the organization. For example, it uses dual reporting, a system that's not found much favor in other circles. Michael Dell explains[30]: "We've discovered that having a common language and effectively sharing common goals actually enhances our organizational structure, which in turn kicks the company into higher gear. In a company that's as large and rapidly growing as ours, you obviously can't have a traditional functional organization, nor a completely decentralized model. The former ends up being a bunch of unconnected groups with unclear accountability; that latter is not a company. You need to maintain functional excellence while injecting business accountability.

"To achieve this, we instituted a system of dual reporting with our people. Most senior-level managers of specific functions, such as finance or human resources or legal affairs, share responsibility with managers of specific businesses, such as particular regions or product lines. Our lawyers in Europe, for example, report both to the head of our European business, as well as to our general counsel at our headquarters in Round Rock."

As Roger Eacock, Senior Manager of Supply Chain Integration at Dell says[31]: "In terms of supply-chain metrics, Dell metrics everything! The net result is this allows us to understand cost drivers, areas for improvement etc. Today we are by far the lowest cost PC manufacturer, and as a result the only company still making a profit on PC sales."

And, from IT-Director.com[32]: "Dell is a tough competitor because its manufacturing operations are brilliant. This is no secret of course, but a trip round a Dell manufacturing plant provides food for thought. Here's the flavor: All of Dell's plants are run on the basis of the continual monitoring of critical success factors. The ones used are:

- "Hours of Sales Inventory: This is the amount of inventory held in production and you want it to be as low as possible. In the Austin (Texas) factory I visited the figure was a remarkable 22 hours for the servers they build, but in Dell PC plants it is more like 7 hours.
- "Actual Uptime: The amount of time that the plant as a whole is unavailable because of failures of any kind from machine failure to lack of supplies. The target is 97 percent but most Dell plants run at 99 percent.
- "Ship to Target: In the server plant in Austin, the target is 5 days from order to shipment. When the factory is really humming it can get down to 2 days, but that's exceptional.
- "Deliver To Target: This is the same as above except it measures when the customer receives the goods, so it monitors the delivery process."

Streamline

Dell always goes for speed and efficiency, and that translates to increased ROIC. In 1998, Dell produced $745,000 of revenue per employee; in 2005, it's $900,000 per employee—HP, by contrast, is at $540,000.[33] That's not just from revenue growth, but also from streamlining its operations and cutting costs. And Dell does that like no other.

Streamline the Supply Chain

You're already familiar with Dell's hatred of inventory. When *Fast Company* magazine[34] asked Kevin Rollins, "Dell is constantly trying to build speed and efficiency into its supply chain. Why is speed so critical?" Rollins' answer was predictable: "Whenever you compress time you end up with lower cost. So we do everything we can to cut inventory and reduce the cycle time from order to delivery. That ends up being a cost and performance advantage for the company."

Dell has long been working to replace inventory with information, and it is outsourcing its inventory problems. The success it's achieved has been due to its superior execution in this area. From an article by the Wharton School[35]: "Other companies, most notably Gateway, have tried to copy the Dell model. But none has matched Dell's 'operational excellence,' says Wharton professor David Croson. (Gateway, in particular, has also never matched Dell's power in the enterprise market or its leadership in notebook computers, analysts point out.)

"'It's not simple to streamline your supply chain to have reliable sources of high-quality parts, to have very efficient manufacturing techniques, to have very tight quality control tolerances and to be able to communicate this to customers so they're willing to pay a premium all at the same time,' Croson says."

Streamline Manufacturing

Dell also has become an expert in manufacturing, streamlining the process like nobody's business.

Manufacturing is a very capital-intensive operation, so you can be sure that Dell has spent a great deal of time tuning it. Despite the fact that others have outsourced much manufacturing, Dell customizes all the PCs it sells (and estimates that something like 650 million configurations are possible) and so it has to handle this part of its operations entirely by itself—or does it? The remarkable thing is that Dell has convinced suppliers to handle a great deal of the work.

Dell's manufacturing optimizations run from the very layout of the manufacturing floor to the number of screws used. IT-Director.com describes the TMC plant like this[36]: "The plant is automated by a large manufacturing system, built by Dell itself from various packages and a good deal of custom code. This picks off the orders to be built and sends a request for pieces to the inbound supplies area of the plant. The bits are picked and routed to an assembler, with the more difficult assemblies going to the more experienced staff.

"Once built the computer goes to a load and test area, where the requested software that was ordered with the system is automatically loaded and the whole assembly is tested. Then it goes to packaging where it is put in boxes along with documentation and other accoutrements and is shipped. There are just four steps in all this; pick, assemble, load and test, and box—so the plant is laid out in that fashion."

Fast Company magazine[37] is also all praise when it comes to Dell's manufacturing abilities. Here's its description of the TMC: "Inside the TMC, amid the whir of positive-force ventilators blowing dust and grit back out onto the Texas hills and the rush of forklifts plying the factory floor, multiple assembly lines snake and swerve through the plant like Coney Island roller coasters, cranking out more than 700 corporate and consumer desktop PCs an hour. Dell has brought a maniacal focus to shaving minutes off the time it takes to assemble and ship a computer. By studying videotapes of 'the build,' as they call it, factory managers have slashed in half the number of times a computer is touched by workers. They've counted the screws in a PC and redesigned it so that the major components—hard drive, graphics card, CD player—simply snap in place.

"In a blur of synchronized movements, a veteran builder can piece together a Dell OptiPlex or Dimension PC in three minutes. The software burn and testing, which is powered by Dell servers with enough bandwidth to download the entire *Encyclopedia Britannica* in eight seconds, takes several hours, depending on the amount of customization that's required. The entire process, from the time the order is taken to when the finished PC exits the factory, is wrapped up in four to eight hours.

"While the TMC takes up less than half the space of its predecessor, it boasts three times the output. And even that's not good enough. Dell is always on a mission to outdo itself, and the factory is expected to increase its production by some 30 percent by year's end. Michael Dell himself drove that point home when he recently toured the plant. A group from one of the packing lines showed him how they'd upped their processing rate from 300 to 350 boxes an hour. 'Michael congratulated them, and there were high fives all around,' recalls [Dick Hunter, Dell's supply-chain chief for the Americas]. 'But then he issued a challenge: "How can we improve to 400?" He's pleased, but never satisfied.'"

The attention to detail never stops, from top to bottom. To streamline, Dell started using one family of chassis for its entire Optiplex, Precision, and Dimension PC lines. The goal was not only to streamline inventory and manufacturing, but also to design the new chassis, the Optiframe, to make PC construction faster.

Mechanical Engineering Magazine[38] did an in-depth study of the Optiframe development and has this to say: "Eliminate five screws, save 40 seconds, multiply by 10 million: A computer's new development path pays off....the Optiframe design had reduced assembly time an average of 32 percent from earlier frames. It was so easy to put together that Dell could postpone constructing several new factories.

"In a Dell computer motherboard, a metal plate, called a tempan, holds the board rigid for shipping and installation. The one-piece solution that eliminates a screw reduces the potential for damage. The chassis had to come in three sizes and had to accommodate the characteristic variations of the three Dell desktop PC product lines....

"Dell calls its approach to product development Design for X. The 'X' can stand for manufacturing, logistics, ergonomics, service, or just about any other practical consideration. Teams comprise mechanical engineers and experts from other parts of the business, including logistics, shipping, and the supply chain. They start by listing most of the features of a new design, and then look at the product's expected life, from manufacturing through warranty service. The teams chart their progress along a defined product development path....

"A key goal was eliminating fasteners," said Dwight Stimson, a senior DFX engineer. "If you look at a DFA analysis, you'll see that every screw you design out of a product reduces assembly time by approximately eight seconds."

In fact, the Dell teams considered removing fasteners altogether—letting their machines be assembled simply by snapping components like drives and CDs in place. And, it turned to suppliers to do some of the work. As *Mechanical Engineering Magazine* says, "Dell developed a patented design using shock-absorbing material for the rails. Suppliers agreed to fasten the rails onto the components, so the screws for those parts were moved to an earlier stage of manufacture."

As it turns out, the supplier could do more, such as installing cables: "Another targeted task involved routing the integrated drive electronics cables inside the chassis and plugging them into the appropriate components. 'Once you start combining features, it's hard to stop,' Stimson said. 'The [chassis] design included the cable routing and allowed us to receive the cables preinstalled by the supplier. Plus, we color-coded the cables to make plugging them in even easier for both the factories and service.'"

The new chassis not only opens without tools, it actually locks into place at a 90-degree angle for the easy insertion of components. It was also smaller than previous chasses—shaving as little as half an inch off the size of packing cartons lets Dell shave hundreds of thousands of dollars off its shipping costs. Because components and features are shared by all three desktop lines, Dell can save inventory and assembly training.

Dell doesn't spend that much on product research and development compared to some of its competitors. But it has many patents (listed on its web site), and a large fraction of them are for manufacturing processes, not tech development, which reveals something about Dell's priorities in this area.

Streamline Customer Interaction

Dell is always looking for ways to streamline its customer interaction, as we've already seen. Dell is a direct-sales company, but it's always refining the customer interaction, in many ways: customer segmentation, online support, outsourcing tech support, and so on.

A large part of that streamlining process, of course, involves using the Internet. The benefit of the Internet for customer interaction is that software can handle the process, not paid employees. Dell has always excelled at using the Internet—and more important—getting customers to use the Internet. Like every other facet of its operations, Dell works on and refines its interactions with customers continuously.

Get the Best People

Dell has always emphasized getting the best people it can, even from the very beginning, as soon as Dell Computer could afford it. Like many other corporations, Dell has hired the best people away from other large corporations; in Dell's case, that includes Sun Microsystems, Novell, Apple Computer, Wal-Mart, and many others. Kevin Rollins is a prime example: Before joining Dell in 1996, he was vice president and partner of Bain & Co. management consultants. While at Bain, Rollins was instrumental in developing direct-selling strategies and services that helped move Dell in its relentless march up the charts. Michael Dell recognized talent when he saw it, and now he and Rollins effectively share the top spot at Dell.

Michael Dell says[39]: "A company's success should always be defined by its strategy and its ideas—and it should not be limited by the abilities of the people who are running it. As a manager and CEO, I was aware of my strengths and my weaknesses....

"By the end of 1993, it was apparent that there was too much for me to handle on my own. There were customers who I wanted to spend time with. There were management meetings and operations reviews I wanted to attend. There were speeches I wanted to make. I wanted to have the time to spend with our employees, in order to better understand their challenges and provide whatever help or insight I could on how they might improve different parts of the business."

So, he turned to getting the best help he could. He says[40]: "I've always tried to surround myself with the best people I could find.... The more talented people you have to help you, the better off you and your company will be."

Besides going out and finding the talent it wants, Dell also has the habit of hiring former CEOs for its operations. From the *Wall Street Journal*[41]: "Dell has used former CEOs and chief operating officers as key players as it has bucked the computer-industry trend and turned in double-digit sales growth despite the technology slump. This year, Wall Street projects the company's profit will rise 22 percent, to $2.58 billion, on revenue of $40 billion. Its personal-computer development, service, sales and marketing groups all have, at one time or another, included managers who once were presidents or CEOs elsewhere.

"In part, Dell's ex-presidents' club has grown because of the company's insistence on managers with strong financial know-how. [Joseph A.

Marengi, formerly Novell Inc.'s president and chief operating officer, who joined Dell in 1997] says he recruits managers who have experienced business ups and downs, and can still hit profit targets despite sales slumps. 'Profit-and-loss management is critically important here,' he said. The company needs managers who see the bottom line, not those who merely know how to stay within a budget...."

How does Dell find talent? It turns out that's another thing that its suppliers supply. From the *Wall Street Journal* article: "Dell says it doesn't go looking for top executives. Rather, it tends to recruit managers who impress its current executives through business dealings."

Target Your Competition Carefully

Part of adapting involves keeping close tabs on your competitors and adapting to what they're doing. Dell has a history of doing that and devastating its competitors at their own game.

Dell is so good at this that sometimes the media thinks that the process is personal, some kind of grudge match. Take a look at this *BusinessWeek*[42] article on how Dell has been moving into the printer business: "This drive is part of Dell's strategic plan to diversify beyond PCs into everything from corporate data storage gear to Internet music downloads. But there's also a more Machiavellian motive: draining profits from rival HP, which gets 70 percent of its operating profit from printers and ink. Dell believes its low-cost, direct-sales approach will allow it to torpedo prices in the printer market—especially for ink cartridges, which can cost as much in a year as the printer itself. If lower prices start luring HP customers to Dell, HP will have to cut its own prices or give up market share. Either way, HP would risk slippage in the rich profits that have bankrolled price wars with Dell in PCs and servers. 'We're going to keep the pedal down,' says Dell President Kevin B. Rollins."

Behold, the Dell Effect at work. Dell may indeed be targeting HP and the "rich profits" it uses to subsidize its fight with Dell in the PC and server market, but that's just business as usual.

Outsourcing

One of the most controversial ways that Dell streamlines its operations is through outsourcing. The long-term effects of outsourcing are as yet unclear, although Dell has been struggling with quality control in its Indian tech support centers. An article in *Enterprise Innovator*[43] notes that Dell is now creating other call centers as well: "TBR says it believes Dell 'now employs 12,500 people in its global technical support operations,' of which it estimates 'more than half of these individuals are located in India.' TBR adds Dell 'expects to grow its call center and engineering teams in India to upwards of 10,000 employees by year-end 2005,' though while 'India has become the primary country for the company's customer support infrastructure today due to its low labor costs,' Dell's also 'building out its infrastructure in many other geographies,' with 'recently opened customer contact centers in Germany, Holland, Glasgow, Alberta, Edmonton and Oklahoma City.'"

Another trend is more ominous; Dell and other companies increasingly appear to be outsourcing the design and engineering processes as well. From *CIO* magazine[44]: "U.S. computer makers such as Dell, Motorola and HP are outsourcing not just the manufacture but the design of new products to offshore companies. Could this be the end of America's innovative edge in electronics?

"Outsourcing has reached the highest level of the manufacturing supply chain: R&D. By outsourcing R&D offshore, original equipment manufacturers (OEMs) can freeze a portion of their R&D budgets while growing their product offerings. Even R&D powerhouses such as IBM, HP and Motorola have frozen—or even reduced—their R&D budgets since 2000. "[Outsourcing] is a tremendous opportunity for cost savings on R&D," says Jack Faber, vice president of operations, enterprise systems for HP.

"But there may be a downside to all this R&D reshuffling. Some economists say the outsourcing of manufacturing—and now design—is the leading edge of a longer-term trend toward reduced innovation and competitiveness among U.S. companies. As OEMs turn over the development of new products to outsourcers, it could have a withering effect on these companies' ability to create the next breakthrough, especially as many freeze R&D spending."

What's going to happen here? Time will tell.

Chapter 7

Value Information

∾∾

Information is the key to any competitive advantage.

—Michael Dell[1]

This chapter is all about Dell's use of information and metrics, something that it excels at and something that raises it above its competitors. To be nimble, as Dell Inc. has to be, you have to have more than just corporate will, you have to have information flow. As Michael Dell says, "In leadership, it's important to be intuitive, but not at the expense of facts."

You have to jump quickly in the tech field but, before you jump, you have to know as much as you can about where to jump. Dell prides itself on its information handling, and it's known for measuring just about everything. As *Fortune* magazine notes[2]: "Today, by every unit of measure (and the folks at Round Rock love to measure), in the computer hardware business, Dell is irrefutably the No. 1 company in the U.S."

The information flow that rockets continually around Dell is part of its direct model. Dell often gives the impression of a company that's been designed by engineers rather than by using traditional business principles. Part of that means using an engineer's love of data to design your company around information flow. There's a feeling you often run into at Dell that standard business structures only get in the way, because you need to be able to react fast, and you have to know what you're doing. It's not too much to say that Dell Inc. redefines the business model for the tech age.

One way that Dell sends information flying around the organization is to use both the Internet and Dell's own internal intranet. This chapter covers Dell's use of the Internet and intranet; without that use, Dell would be nowhere when it came to efficient information handling. Internet and intranet use is one of the themes Michael Dell likes to harp on, and people who hear him often don't understand why. This chapter explains why: They're the backbone that lets the information Dell Inc. so desperately needs to maintain its competitive edge keep moving at light speeds. Dell says,[3] "We wanted the Internet to become a key part of our entire business system. We wanted to make the Internet the first point of contact for every customer and prospect, and we planned for 50 percent of all customer transactions to be online within a few years."

Dell trims fat anywhere it finds it, and that includes the speed with which information moves. It's one of the things it needs to maintain its advantage. Michael Dell is explicit on this point[4]: "Dell is not the kind of company in which messages languish. We have to 'talk' in real-time through messages, over e-mail, and on the intranet because we're in a real-time business. Things happen in the morning that you have to react to by the afternoon. We have to be competitive twenty-four hours a day, 365 days a year, or else we lose business. A sense of urgency about communicating and solving problems is imperative."

Central to Dell's information flow are the many metrics it uses. The Dell metric that is going to get a significant amount of attention in this chapter is Return on Invested Capital (ROIC). Many corporations use many different metrics, such as profit, margin, price-to-earnings (P/E) ratio, and so on, but I'm going to argue in this chapter that Dell has pinpointed ROIC as the most significant one for effective business application. This focus on ROIC has let Dell trim its operations and reduce inventory. Essentially, the ROIC of a business or a business unit tells you how effective that business or business unit is at doing business; it tells you how fit that unit is. That's the measure you want. You might not be able to predict future business conditions, but you know that a company that focuses on ROIC—that is, on doing the most with the least—is going to be the best suited for the task.

Information Flow and Your Corporation

Much of the Dell culture relies on information flow. There's an understanding that, when you do something new, you also must have some way to measure it. That's a way of life at Dell.

It wasn't always that way. Like many corporations, during its formative days, Dell operated in the dark when it came to internal metrics and information flow. Dell says[5]: "It was clear that in 1993 we didn't have the information we needed to run our business. We didn't fully understand the relationship between costs, revenues, and profits within the different parts of our business. There were internal disagreements about which businesses were worthwhile and which were not. We were making decisions based on emotions and opinions." That's an accurate description of how too many companies function internally.

Today, the situation is different; Dell uses financial metrics for all aspects of its business. And that's infused the entire organization. *CFO* magazine interviewed Dell CFO Jim Schneider,[6] who was happy to find that everyone at Dell was already focused on finances: "Fortunately, Schneider says, Dell's staff understands [the burden of reporting financial forecasts]. 'Everyone here is very analytical and has a good finance bent,' he says. 'They know that if they're not focused on finance, we can't survive.'"

"It's important to be intuitive, but not at the expense of facts."

1993 was a crucial year for Dell. They had been using standard business practices and structures, but they were growing too fast, and they were overextended. *CFO* magazine sums up the situation[7]: "That year, Dell was enjoying heady growth as a direct seller of computer systems, but inventories were ballooning, cash reserves were in danger of going dry, and accounts receivables were rising faster than the revenue growth rates. In the first six months of 1993, Dell had a $66 million loss thanks to inventory write-downs."

Michael Dell realized at the time that a large part of what was missing was information. Dell had the corporate will, the ability to execute, but didn't know what to do. He says[8]: "In leadership, it's important to be intuitive, but not at the expense of facts. Without the right data to back it up, emotion-based decision-making during difficult times will inevitably lead a company into greater danger. That's precisely what was happening to us [in 1993]."

He knew it was time to bring in some outside help to clarify the picture. Enter Kevin Rollins. As Dell says,[9] "In August of 1993, in the middle of one of the most challenging periods in our company's history, I outlined a blueprint for the company's recovery for our Board of Directors. One of the items on the list was to get some outside help.

"We knew by now that there were areas where we were making money, and areas where we weren't. But we hadn't evolved enough to know exactly where, company-wide, nor did we know the magnitude of this disparity. So we called Bain & Company, with whom we'd successfully worked before, to help us out again. It was at this point that Kevin Rollins, the lead partner at Bain for Dell, became an integral part of our executive team.

"In keeping with our P&L plan, we worked with Bain to further dissect the business into its component parts. Based on this, we were able to develop a set of metrics that determined which business units and which weren't.

"We could compare one group's metrics to another's, identify performance opportunities, and accelerate growth in areas that made money. Once we determined which groups weren't performing as well, we could study the groups that were, and make an informed decision about if and how we could study the groups that were, and make an informed decision about if and how we could improve the lower performers—and if not, whether to cut our losses and close them down.

"It was a wonderfully efficient, liberating framework."

So, Dell started to examine its information flow, and it began to make progress. But, the real inspiration here ultimately came from a new CFO at that time, Thomas J. Meredith, now a former Dell CFO. It was Meredith that really introduced the ROIC metric to Dell. Tom Meredith was an evangelist for ROIC, so much so that he put ROIC on his license plate. His enthusiasm paid off for Dell.

Enter the Internet and Dell's Intranet

After the 1993 pothole, Dell Inc. became a big convert to information flow and metrics. Michael Dell's inspiration was that the Internet, and Dell's own intranet, were going to become central to that information flow. He has said[10]: "The Internet—and the company's internal intranet—let us shrink the amount of time it takes for the organization to get up to speed on a new topic or to share best practices across the company. It eliminates the physical forms of information that take more time and cost more money to deliver.

"We used to attach files to e-mail documents when we wanted people to review information. Then one day, I was in a meeting and said, 'Gee, wouldn't it be great if we could review information over the Internet so our network capacity wasn't strained by all of these charts and graphs flowing back and forth?

"Today, we put an Internet or intranet address in the e-mail, so that people can click the hyperlink to access the information. We used to get performance reports once a week. Now we can go to the net and get the information in real time."

What's better at disseminating and sharing information better than the Internet? Around this time, using the Internet became one of Michael Dell's passions. And www.dell.com appeared in June 1994. Like ROIC, using the Internet and intranet is a repeating theme in this chapter.

A Passion for Information Flow

The Internet and Dell's intranet are not the only way Dell sends information around. Information flow is a passion at Dell, and no one is an advocate of that more than Michael Dell himself[11]: "We also learn a lot by asking the same questions in similar groups across the company and comparing the results. We do this to share the best ideas throughout our various businesses because we're all working towards the same goal. If one team is having great success with medium-size companies, we cross-pollinate their ideas around the world. If another team has figured out how to sell into law firms, we share their learning throughout the organization. Our best ideas can come from anywhere in the world and be shared instantly…. We exchange ideas through e-mail and the web, and through councils where we bring different groups from around the world to exchange information."

Dell also puts emphasis on making meetings functional. As Michael Kanellos, CNET news.com editor-at-large, says, "One thing they really discourage is long meetings. Meetings can only last 50 minutes. In the older days, a lot of conference rooms didn't have chairs—it cut down on any desire to keep it long."

Segmentation Helps

One thing that has helped facilitate information flow at Dell is its use of segmentation. Segmentation, which divides monolithic structures into smaller ones, makes for smaller feedback loops. As a result, investing in segmentation has let Dell measure the efficiency and effectiveness of each of its units in a way that wouldn't be possible without that segmentation.

You can measure metrics more sensitively if your organization is segmented. Want to see which units are doing well? Check the metrics. Want to see which are doing poorly? Same answer. As we saw in Chapter 6,

Dell says[12]: "One of the great things about segmentation is that it has allowed us to see growth rates, profitability, service level performance, and market share in each unique segment, and adjust our activities accordingly."

Information Flow and Customers

The Dell Direct model is well known to us at this point. Dell's connection to its customers is legendary, as are the efforts it puts in to maintain and hone that connection. Not only does it collect information continually and directly from customers following each sale, but it also uses face-to-face contact, as with its Platinum Councils.

Michael Dell has said[13]: "We have set up a number of forums to ensure the free flow of information with our customers on a constant basis. We arrange technical briefings at briefing centers designed specifically for this purpose at each of our regional headquarters around the world (Limerick, Ireland; Penang, Malaysia; Xiamen, China; Alvorada, Braxil; and Round Rock, Texas). We'll often run two or three briefings every day in each facility. We also have one on one meetings in our offices and out in the field."

What's also worth talking about here is the emphasis Dell puts on the Internet as a conduit for information in connecting with its customers. The emphasis on Internet use at Dell is fundamental, although many businesses shrug it off. Dell was a pioneer in going to the Internet; www.dell.com appeared on 1994, and e-commerce capability appeared in 1996. The year after that, Dell became the first company to have over $1 million in daily sales. Today, www.dell.com is one of the highest-volume sites on the Internet. These days, that site (which, as you'd expect, runs on Dell PowerEdge servers) gets more than two billion hits per quarter. There are 84 country sites in 20 languages or dialects and in 26 currencies.

Dell relies on the Internet for procurement, customer support, and relationship management of all kinds. At the www.dell.com site, customers can configure systems and get price quotes, and, of course, they can order systems directly and track their manufacture. Many thousands of business customers use Dell's Premier.Dell.com web pages to perform the same kinds of operations. Want technical support? Just double-click the Dell Support icon on your screen: no problem.

Dell says[14]: "As I saw it, the Internet offered a logical extension of the direct model, creating even stronger relationships with our customers....

"In addition to researching, configuring, pricing, and ordering our products online, customers could use the Internet to check the status of their order as it moved down the manufacturing line. If they had questions about how it worked, they could go to our technical support page, where they would have access to all of the same information that our own technical support teams did. The Internet would make the direct model even more direct."

And[15]: "The direct model also affects our suppliers in other ways. Dealing directly with customers enables us to provide fast feedback to our suppliers—a plus they don't get from other computer companies. Because customers tell us almost immediately what's working for them— or what's not—the supplier is able to benefit and adjust quickly, making appropriate improvements or adjusting output if necessary."

And[16]: "We can put complex white papers online that explain new technologies and provide diagrams of how machines are configured. This way, users can get a great feel for what our products do—much better than they would get from some static brochure or some other noninteractive form of information. They can get as much detail as they desire. And we know that they've read it.…

"The ability to measure customer response in a scientific way is just remarkable. We can do some of this in the physical world with dedicated toll-free numbers for specific advertisements that tell us which ads generate how many calls and how many of those calls translate into sales. But on the Internet, you can do real-time experiments. You can present an offer to customers and within two hours you know whether that offer is successful. You can even change the offer slightly and compare the results of the different offers in real-time, then switch to whichever one seems to be the most effective—literally within minutes." Watch the Dell site at the end of any given month—you're going to see all kinds of good deals appearing as the factory wants to hit its target sales.

Information Flow and Suppliers

The Internet is also a huge part of moving information between Dell and its suppliers. Michael Dell says[17]: "Just as the Internet increases customer intimacy, it can also be used to enhance supplier intimacy. The idea is to connect with your suppliers in much the same way you connect with your customers. We use our supplier connections to share inventory data, quality data, and technology plans; to give our partners immediate visibility to the field; and to serve as a central repository for information we all need—which we can access simultaneously, in real time.…

"To do that, we are creating web-based links for each of our suppliers, just as we did for our customers. These will further facilitate the rapid exchange of information, including component quality as measured by Dell's own metrics and current cost structures, as well as current forecasts and future demand. For example, a web-based link we designed for Intel allows us to more quickly and efficiently manage order flow and just-in-time delivery of inventory. In that same vein, we're currently conducting pilot programs that will link our internal management systems to suppliers overseas and, ultimately, directly into the very factories that are producing the components....

"By using the Internet to maintain a continuous flow of materials from our suppliers into our factories, our people spend less time placing orders or expediting parts and more time adding value."

Dell also says[18]: "The link between the day-to-day demand trend and the incoming material from your suppliers is absolutely crucial to your success—so the shorter you can make the link, the better off you are. Today we have access to technology that greatly facilitates the exchange of this information. We can share methodologies with supplier-partners in ways that just weren't possible five or ten years ago, which results in dramatically faster time to market."

Enterprise *Innovator* comments on the sheer volume of information[19]: "[Michael] Dell noted how Dell gets around '120,000 to 140,000 computers sold [worldwide] on a daily basis,' and that orders 'come in a variety of ways' whether by 'phone, Web, fax, all sorts of ways that orders come in.' He added, 'These orders come in, and the minute we get a signal from customers that they want to buy something, it propagates back through the system to the suppliers,' which 'deliver components to our factory every 90 minutes based on the orders that come in.' In this way, the Web provides a mechanism for real-time inventory control, 'so we don't have all this guessing.' Dell explained, 'If I know exactly what you want to buy, I don't need a whole lot of material at all,' and with the Web, Dell was able to replace stockpiles of components with information, creating a 'tightly integrated supply chain.'"

Dell's tight connection to its suppliers is a given, but it's crucial to bear in mind the role that information flow plays in that process. The tight coupling provided by instant data access allows Dell to work with suppliers as it does and permits Dell to maintain almost zero inventory.

Information Flow and Employees

Information flow permeates Dell, and employees are included in that loop. There's an effort to keep people in touch with what's going on, providing overview information that helps align the company's goals and the workforce. That happens in most major corporations; you see signs and placards frequently, but most employees shrug them off. Corny slogans and goofy cartoons don't hack it.

Dell is different: By focusing on financial metrics, by genuinely working to make everyone feel like an owner, it seems to have significantly aligned corporate and workforce goals. That's not to say there's anything like 100 percent management–workforce alignment at Dell. But there's significantly more alignment at Dell than in most other corporations.

The big names make company-wide appearances, of course; Michael Dell says[20]: "I go to brown-bag lunches two or three times a month, and meet with a cross-section of people from all across the company." Meetings and answer sessions are held, and there are memos and so on.

Dell says[21]: "Every year, we have town hall meetings at which I describe how the company is doing, what our strategies are, where we stand in the market, and what our plans are. Then I answer lots of questions. Any question is OK.... It's such a great opportunity to reiterate the objectives and mission of the company that we post a transcript on our intranet for anyone who has to miss the meeting.

"We celebrate successes both in person and electrically. We send out mass e-mail messages congratulating our teams on big wins, elevating their win to a company-wide accomplishment. It's exciting for people to hear about what's going on in different businesses or teams, and it also helps to share best practices, because one group benefits from what's working for others. It also helps build confidence throughout the organization."

And[22]: "We went into high gear to communicate the necessity of achieving our goals in servers. We sent out company-wide 'Message from Michael' e-mails, put up posters in high-traffic areas, and talked through the strategy at numerous brown-bag lunches and company get-togethers. We staged a huge event—'The Great Dell Torch Event'—for seven thousand employees in an auditorium in downtown Austin just to drive the point home. Someone dressed up as Server Man, complete with a cloak and tights and a big red 'S' on his chest, and went around to all the buildings to get people revved up about attending the event. I opened the evening by running into the auditorium carrying an Olympic-sized torch."

Standard, and fairly embarrassing, corporate fare. But unlike a typical corporation, the focus is not on aligning work goals so much as it is on aligning a business philosophy. That's why it works. In a typical corporation, employees understand that the gung-ho nonsense they get on the latest project targets is more or less just that—nonsense. It doesn't change the underlying relationship—you employee, me boss. You're trying to get me to get all wrapped up in your project, the employee says, and I will, but for myself. You're obviously very excited about this, so I'll play along. Maybe I'll get a promotion out of it.

Dell Inc. makes an effort to be different here, because it focuses on the business strategy. And it communicates that strategy to employees, which fosters a sense of shared goals that actually works. Rather than talking down to employees, as at so many major corporations, Dell—despite Server Man—treats them like adults when it comes to a sense of corporate mission. Everyone knows what Dell Direct is all about, and most people share that sense of a winning culture. The idea of creating a company of owners isn't just talk at Dell; business and financial strategies infuse the company far more than at other corporations I've studied.

As a result, Michael Dell is able to say[23]: "Almost anyone at Dell can explain the fundamental concepts that our business is based on. That's because we spend a tremendous amount of time communicating what's going on, what we're planning to do, and what everyone needs to do to help us achieve our goals."

As you'd expect when you have as many employees as Dell has, the results are not 100 percent alignment, but they're still good. By treating its employees as adults, by involving them more in the idea of a shared and winning business philosophy, Dell gets significant alignment. That's far better than watching thousands of employees yawning their way through yet another motivational presentation from upper management, where the underlying and subtly antagonistic me-boss-you-employee stance keeps those on the podium very far apart from those in the folding chairs. If you've been through as many of those as I have, you know that employees like these events mainly because it gives them the chance to get off work for a while and maybe to grab some refreshments.

Dell's employees also are immersed in the metrics specific to their jobs, as you'd expect. Dell is a real convert to information flow and, if there's any feedback loop that must be implemented, you can bet it already is at Dell. For example, *Industry Week* tells us[24]: "Three critical metrics that Dell employees focus on are customer-centered: ship-to-target rates (the percentage of shipments made within five days of receiving an order); the combined initial field incident rate; and 'on-time, first-time fix' by customer-service technicians.

"Employee profit-sharing bonuses are tied to the three key metrics, which must show a 15 percent year-to-year improvement in order to generate a bonus equal to that given in the prior year. Typically, profit-sharing accounts for up to 20 percent of Dell employees' annual compensation."

Michael Dell says[25]: "On our factory floor, for example, people work in teams of two to receive, manufacture, and pack an order for delivery to a customer. Their profit-sharing incentive encourages them to be productive as a team. Hourly metrics (or data) are posted on monitors on the factory floor so that each team has a sense of how it is doing against our goals. The more efficient our manufacturing teams are, the more they stand to gain."

The information that employees need to perform is available on the Internet or intranet as well. Dell says[26]: "It's impossible for any sales organization to understand the breadth and depth of all the products a company offers. But it's easy to describe and explain them on the Internet and to update them as frequently as necessary so that salespeople have a readily accessible reference guide. If we have a new product being introduced in the next few months, we can provide information to our sales and support teams immediately. We no longer have to sit around the proverbial campfire and tell one guy to pass it on to the next."

Because this is Dell, employees themselves are also measured with great thoroughness. Dell conducts not just employee reviews, but "360-degree performance appraisals." These appraisals involve talking to everyone who works with an employee, and the flow of information is two way. Michael Dell describes the process this way[27]: "The principle behind the 360-degree performance appraisal [also emphasizes how it is more beneficial to work together than apart]. Instead of gauging an employee's annual progress against the subjective views of one person—usually [their] direct supervisor—this full circle review solicits input from everyone an employee works with. It's a great measurement for identifying those areas that might require further development or improvement, and it keeps people focused on achieving their goals as a team. It's the closest we've come to objectifying the data on our people, minimizing interpersonal politics."

As you already know, Dell often uses dual reporting, having some employees report to at least two other persons.

Information Flow and Managers

Managers, like others, are subject to 360-degree performance appraisals. And there's another standard mechanism for rating managers from the employee perspective: the "Tell Dell" surveys. Employees rate their bosses every 6 months using those surveys.[28]

Dell is metrics-obsessed when it comes to the parts it uses in manufacturing, and it's also metrics-obsessed when it comes to its people, which can sometimes make those people feel like one of those parts. At Dell, a lot of scrutiny goes on, and you can end up feeling like a PC during the assembly process.

There's no doubt this helps monitor performance, but it also can engender a feeling of quasi-paranoia. Michael Dell says,[29] somewhat optimistically, "Challenging the current state of affairs ensures that you don't get too wrapped up in your success. By now, self-criticism is ingrained in the Dell culture—we're always ready to question our own ideas, looking for the ways things can be improved. We try to model this behavior from the top down. We hire for, and develop, leaders who are open-minded and can accept being disagreed with publically or corrected when they've got their facts wrong. This helps promote open debate and encourages an intellectual meritocracy." Hearing that from the employee side of the equation might make someone think that it's easy to say that when you're the boss and your name is on the front of the building. As far as that feeling of quasi-paranoia goes, Dell is known for quickly shuttling people out if they don't work out.

But Dell also genuinely wants his managers to get out there and collect information and feedback. He adds,[30] "As managers, it's not enough to sit around theorizing and reviewing what those who report to us do. We frequently meet with customers and attend working-level meetings about products, procurement, and technology, to tap into the real source of our company's experience and brainpower."

The Profitable Growth Metric

Dell is wise about the metrics it selects, and one of them is profitable growth. In its early days, Dell went after growth, period. But growth at any cost can become a serious problem. Everyone's familiar with stories about companies and CEOs who went after acquisitions and mergers that proved untenable, so that, while the growth was there for a while, it was ultimately costly and unsustainable. Or, of stories of how growth was achieved on razor-thin margins so that it involved a massive capital investment to get there.

Dell no longer simply goes for growth; that was its problem in 1993. It goes for profitable growth; hence, industry-watchers sometimes misunderstand its motives, as in the case of China, where it's substantially pulled out of the entry-level PC market, at least for the moment. The growth was there, but not the profit. To outsiders, Dell is a company that focuses on offering low-cost tech products. But Dell emphasizes profitable growth and doesn't feel constrained to stay in an unprofitable market sector. That's why Dell is nimble about pulling out of a sector when products become commodities. Outsiders think it's retreating, but it's staying true to the profitable growth metric, which in China has meant pursuing higher price-point markets, especially corporate customers.

Growth is important for any public company with stockholders clamoring for share price appreciation; it's a matter of grow or die, and Michael Dell has said as much.[31] But growth for its own sake doesn't make sense if it's going to end up dragging you down. So, Dell attempts to grow where it makes sense. From *Forbes Magazine*[32]: "Standard & Poor's Equity Research reiterated a 'strong buy' rating on Dell, saying the hardware company's revenue growth levels are 'attractive' versus peers.' The research firm said it sees 16 percent or higher revenue growth for Dell over the next two years, down slightly from the fiscal 2004 to 2005 period, as the company becomes more disciplined in pursuing only very profitable growth areas."

Pursuing *profitable* growth is one reason Dell consistently increases its margins, despite industry dips. From Dell's web site[33]: "Dell is extending its trend of winning new customers and achieving profitable growth even without broad industry recovery, and raising its expectations for revenue in the third-quarter. The quarter would be the seventh consecutive in which Dell has met or exceeded its sales and earnings guidance."

Why move from PCs to include servers? Profitable growth. Why move on to LCD TVs, printers, services, and even portable music players? Same answer.

If you look deeper into this story, however, you'll realize that profit and growth are only two of the three parts of a mantra that Dell adopted shortly after its 1993 problems. Michael Dell puts it this way[34]: "We had been operating under the assumption that we would grow faster than the market, but that we would still achieve a return on sales of 5 percent. But we had grown too quickly. We realized our priorities had to change. We needed to focus on slow, steady growth, and liquidity. Once we got our cash situation in order, we could then turn on the profit valve and eventually reaccelerate our growth. Instead of 'growth, growth, growth,' the new order of business at Dell would be 'liquidity, profitability, and growth'—in that order.

"Achieving this was a laborious but revealing process. We analyzed each and every segment of our business carefully, with the hope of coming up with a profit and loss statement for each *part* of it. By understanding the economics of each segment of our business, we could appropriately target our best opportunities and where we needed to improve."

Dell's internal business strategy shifted to that triumvirate: liquidity, profitability, and growth. Growth for its own sake was out; liquidity, profitability, and growth were in. In fact, Michael Dell started handing out pyramidal Plexiglas paperweights inscribed with "Liquidity," "Profitability," and "Growth" on each side at management meetings.

You'll find "liquidity, profitability, and growth" in many places throughout Dell; the following is from the Dell at a Glance web page on Dell's web site[35]: "Dell's high return to shareholders has been the result of a focused effort over time to balance growth with profitability and liquidity. Dell has consistently led its largest competitors in each of those categories."

From a 2001 article on news.com[36]: "Analysts described Dell's gambit—trading some profitability for big market share gains—to playing the board war game, Risk. By expanding its lead in more markets—or in Risk controlling enough countries—Dell hopes to overrun competitors.

"What Dell is try[ing] to do is use the bad climate to gain share, and from an enhanced share position rebuild the liquidity, profitability, revenue growth triumvirate that is their kind of mantra," [IDC analyst Roger] Kay said. "They can't abandon that model."

But, despite that prediction in 2001, things have indeed shifted. "Liquidity, profitability, and growth" has not been abandoned, and it was a far better orientation strategy for Dell than simply "Growth, growth, growth." But the even this three-part philosophy morphed into something more powerful—a single metric that has become a real corporate focus. And that metric is ROIC.

The ROIC Metric

The supreme corporate metric at Dell is Return on Invested Capital (ROIC), the metric Thomas J. Meredith stressed during the 1993 panic days. From a 1997 *BusinessWeek* article on that episode[37]: "It wasn't that long ago that the PC cognoscenti were predicting Michael Dell and his mail order model would hit the wall. It certainly came close. In the first six months of 1993, Dell had a $65 million loss from inventory write-downs and an industrywide price war started by Compaq.

"But the close call was transformed into a lesson on the dangers of growth at all costs. Dell wised up and recruited operations-savvy managers from Motorola, Sun Microsystems, and Western Digital. Financial teams fanned out to talk with employees about new metrics for running the business—minimizing inventories and increasing return on capital. Today, the financial nitty-gritty is deeply ingrained in Dell's 10,350 employees. The marketing department calculates the return on invest-ment for each mailing; purchasing managers figure the cost of unsold inventory each day. "We spent 15 months educating people about return on invested capital, convincing them they could impact our future,' says [now former] Chief Financial Officer Thomas J. Meredith."

CFO Magazine gives us more of the details on how Dell came to emphasize ROIC[38]: "Balance is especially important in performance measurement, says Meredith. 'Wall Street rewards companies that balance growth, liquidity, and profitability,' he says. 'In 1993, however, our bal-ance was out of whack.'...

"To bring about a better balance, Meredith identified the cash conver-sion cycle (CCC) as a key performance measure—one that, not coinciden-tally, has the concept of speed at its heart. 'The balance between profitable growth and liquidity management is all about velocity,' he argues.

"Using the metrics of days sales outstanding (DSO), days sales in inventory (DSI), and days of payables outstanding (DPO), Dell added DSO and DSI, then subtracted DPO, to determine the cash conversion cycle. During 15 months of what Meredith calls 'impassioned evangeliz-ing,' he focused Dell employees on how they could influence the CCC equation: accelerating inventory turns and collection activities, slowing down supplier payments, and the like. In late 1994, the cycle stood at an acceptable 40 days; today it is a phenomenal negative 8 days.

"In 1995, to drive home further the need to optimize the 'Golden Triangle' formed by growth, liquidity, and profitability, Dell began using return on invested capital (ROIC) as a broader measure of value creation, and linked the ROIC metric to the variable pay of all executives. Bonus eligibility, as well as receipt of the maximum payout, is now based on a matrix that reflects an appropriate balance between ROIC and revenue growth. In three years, Dell's ROIC has more than quadrupled....

"What makes Meredith positively crow, however, is that Dell's com-petitors have recently adopted similar metrics. "These companies have had to respond to a landscape shaped by Dell," he says. None, he adds, can touch Dell's numbers."

It's not only executives that are directed to remember ROIC; every employee in every unit is also. Michael Dell has said[39]: "ROIC became a focusing device. We introduced it in 1995 with a company-wide push to educate everyone about the benefits of a positive ROIC, with articles in the company newsletter, posters, talks by managers, and 'Messages from Michael' devoted to the topic....

"We explained specifically how everyone could contribute: by reduc-ing cycle times, eliminating scrap and waste, selling more, forecasting accurately, scaling operating expenses, increasing inventory turns, collecting accounts receivable efficiently, and doing things right the first time. And we make it the core of our incentive compensation for all employees. We decided to reward employees around a matrix of ROIC and growth; higher performance directly correlated to higher ROIC, which came back in the form of higher compensation."

Meredith was right on with the emphasis on ROIC, and it helped turn the company around. From the *CFO Magazine* article: "Back in 1993, Dell Computer Corp. chairman and CEO Michael Dell was ambling through London's Heathrow Airport with his newly minted CFO, Thomas Meredith, and was increasingly puzzled by the optimism in the finance executive's words. Those days, after all, couldn't have been darker for the Round Rock, Texas-based computer maker. The company was growing too fast, burning cash at a breakneck pace; it had posted a $39 million loss the previous fiscal year. Under attack by securities analysts for its hedging practices, its stock price was plummeting from $49 per share to $16 per share.

"Dell, a glass-is-half-empty kind of guy, listened gloomily as Meredith went on about how the company would recover, how everybody would learn so much in the process, and how only good things would follow from the experience. Then, as the two approached their gate, he shot his CFO a crooked grin. 'Tom,' he quipped, 'you have a really distorted sense of humor.'

"But Meredith was deadly serious—and right on target, as Dell notes now. 'I give Tom credit for seeing through the stormy times and realizing we'd come out better on the other end,' says Dell. And that foresight, among other qualities, prompted Dell to nominate Meredith for the CFO Excellence Awards. The judges concurred, naming Meredith the only two-category winner, with the top prize in both performance measurement and risk management."

What's so special about ROIC? Why is it such an important, yet such an overlooked, metric? Fundamentally, ROIC is a measure of how *fit* a business or a business unit is. It tells you how well an entity can take $1 and turn it into $2. What's missing in all the standard talk about profits and growth is how much it takes to produce that profit or that growth. By emphasizing ROIC, both the *return* and the *invested capital* are taken into account.

Emphasizing ROIC by making it the chief metric takes into account how you get the return you're reporting on. So, you not only maximize return, you also minimize the invested capital. Watching ROIC is how Dell came up with the idea of minimizing inventory—now *that's* a metric that works.

From an article on slate.msn.com[40]: "Finally, a simple focus on the P/E blinds investors to the most important number to consider in evaluating a company, namely its return on invested capital (ROIC). What you really want to know about a company, after all, is how efficiently it's using its capital. You want a company to turn $1 in capital into $2 in cash, not $1 in capital into $1 in cash. And no company in America is better at doing the former than Dell. Its return on invested capital is historically above 200 percent, and has occasionally bettered that number. By getting money from customers before paying money out to suppliers, and by keeping inventories incredibly lean, Dell effectively lets its suppliers fund its operations. In effect, Dell is selling $18 billion of computers and servers a year while investing almost no money in the business."

ROIC measures a business unit's abilities, which are a combination of both nurture (the personnel and corporate structure) and nature (the business environment). If the personnel and the structure of the unit come up short, you'll see that in the ROIC, which tells you how well the unit is able to handle resources and turn them into results. If the business environment isn't a good one to be in (say, you're selling outright commodities like toasters—or low-end PCs in China), your ROIC will tell you that there's a problem. Either way, ROIC tells you how well adapted and how effective a business unit is. If it's not well adapted or effective, it's time to make changes.

In other words, maintaining a good ROIC is all about the survival of the fittest, about being the corporation most able to do the best. If you want to be the fittest in the fight for corporate life, ROIC is the metric to watch. It's a measure of a business unit's resilience, effectiveness, and placement—that is, how fit it is as far as your business goes. (If a good business unit has been placed in an underperforming environment, or a dysfunctional market, that's going to lower its ROIC.)

J. William Gurley wrote *Above the Crowd/Productivity Paradox*, which emphasizes the importance of the underutilized ROIC and describes it using exactly those terms. From the book[41]: "In evolution-speak, the term 'fitness' is often used to describe a species' capacity for survival. From a corporate perspective, the best measure of fitness is return on invested capital (ROIC), which measures a company's true cash output relative to the total cash value of the assets deployed in the business. The reason this measure matters most is that, over the long haul, capital flows away from investment opportunities with a low ROIC, and toward investment opportunities with a high ROIC. Inefficient companies are eventually starved from the cash that they need to survive.

"To truly understand just how indispensable technology has become, you have to break down ROIC into its two key components: The numerator is its cash-adjusted operating profit, while the denominator is the cash value of the company's net capital investments. Divide both numbers by sales, and you'll see that ROIC can be restated as operating margin multiples divided by asset turnover.

"In other words, the two critical components that define a company's fitness are an ability to charge a higher spread between price and actual cost, and the ability to generate more sales from a smaller base of invested capital."

Although Gurley writes in terms of a company's ROIC, Dell uses ROIC for each of its internal segments, as well as an overall one for the company as a whole. Each segment must continually justify itself in terms of ROIC, and that metric is made known to the employees in the unit. Using ROIC in this way transformed Dell. It's an easy move to have made in retrospect, but in 1993, the way forward was cloudy: Dell lacked some way of measuring the specific performance of its various units. Some were making a lot of money while consuming a lot of resources, so it was hard, in a business sense, to know what was going on.

ROIC changed all that and got Dell onto a business footing. It's a true business measure and, for Dell, just about the best possible one. It's a point many of Dell's competitors have yet to fully appreciate—to come out on top in terms of ROIC, you have to have both profitable growth and run a very tight ship. Once you realize how well that describes Dell Inc., you can see how greatly the ROIC metric is responsible for what Dell is today. And you can see why cutting costs is so integral to Dell's operations; growth isn't enough, profit isn't enough—not even margin is enough. It's how much you get for what you put in that counts. That's what will drive your business.

Dell shapes its internal structure using ROIC, and it's not shy about cutting units that don't measure up. Most corporations don't use this kind of internal metric, which is a mistake. If they use ROIC at all, they use it for an overall corporate measure, which obscures the internals. For example, the *BusinessWeek* article[42] mentioned in Chapter 6 says that HP has been using the profits from its printer division to shore up the fight against Dell in PCs and servers: "Either way, HP would risk slippage in the rich profits that have bankrolled price wars with Dell in PCs and servers." Obviously, that's not a sustainable business strategy; you would expect Dell to do something like enter the printer market after a quick glance at HP's annual reports, and that's what Dell has done. Watching unit-by-unit ROIC makes sure that something like that doesn't happen unintentionally; you know where the money is coming from and where it's going to. If you don't know that, a company that does, like Dell, is going to pop your bubble.

Relatively few other corporations are steered by ROIC in all operations, and this often confuses the media when it comes to understanding what Dell is doing (as in the media storm about its China operations). So, if you can't understand a move Dell makes, take a look at what's going on in terms of ROIC. The clouds will often part at that point, because Dell doesn't hesitate to exit market sectors where there's no ROIC, as when it abandoned the big retailers. Many other metrics are in constant use, but the one you can't argue with at Dell is ROIC.

As Michael Kanellos, CNET news.com editor-at-large, says, "Another important point is that ROIC gives everyone a convenient point for framing debates. It's one way everyone can look at the same problem without getting into philosophical arguments. In turn, that helps the whole sense of coherence at Dell. Everyone pretty well knows what they are doing—that is one of their big assets. HP is confused often. The R&D departments work on projects that may only have tangential relationships to actual products. Chip departments lobby for survival. Most companies are more balkanized."

A case study[43] on Dell at the Tuck School of Business at Dartmouth reviews the internal metrics in use at Dell: "Turning Michael Dell's concept into reality meant rallying a large and dynamic organization around a common purpose and measuring its performance by relevant and concrete measurements (or metrics). In August 1993, Dell engaged Bain & Company, Inc., a global business consultancy, to help it develop a set of metrics to judge business-unit performance. Reflecting on that experience, Michael Dell said, 'It was all about assigning responsibility and accountability to the managers.... Indeed, there were some managers within Dell who resisted the use of facts and data in daily decision making, and, painful as it was for all of us, they eventually left. But for the most part, people were energized by the change. We carefully communicated what this meant for the company's future to our employees, customers, and shareholders. It was met with an overwhelmingly positive response because of the clarity of vision it afforded. "Facts are your friend" soon became a common phrase at Dell. We were still the same company, marked by the same Dell drive and spirit, but we were better armed to make important decisions.' Dell recognized early the need for speed, or velocity, quickening the pace at every step of business. The company learned that the more workers handled, or touched, the product along the assembly process, the longer the process took and the

greater the probability of quality concerns. Dell began to track and systematically reduce the number of 'touches' along the line, driving it to
zero. The company took orders from customers and fulfilled them by
buying and assembling the needed components. Customers got exactly
the configuration they desired, and Dell reduced its need for plants,
equipment, and R&D. As a result, Dell turned a product business into a
service industry. The primary financial objective that guided managerial
evaluation at Dell was return on invested capital (ROIC). Thomas J.
Meredith, former Dell CFO, even put ROIC on his license plate.

"Dell's scorecard included both financial measures (ROIC, average
selling price, component purchasing costs, selling and administration
costs, and margins) and nonfinancial measures (component inventory,
finished goods inventory, accounts receivable days, accounts payable
days, cash-conversion cycle, stock outs, and accuracy of forecast
demand). The scorecard was generated on a real-time basis, and relevant
performance measures were broken down by customer segment, product category, and country." When you watch ROIC, you turn your corporation into a business machine; you're no longer tied to a specific niche.
This is the point at which Dell Computer became Dell Inc.

The emphasis on ROIC gives some interesting results and, occasionally, some creative numerics that seem to come close to book-cooking.
Whitney Tilson, a columnist on The Motley Fool web site, innocently
took the numbers that Dell publishes about its operations—as those in its
annual reports, freely available on www.dell.com—and tried to calculate
its corporate ROIC. He wanted to compare his result with the ROIC Dell
makes public.

The results were nowhere close, and Tilson couldn't understand the
difference. Dell's published ROIC was far higher than Tilson's calcula-
tions, and it took a good deal of communication with Dell to resolve the
difference, which Tilson discusses in an article on The Motley Fool web
site.[44] The discrepancy centered around such items as what should be
considered invested capital and what was merely excess cash, for example. In nearly every case, unsurprisingly, Dell went to pains to raise its
ROIC. With the corporate focus on this metric, that's not exactly unexpected.

An article[45] in *Slate* magazine discusses this aspect of calculating
ROIC: "In essence, what ROIC looks to capture is the amount of cash
generated by the company's ongoing operations relative to the capital
needed to generate that cash. As a result, return on invested capital is
simply the company's net operating profit after tax (NOPAT) divided by
its invested capital. NOPAT is equal simply to sales minus operating

expenses minus taxes. (Keep out interest earnings or one-time deals from the sales number.)

"To find 'invested capital,' just take a company's assets, subtract its current liabilities, then subtract the cash it has on the balance sheet. This is the amount of money the company has spent on working assets less the normal cash that flows in and out. (To figure out a company's ROIC for a given period, you need to calculate these numbers at the beginning of the period and at the end, and average them.) A company like Dell has few assets—relative to its sales—and high liabilities, since it waits to pay its suppliers until after it gets paid by its customers. As a result, its return on invested capital is astronomical. This is a good thing if you're a Dell shareholder.

"There are, of course, other ways of calculating ROIC. Some people think you shouldn't subtract cash at all, since it is being 'invested' even if it's not being put to work in the business. Others think you should subtract 'excess cash'—say, cash in excess of 20 percent of revenues—from total assets. And there are also modifications you can make to NOPAT involving uniform tax rates and the like, modifications that you should worry about only if your parents cruelly blocked you from your dream of being an accountant."

Watching ROIC makes Dell one nimble corporation, able to handle the industry dips better than anyone else. As *BusinessWeek* says[46]: "'Dell gets its ROIC because it can turn an asset faster than anyone,' says Kevin McCarthy, an analyst at Donaldson, Lufkin & Jenrette, referring to Dell's inventory model. That's why Dell has done so well even as PC prices have dropped rapidly." Low inventory, high ROIC.

Watching ROIC encourages Dell to be effective and efficient in everything it tackles. From a speech Dell made to The Chief Executives' Club of Boston[47] on Internet use: "Dell has seen first hand the benefits of Internet integration. If you examine Dell's ROIC, you will see the financial Return on Invested Capital in our 1996 fiscal year was 34 percent. In 1999, we aggressively increased our Internet integration for supply-chain management, and reaped the benefits of that in our fiscal year 2000. Our financial ROIC in the second quarter of this year increased to 294 percent. Dell's ROIC has been a reflection of our commitment to infrastructure computing. The acronym ROIC has traditionally meant Return on Invested Capital. Because of the importance of Internet infrastructure to a company's operations, I propose a new way of looking at this metric: Think of it as Return on Infrastructure Computing. The new ROIC is a subset of traditional financial metrics used to measure performance. This University of Texas and Dell sponsored 'E-Census' clearly indicates that the further companies integrate the Internet to meet their operational objectives, the more financially successful they will be."

Want to understand Dell's business model?

Think ROIC. It's the guiding light.

Metrics, Metrics, Everywhere

Everything Dell does is infused with metrics. A case study from Knowledge Advisors, a learning measurement and analytics technology company, has this to say on how Dell requested customer training classes be set up—note that it's typical that Dell would request a system of metrics to see how well people were learning.[48] "Dell provides value-added training to assist its customers in optimally using the products and services they purchase from Dell. Customers ranging from corporations to individuals can access a comprehensive listing of course titles from which they can learn the best practices and supporting tactics to help them get the very most out of their new Dell purchase. Training from Dell's perspective is an essential part of the customer experience.

"Dell requested a scalable and flexible approach to measure the investments they make in learning programs. They wanted to ensure the approach encompassed sound learning methodologies while being practical to use in the real world. Dell worked with their training partners including Netg, an eLearning content provider, GeoLearning, a learning management system, and KnowledgeAdvisors to create a seamless, integrated, customer facing interface where all systems work together to register participants for the training, present the training, and measure the training. The measurement solution is a Dell branded interface that seamlessly directs respondents to [Knowledge Advisor's] Metrics that Matter™ to complete their learning evaluation. Once all the data is collected, it is stored, processed and reported in the reporting interface of Metrics that Matter™. From this powerful site, Dell can access real-time metrics covering key performance indicators on learner satisfaction with training, knowledge and skill transfer per course, training impact on the job, training impact on business results, and a hard and soft ROI[C] metric. Further, these indicators can be filtered in multiple ways including learning vendor, location, client name, learning modality, course, class, curricula, and program....

"The value for Dell is the real-time access to business intelligence to help them 1) monitor their learning day to day for quality and customer satisfaction, 2) use the metrics proactively for continuous improvement purposes, and 3) use advanced indicators such as job impact, business results and ROI[C] to showcase the overall value of learning when purchasing Dell products."

If Dell does it, and it can be measured, you can be sure it will be.

Chapter 8

Get Others to Do More of the Work

∾

Choose what you want to excel at, and find great partners for the rest.
—Michael Dell[1]

This chapter is all about how Dell chooses and works with its partners. More than almost any other similar corporation, Dell is partner-based. It treats its customers as partners, its suppliers as partners (which often translates into those suppliers doing more of the work than they originally thought they would), and its own people as partners.

Dell makes a study of choosing the right partners when it comes to choosing the right suppliers, the right customers, and the right personnel. It pays off for Dell, making it a smart organization, built of components it can rely on. Choosing the right partners is a vital part of the Dell model, and that's the subject of this chapter.

Choose Your Customers Carefully

Carefully choosing your customers is not a luxury most companies have, but you might actually think of this as carefully choosing the market segments you enter. Over and over, industry watchers have not understood this facet of Dell, and it bears examination. Dell examines markets with greater scrutiny than most corporations, and it selects its fights carefully. When it jumps, it goes for good ROIC, good margins, and profitable growth.

Dell is a market penetrator, not a market pioneer. It goes after established markets where its model will work well, and it stays true to that model. To do that, it needs to start by staying in touch with the markets.

Keep in Touch

Dell watches the markets obsessively, because this is its playing field. It doesn't strike out into new territory where no one has gone before: You're not going to see Dell putting huge resources into selling PCs in war-torn, poverty-stricken regions without viable markets. Dell follows the markets and disrupts them with its own effective direct sales engine.

As a market follower, Dell certainly watches and defines itself to a good degree in terms of its customers. As Kevin Kettler, Dell's Chief Technology Officer says,[2] "At Dell, our approach to innovation focuses on customer requirements. Customers define what is important."

From *Industry Week* magazine[3]: "Where most companies segment by product, Dell segments by customer. Dell figures it refines and intensifies the relationship with the customer. "Knowing what the customer needs is a very effective inventory-fighting tool," adds [Sharon Boyle, the Austin plant's operations manager] Boyle."

To watch customers, Dell segments deeper and deeper; from *Enterprise Innovator*[4]: "SMB Sub-Categorization: William Blair & Co. analyst Bruce Simpson asked how Dell sub-categorizes the SMB segment, and Parra replied that Dell uses 'multiple segmentation to gauge our different customer segments,' with companies with from 1-500 employees in 'SMB' and companies with 500-1000 'called medium,' but within SMB, Dell has 'further segmentation' of '1-100, 100-250, and 250-500,' as the 'economics of those is dramatically different.' As far as sales accounts go, as the size of the company represented increases, the number of companies in an individual sales account declines. Parra noted that Dell divides its accounts into 'retention' and 'development' accounts and thus 'we really look at accounts in two ways.'"

So, it's certainly true that keeping in touch lets Dell know what's going on with its existing customers. And, it lets Dell know, to some extent, what those customers want in other areas, giving it some insight into lateral market penetration.

But, as far as choosing the market segments that it wants to penetrate goes, it's a different story. Dell is a great fan of exhaustive market research, and very few can fault Dell's analyses. As a result of that research, Dell has near-perfect timing on when to enter markets; as *USA Today* says[5]: "Some of Dell's soul is obvious—namely the much-publicized manufacturing process that allows Dell to hold virtually no inventory of parts and make computers more quickly and cheaply than any other company.

"But a part of Dell's soul is often overlooked. It's the company's ability to know when to enter a new market so it can ride it like a surfer on a perfect wave."

Here's a similar analysis from *CFO magazine*[6]: "In addition to partnerships, Dell's fortunes may hinge on its ability to simply bide its time. Consider network switches, yet another area in which Dell's value proposition is low price. 'They're offering a commodity line of stackable switches, which have all the features a midrange enterprise needs to get by,' says [Cambridge, Massachusetts-based Forrester Research's analyst Galen] Schreck. 'They don't really compete against Cisco, which supplies the giant pipes. But when you open the door to the wiring closet, you might see Dell switches reaching out to the cubicles. That's their play. For now.' But as the networking business becomes more commoditized, Schreck predicts that Dell will 'chew its way into more expensive gear. They've always been disciplined about knowing when to enter a market—it's the thing that really sets them apart.'"

In other words, when Dell keeps in touch with the markets, it does so through its customers, but it's also crucial to understand how closely Dell watches the tech markets to know when to make its moves.

Go for Good ROIC

With all due respect to Galen Schreck at Forrester Research, there's much more than timing at work when Dell chooses its market segments and, thus, its customers. It's all about finding opportunities for good ROIC and selecting your customers to match. Dell has known from the beginning that many different types of customers exist in the marketplace, and it gives those with higher ROIC special care. From a *Business2000* case study on Dell[7]: "There are several differences between domestic customers and business customers.

- "Businesses often have dedicated budgets for the purchase of computers.
- "They usually spend more.
- "They buy at regular intervals and are usually repeat purchasers unlike domestic customers who often buy just one home computer and purchase another only when the original one is outdated.
- "They will normally purchase to an agreed plan. Domestic customers often purchase for highly personal reasons, e.g., they want to e-mail family or play games. Businesses often have a specialist staff member who looks after these purchases. They may purchase more complex machines such as servers.

- "They are focused on more than just the price—they look at other factors such as how easy is it to upgrade the computer or to service it. This is called Total Cost of Ownership (TCO).
- "In view of these differences, Dell appoints an Account Manager to look after the interest of a larger business. An Account Manager will build a long-term relationship with the business customer. The customer will be able to make contact with their Account Manager to get advice, to solve a problem or to place an order."

Dell is no dummy when it comes to focusing on those segments where it will have the best returns. It makes partners of its best and often largest customers. As a case study from the Harvard Business School[8] discussing Dell notes, "Make Your Customers Partners. Segment customers. Focus on groups you can serve with the largest gross margins. 90 percent of Dell's sales go to institutions, 70 percent to customers buying $1 million+ in PCs annually.

"EXAMPLE: Dell's direct selling revealed a new customer segment: Experienced consumers looking to purchase their second or third computer. While first-time buyers purchased at rock-bottom prices from competitors, Dell built a billion-dollar business by serving the more savvy buyers. Communicate closely with customers to forecast needs and keep inventory down.

"EXAMPLE: Dell's senior technologists regularly meet with customers to exchange views on trends, needs, products. The practice has fueled multibillion-dollar ideas; e.g., notebooks with longer-life batteries, strategies for satisfying institutional customers' need for product stability over speed. Give customers unique value.

"EXAMPLE: Eastman Chemical used to order PCs and then load them with its own software, one employee's computer at a time. This two-hour, $200-$300 nuisance was multiplied by hundreds of employees. NOW Dell loads Eastman's software onto workstations it has purchased as they come down Dell's assembly line—saving Eastman major time, money, and hassle."

In this sense, Dell makes partners of its customers by selecting them, moving into areas where it can expect the largest ROIC. Going after ROIC is Dell's guiding light when it comes to growth; as a *BusinessWeek* article on how Dell is operating in the world of services says—note the ROIC for Dell compared to others[9]: "For now, Dell is wisely exploiting the easiest opportunities. It is selling primarily to existing corporate customers, particularly those that don't ask it to support products from its rivals....

Dell generates $254,000 in revenues for each services employee, compared with an industry average of $151,000, according to TBR."

Dell's emphasis on higher ROIC segments is very obvious at times; the same *BusinessWeek* article also notes that when it comes to services, "In 2003, complaints against the company piled up, in part because it was routing support calls to India. That November it discontinued the practice for most corporate customers."

From an article in *Enterprise Innovator*[10] on Dell in China, which again spotlights Dell's emphasis on ROIC: "Rollins explained that 'we've got to be careful with what we want to do' and reiterated that Dell has 'never focused on the consumer segment as a company,' and while it has a 'consumer business in the U.S.,' outside the U.S. market it represents 'less than 10 percent of our business around the world.' Rollins believes that it is 'not in our interest to get into third-tier cities in China,' and notes that 'Lenovo does not have an enterprise business' so they 'have to go after new challenges.' But he said 'if I were running Lenovo, I would not be going to third-tier cities to do that,' and while it 'may work for them,' he said he is 'a little skeptical—but we'll see.' In contrast, 'Dell has bigger fish to fry,' and will 'focus on major cities long before we consider third-tier cities.' He added, 'As I look at our overall profitability and growth probability in China—I think ours look better than Lenovo....

"Rollins said Dell wants the market to know it will be 'going after good profitable growth and not volume growth at decreasing profitability.'" (Parenthetically, one might note that now that Lenovo has bought IBM's PC unit, Lenovo does indeed have an up-market business sector, and at some point, Dell is going to have to confront that.)

Industry watchers stereotype Dell as a lost-cost PC provider, and so miss the point. As Rollins says, Dell has "never focused on the consumer segment as a company" and that's true. The focus is on ROIC in choosing its customer partner segments. Dell finds that ROIC by being a market penetrator, not a market pioneer, another thing that analysts don't seem to fully understand. For example, a recent *BusinessWeek* article missing the point on Dell states[11]: "Increasingly, industry analysts believe it's time for Dell to tweak its sales model. After all, times have changed...."

The article argues that emerging markets in Asia are different from what Dell's been used to working with in the United States. Here's what *BusinessWeek* says: "About 80 percent of total PC unit sales from now to 2010 will come from developing markets like China and India, according to tech consultancy Forrester Research. But Dell is struggling there.

"Here's why: Because of cultural and technological reasons, customers in those markets buy computers from stores and system integrators, says Forrester analyst Simon Yates. That's not surprising, considering that in India, where PC ownership should jump from 7.9 million units to 78 million by 2010, most people don't have Web access. Many rural areas lack phone lines, and most people know little about computers. So they go to local stores or computer specialists to ask for advice and to make their purchases.

"And because Dell doesn't have a strong presence there, consumers buy their computers from local heavyweight HCL Technologies, HP, and IBM, whose PC division is now owned by China's Lenovo. As a result, Dell gets a measly 4 percent share of China's PC shipments, according to tech consultancy IDC...."

The author here assumes that Dell is simply after market share, without apparent thought for margin. But having read as much as you have about Dell in this book, you know that's not true. You'd expect Dell to stay in those new markets, such as enterprise servers, going after the segments where they can get the ROIC they want. In time, as the rest of the market matures, and customers are better supplied with web access and credit cards, Dell will step in. To its credit, *BusinessWeek* recognizes this as a possible path for Dell, saying: "Bottom line: Dell has three options. One, it could stick with the direct-sales model, waiting for markets like India and China to mature technologically. Two, it could exit the PC business, as IBM has done. Or three, it could establish more of a retail presence in developing countries to ensure that it grabs a chunk of their PC sales in the next few years. That can be done through a partnership with or purchase of a local manufacturer already commanding a substantial market lead over U.S. companies in countries like India and Russia. Or, Dell could set up relationships with retailers and system integrators in these countries."

Dell's response, as given in the same article? As you'd expect: "For the time being, however, Dell says it's sticking with option No. 1 [the direct-sales model]. 'We're completely committed to the direct-sales model and have no plans to go retail outside of the U.S.,' says a Dell spokesperson." Is that going to stem the flow of articles on how Dell is "losing its edge" in emerging markets? No.

For those who do see it, however, the lesson from Dell is clear: When it comes to choosing your customers, go after those customers who will give you the ROIC you want.

Customize the Customer

Dell also likes to customize the customer to the extent that it can. As mentioned in the previous chapter, Dell performs real-time experiments in prices on its web site in an effort to move products that aren't moving. And it runs sales frequently.

But, even longer-term goals are at work here, at least from Dell's perspective. An article in *Enterprise Innovator*[12] says, for example, "[Dell's Joe Marengi] went on to explain that on the consumer side, there are 'a couple of different avenues that exist out there,' but noted that as the 'core price of PCs falls,' Dell must help to adjust consumer 'services expectation,' and that 'we have to do better job of resetting services expectations.' He noted how on a $2,500 TV customers expect to receive 'no service' while on a $250 PC, they 'expect lifetime service,' and that is something that 'has to change.' But 'all in all,' Marengi believes that 'we made significant improvement in the last 18 months.'"

How Dell plans to change customer's expectations on "lifetime service" wasn't made clear in the article.

Choose Your People Carefully

As important as carefully choosing your customers is carefully choosing the people in your organization. Dell works to get the best people it can. Keeping the energy that comes from your people is always a challenge, including at Dell, and it wants to get the best people it can. Michael Dell says[13]: "I'm often asked how we manage to maintain the attitude of a challenger, even as we continue to grow at record speeds. Culture is, by far, one of the most enigmatic facets of management that I've encountered.

"It is also one of the most important. Once a reporter asked me which of our competitors represented the biggest threat to Dell. I said the greatest threat to Dell wouldn't come from a competitor.

"It would come from our people.

"It hasn't been easy, trying to maintain the entrepreneurial spirit that has characterized Dell as our company has grown bigger (in terms of head count) and more complicated (by way of infrastructure). Nor has it been easy to maintain the energy of a focused team, as we've expanded around the world. But my goal has always been to make sure that everyone at Dell feels they are a part of something great—perhaps something even greater than themselves."

He says[14]: "Mobilize your people around a common goal. Help them to feel a part of something genuine, special, and important, and you'll inspire real passion and loyalty." As mentioned earlier, Dell likes to hire ex-CEOs[15]: "I'm always actively looking for good people, and I expect others on our team to do the same"

From the "Soul of Dell"[16]: "We believe our continued success lies in teamwork and the opportunity each team member has to learn, develop and grow. We are committed to being a meritocracy, and to developing, retaining and attracting the best people, reflective of our worldwide marketplace."

From Kevin Rollins[17]: "We are committed to winning, and in fact feel an ethical imperative to compete as hard as we can, on behalf our shareholders, customers and employees. We idealistically believe it is a better way to operate and will enhance our ability to win and attract the best people."

Dell works hard on getting the best people. Michael Dell is a CEO who knows how to delegate, and that means he relies on getting the best possible people in his organization. Long ago, Dell realized that he would go nuts trying to do everything himself, and he's made it a priority to get people whose skills and loyalties he can count on. Many CEOs try to do it all, and so burn out, but Dell knows the advantages of enlightened delegation.

On this point, he's said[18]: "The ability to find and hire the right people can make or break your business. It is as plain as that. No matter where you are in the life cycle of your business, bringing in great talent should always be a top priority. It's also one of the hardest objectives to meet....

"People who thrive at Dell are results oriented, self-reliant, and driven to lead. We give them the authority to drive the business in a particular direction, and provide them with the tools and resources they need to accomplish their goals.

"Whether you're hiring someone in an entry-level position or to run one of your largest groups, that person must be completely in sync with the company's business philosophy and objectives. If the person thinks in a way that's compatible with your company values and beliefs, and understands what the company does and is driven to do, he will not only work harder to fulfill his immediate goals, but will also contribute to the greater goals of the organization."

Dell's become known for its acute hiring skills; Michael Kanellos, CNET news.com editor-at-large, says, "Here are some examples of good recruiting decisions: Alex Gruzen, who used to run HP's notebook division, got recruited away in 2004. Hurt HP quite a bit. [Joe] Marengi also has seen his career revitalized there. The ultimate pickup way back was with Mort Topfer."

Hire for Growth

Dell's fast growth presents particular problems when it comes to finding the right personnel, because most people will come from environments in which handling such growth is not an issue. An article[19] in *HR* magazine, on Dell's hiring practices, comments on the growth issue: "The company's growth...forces its human resources staff to constantly raise the bar by which it measures success. The challenges HR faces include selecting and developing a workforce that can meet constantly changing requirements without losing Dell's market and customer focus, or its culture.

"When you're growing this much, HR clearly has to have its hands around the selection of people," says [Vice president of human resources for Dell's Public and Americas International Group (PAI) Steve] Price, "What will stop growth will be the inability to hire people."

"But hiring quickly is not enough. Rapid growth, Price points out, can cause organizations to sacrifice quality for quantity. 'Unless you have good processes in place, you run the risk of not always hiring the best people. There can be a tendency to say 'We need people so badly, a fresh body is better than no body.'"

The article also mentions that "[Vice president of staffing Andy] Esparza notes that Dell's growth presents challenges and that HR is taking on new initiatives to achieve greater results. The company, he says, is "still trying to develop more expertise on planning, which is hard at the rate we're growing."

Because of this growth, Dell Inc. makes an effort to hire people who will grow flexibly as well. This is a tricky process, but a crucial one. Michael Dell[20] says: "It's not enough to hire to fill a job. It's not even enough to hire on the basis of one's talents. You have to hire based upon a candidate's potential to grow and develop....

"Today, we hire people with the long-term in mind. We're not bringing them in to do a job; we're inviting them to join the company. If it's a great match, their jobs are likely to change many, many times as we segment the business, and as we focus more heavily on some areas rather than others...."

He went on to add something remarkable: "We recruit for succession. And, in fact, we institutionalize it. Everyone's job includes finding and developing their successor—not just when they are ready to move into a new role, but as an ongoing part of their performance plan." It's hard to think of anything that will make people more aware that they can be replaced than a institutionalized replacement plan like that.

Segment Your People

To manage hypergrowth, Dell has turned to segmentation, and it lets the market lead the way, making the organizational growth of the company an organic process. In this way, Dell has been able to not only manage growth, but has found balance between centralization and decentralization. At Dell, part of the segmentation process involves segmenting the responsibilities of your people.

Michael Dell is quoted[21] at 1000ventures.com as saying, "Cultivate commitment to personal growth. Success isn't static—and your culture shouldn't be either. Pay attention to what your best people are achieving, and build an infrastructure that rewards mastery. The best way to keep the most talented people is to allow their jobs to change with them. Sometimes, reducing their responsibilities will give them the space to tackle new opportunities and to expand—and your business will expand too."

Reducing people's responsibilities has become an accepted thing to do at Dell, when those responsibilities become too large because of growth. Dell says[22]: "The best way to keep the most talented people is to allow their jobs to change with them. Sometimes, reducing their responsibilities will give them the space to tackle new opportunities and to expand—and your business will expand, too."

Michael Dell explains the process[23]: "The right people in the right jobs are instrumental to a company's success. Traditionally, when a talented employee masters a job, he gets promoted to a new job that has broader responsibilities, a larger staff, and a bigger budget. But what do you do when job responsibilities are increasing half again every year, simply as a function of the company's growth?

"If you assume that your people can grow at the same rate as your company—and still maintain the sharp focus that is critical to your success—you will be sadly disappointed. When a business is growing quickly, many jobs grow laterally in responsibility, becoming too big and complex for even the most ambitious, hardest-working person to handle without sacrificing personal career development or becoming burned out."

"Our solution is segmentation.… Segmenting a job happens a couple of ways. We'll bring in additional talent and/or divide a business unit, product organization, or functional unit in some way that makes the newly segmented structure more manageable and more sharply focused to the business opportunity. This allows us to keep our people happy and thriving and maintain a high growth rate.

"When we first started doing this, some people were confused—and understandably so. Traditionally, narrowed responsibilities are a sign of demotion, disapproval, or failure. At other companies, people are evaluated by the size of their staff or how many dollars they generate. At Dell, success means growing so fast that we take half your business away....

"Job segmentation is completely counterintuitive to conventional business practice. But the underlying logic makes perfect sense: We want good people to thrive and help us continue to prosper. It's the best way we know to create meaningful jobs that more precisely match an employee's skill set."

The *HR* magazine article[24] describes this way of doing things: "To prevent its growth from spinning out of control, Dell uses a strategy that splits off business segments once they reach a certain threshold. Managers take charge of these smaller pieces of the business and attempt to grow them to the point where they can be split again—much in the way that a cell divides over and over to grow a human body.

"Steve Price...gives the following example to show how the process works: 'Our education market is comprised of a higher education component and a K42 component. Today, that operates as an education business segment. But now it's gotten so big that we're going to split it and have a business segment called higher ed and a business segment called K-12.'

"The decision to segment is not based on size or number of employees, says Price, but—at least in part—on whether the division has grown to a particular financial measure or threshold. The company couples that measure with anticipated market opportunity, and with the projected profits Dell might reap by focusing on that market opportunity, to arrive at a decision to segment. For example, the threshold number is driving the education split, but the company 'also saw that it needed to approach these two groups differently,' says Price."

Making this work relies on finding people who can grow. The *HR* article emphasizes this point by saying: "To make this segmentation strategy work, Dell actively seeks and cultivates a certain type of employee mind-set. For example, potential employees are told early on that their former titles may not correlate exactly with positions at Dell because the company structure is relatively flat. 'We have to strip the paradigm that titles and levels mean anything,' says Price. 'People have to park their egos at the door.'

"Furthermore, Dell's employees have to move away from the paradigm that more means better. 'It's just the reverse,' says Price. 'When we take half of what you have away from you and tell you to go rebuild it, that's a sign of success.' Dell's compensation strategy carefully backs up this unique measure of success by rewarding managers who grow the business to the point that segmentation is required.

"Such efforts at developing the proper employee mind-set appear to be paying off. Dell employees, according to the company's HR professionals, welcome segmentation.

"'There's an excitement about segmentation,' says Jim Koster, director of HR for customer service, 'because it creates opportunity.' When he was on the sales side, he remembers employees asking him 'We've reached X—when do we split?'

"Erik Dithmer, senior manager of operations for Dell Plus, says that 'When someone says, "Now I don't want you to report metrics for education—I want you to report metrics for higher ed and K-12," everybody does that with a smile on their faces. They're saying "Ah! That's good!"'…"'We typically attract people for whom change is not a problem,' says Koster. 'In fact, most people here thrive on it.' Koster believes there may come a time when HR has to slow down the process a little bit, 'to make sure that everything splits as it should.'"

Splitting off a successful executive's business isn't good for a businessperson's ego. But it's a functional move as far as the corporation goes, giving successful people space to grow without becoming stultified by increased responsibility. It's a bold strategy that will work as long as you have a corporate culture that understands and embraces this mechanism, or when you have people who have placed a significant commitment to the goals of the organization over their own. To some extent, Dell has both.

Make HR a Strategic Partner

At many larger corporations, a significant disjuncture exists between Human Resources and the corporation itself, so much so that candidates understand that, to get the better jobs, you have to bypass HR entirely and go directly to whomever is hiring within that corporation. In other words, you need "contacts" to get anything besides entry-level positions.

But Dell is a tight ship, and HR is significantly more aligned and in-the-loop at Dell than you'll find other places. Dell has a strong emphasis on getting the best people, and the HR department knows what the corporation is looking for. HR is very aware of which people will fit in and which people won't. For example, according to an article[25] by the European Industrial Relations Observatory (EIRO) on the combined Chartered Institute of Personnel and Development (CIPD) and European Association for Personnel Management (EAPM) conference held in Ireland in May 2005, Pat Casey (Dell's vice-president for human resources at Dell EMEA: Europe, Middle East and Africa) "told participants how the building of a shared corporate culture was a strategic priority at Dell, suggesting that it has contributed to the 'bottom line' of the business.... At Dell, the central tenets are said to be clearly articulated and reinforced, and are embodied in the recruitment process, there being definite guidelines for hiring the 'right' staff to fit the Dell culture."

Far from being isolated from the rest of the corporation, as is all too common, Dell's HR department actively works on determining which people fit best into the organization. The article in *HR* magazine says: "HR also tries to spot the qualities its new employees will need by analyzing existing top-performing employees and looking for keys to their success. 'We look at the people who have been given the biggest merit increases, the best appraisals and so forth, and then we interview against these competencies,' says Price.

"To help deal with peaks in hiring demands, Dell's HR professionals reallocate their human resources, says Esparza. 'For example, we have rotational recruiters who come from the IT organization. They have a great perspective on the recruiting process because they're the ones actually doing the jobs. We have a core set of these folks come in at our hiring peaks, spend three or four months helping us recruit, hire and assimilate, and as things retract a little bit, they go back to their IT jobs.'"

The article adds later: "The kind of rapid growth seen at Dell requires an HR department that can partner with the company's business units. Several factors have helped Dell's HR function become more strategic. One is its structure.

"At Dell, HR is divided into 'operations' and 'management,' explains Price. HR operations coordinates transactional functions, such as benefits, compensation and employee relations, through a service center.... Management deals with tactical, rather than transactional issues. These HR employees attend the business unit's staff meetings as consultants; develop the leadership team; produce metrics for such things as turnover, productivity and cycle times; and develop an HR strategy for that particular line of business.

"Dell's HR management team assists in the segmentation planning process by handling HR issues, such as identifying personnel needs, working out lines of reporting and organizational charts, and defining training needs. HR consults strategically with the business unit but also works out the nuts and bolts of putting people where they need to be, with the necessary skills and training.

"Kathleen Woodhouse, an HR manager who supports Dell's preferred accounts division, feels HR is successful there because it has evolved in parallel to the business units."

This being Dell, one way that HR keeps in close contact with the rest of the corporation is through the use of the Internet and intranet. The *HR* magazine article has this to say: "HR has further positioned itself to provide strategic services by letting web-based technology take a lot of paperwork off its hands, Price says. For example, all salary administration is web-based, as are benefits enrollment 401(k) administration and stock options.

"In addition, the company has shifted the power—and authority—for certain tasks to managers. One example is Dell's web-based Organizational Human Resource Planning (OHRP) process, which allows managers to do their own succession planning, key job identification, competency planning and employee development.

"'We've led our customers toward self-help in a number of ways,' says Woodhouse. 'Managers use our intranet to complete HR functions, like appraisals; our appraisal system also feeds into the financial system so they can play with figures if they need to. Managers submit appraisals and recommendations to the next level and on through the approval cycle, online.'"

In many corporations, a wide, wide gulf exists between HR and those groups that need new personnel. To get someone new, you fill out HR forms and then lose all control over the hiring process; HR is its own entity, and the people they send you may be nothing like what you've asked for. That gulf doesn't usually exist at Dell. The company grows too fast, and it's too much into execution, to allow that kind of disjuncture. HR is taken seriously at Dell; the people who do the hiring are not entry-level employees just out of internship who read questions from a script, and they're not clueless.

It's a refreshing change.

Choose Your Suppliers Carefully

At Dell, suppliers also are strategic partners. In fact, Michael Dell says[26]: "Our willingness and ability to partner to achieve our common goals is perhaps seen in its purest form in how we forge strong alliances with our suppliers."

Nowhere is that alliance more evident than when it comes to the costs of innovation, as already discussed. From an article at eweek.com[27]: "With IT spending seemingly coming around again, few are predicting Dell's growth will slow or doubt the company can reach its goal of $60 billion in revenue by 2007. But with the market rebound, Dell faces the challenge of keeping prices down while providing innovation with a research and development budget that is 10 percent that of competitor IBM." For more on this process, see Chapter 5.

Dell in the Driver's Seat

When it comes to suppliers, Dell is in the driver's seat because of its size. From a *BusinessWeek* report[28]: "Rollins thinks Dell also has an edge in how it's approaching this market. For starters, the company isn't trying to do everything—it's focusing mostly on jobs that will help it boost hardware sales. The message, says vice-president of services Gary Cotshott, is that 'to take advantage of the full value of Dell, you ought to combine our technology with services.' Plus, Dell is keeping tight control of costs. It's using its market clout to get great deals from subcontractors such as Getronics and Unisys Corp. (UIS) to handle the workaday tasks."

When it comes to Dell and its suppliers, "market clout" is a good phrase to keep in mind, because it lets Dell write its own ticket. It's not easy to turn down a contract worth billions of dollars. The W*all Street Journal* interviewed Michael Dell on his attitude towards suppliers[29]; note the significance of market clout here: "WSJ: Which end of the rope do you pull first?

"Dell: If we tell our suppliers, 'Hey, look, you need to deliver at 6:20 in the morning, and you got to come to this dock, and it's got to be this many boxes and has to be this high,' they say, 'Yes, sir. You're buying a billion dollars' worth of stuff from us, we'll do it. No problem.'

"*WSJ*: Did you have to use carrots to get people to start communicating with you electronically? Did you have to cull suppliers that weren't making the grade?

"Dell: When we were much smaller, some of them said, 'Well, we're not going to do that.' We had some pretty convincing arguments. For one, we could legitimately say if you weren't selling to Dell, you were losing market share. And it was true, because we were growing much faster than any competitor. So the vast majority of them said, 'OK, we'll play this game.' The ones that did it great got more business, and the ones that didn't got less business or no business.

"*WSJ*: Were there specific tools other than rewards, or the stick, to enable suppliers to do it your way?

"Dell: We had supplier conferences.... We had supplier report cards. We created valuechain.dell.com, which is an internal site that only suppliers and Dell have access to that took the supplier report card online so they knew how they were doing. And we just made it a relentless focus.'"

This puts Dell in the driver's seat and, in consequence, Dell is in a good position to get the best suppliers—best suited to Dell, best suited to the task. Dell always works to get the best partners it can, and suppliers know that if you don't please Dell, you're gone (although some suppliers, such as Intel, are obviously not about to be jettisoned).

This approach does help the supplier. Dell's entry into printers has gone better than people expected, which in turn has helped Lexmark and others who actually make them. Dell squeezes them all in contract negotiations with notorious cheapness, but it can be a huge volume opportunity.

As Michael Dell says[30]: "Traditional industry mentality dictates that if you don't build your own components, you'll never have enough control over the process. But by working with outside suppliers, we've found that you actually can gain more control over the quality of your products than if you were to do everything yourself. How? You can choose among the best providers in the world.

"You can evaluate and select suppliers that have the greatest levels of expertise, experience, and quality with any particular part. If new processes are developed that push quality levels even higher, you can partner with the firm that has taken advantage of them, rather than being held hostage to the investment you've made in acquiring a supplier.

"And, if one firm you're working with is having trouble keeping up with the demand, you can pair with others and add additional capacity. By amortizing this risk among a few suppliers, rather than harboring it yourself, you can get what you need faster and more flexibly, enabling you to expand and focus your energies where you really add value."

What Makes a Supplier a Good Partner?

What makes a supplier a good supplier as far as Dell is concerned? As you'd expect, good quality is high on the list. Dell says[31]: "But just because you're partnering with a company doesn't mean your part of that particular job is done. In our case, just because we're not creating the technology doesn't mean we are leaving things to chance. It's in our relationships with suppliers that the direct model takes on even greater significance.

"When we enter into a relationship with a supplier, we share our clear expectations for quality. When then explain what the direct model is and how it can be beneficial to them. We demonstrate that we've created a business system that is extremely efficient at delivering *their* component technology, or product or service to a large and growing market. They, in turn, are usually pretty happy to provide us with their particular technological expertise."

Obviously, low cost is another important criterion; Dell says[32]: "When we act with our suppliers, we act as an advocate for the customer who uses our products day in and day out, and experiences success or failure in his own business as a result of things we do or don't accomplish with our suppliers. It's incumbent upon us to see that our partners respond to market demand so that we'll all succeed—and with a freer flow of information going from the customer, through us, to the supplier, there's a much greater chance of that happening.

"We spend lots of time explaining our requirements to our suppliers in terms of quality, design objectives, inventory and logistics, service, global requirements, and cost—although cost as a fact in and of itself is less important than knowing whether a supplier can be competitive over a long period of time."

Note the emphasis here; cost is important but, in the long run, being competitive is even more important. In other words, Dell looks for reliability and long-term competitiveness in suppliers. Flexibility is another important aspect; Michael Dell has said[33]: "One of the key attributes we look for in suppliers is flexibility. With our business [growing] over 40 percent a year, we are confronted with dramatic increases in demand."

The Harvard Business School case study on Dell mentioned earlier makes a point of the kind of supplier flexibility you see at Dell, emphasizing that suppliers are even willing to staff personnel in Dell's own plants these days: "Make Your Suppliers Partners. Gotten stuck with obsolete inventory (e.g., a supplier launches a faster computer chip) or overly expensive inventory (while materials costs plummet 50 percent)? Avoid these disasters by making your suppliers partners:

- Have as few supplier partners as possible; keep them only as long as they're technical and quality leaders.
- In real time, communicate your inventory levels and replenishment needs to them.

■ Order from suppliers only when you receive demand from customers.

"EXAMPLE: Dell made a long-term commitment to one supplier for 25 percent of its panel-display requirements—regardless of demand or supply fluctuations. For new products, this supplier also stations its engineers in Dell's plants to fix customer problems immediately. The payoffs? Dell avoids excess inventory costs; the supplier gets predictable business; customers get products fast."

This equation works both ways; a good supplier also opens its doors to Dell. From the *Wall Street Journal* interview quoted earlier[29]:

"*WSJ*: How do you measure supplier performance?

"Dell: We asked our procurement teams to act as almost an extension of the supplier and to get involved in operations, understanding that supplier, and understanding the products and commodities. We go really, really deep into understanding these things: What are the materials involved? Where do they all come from?"

The ability to stay in close contact and constant communication is also important for those Dell considers its best suppliers. Michael Dell has said[34]: "At Dell, we think that our toughest customer is our best customer because the toughest teaches you the most. So, it's probably not surprising that we tend to be a tough customer for our suppliers. We are constantly challenging them to reach new heights of quality, efficiency, logistics, and excellence, which helps improve their processes and enhances their success.

"One of the tools we use to gauge a supplier's performance is our supplier report card. In it, we set our standards very explicitly: We detail the number of defects per million we will tolerate; we outline what we expect to see in field performance, on our manufacturing lines, in delivery performance and in the ease of doing business with them. Essentially, the supplier report card is a full 360-degree evaluation of our requirements for suppliers. We use it to track an individual supplier's progress against our metrics, as well as to compare them with other suppliers who provide similar commodities."

Although it's not a written rule, Dell usually goes for the larger suppliers and avoids the smaller ones. That's more an artifact of what Dell expects from its suppliers than a result of deliberate policy. Dell wants suppliers who have the ability to build and innovate, and to stay on top of the market. That usually means going with bigger suppliers, who have deeper pockets and who will be around in the long term. Larger suppliers will be able to meet other demands by Dell, such as the ability to scale quickly and flexibly, as well as being able to entirely build warehouses and plants near Dell manufacturing plants.

Set Some Rules

As the list of Dell's suppliers expands to include overseas partners, Dell has begun working with suppliers in unfamiliar environments, with customs it sometimes finds hard to take. For that reason, it's put together a code of ethics for suppliers,[35] which reads as follows (emphasis in the original): "To ensure that Dell suppliers around the world understand and embrace high standards of ethical behavior and treat their employees with dignity and respect, the company requires suppliers to adhere to the following standards for employee rights and safety:

1. **Every employee must be a voluntary employee.** Dell will not tolerate use of indentured, slave, convict or bonded labor.
2. **Every employee must be of working age.** Employees must meet appropriate legal age requirements or be at least 15 years of age, whichever is greater.
3. **Every employee must be hired, promoted and rewarded based on ability and performance**, not personal characteristics or beliefs. Discrimination based on race, color, age, gender, sexual orientation, ethnicity, religion, disability or maternity or marital status is not acceptable.
4. **Every employee must be treated with dignity** and be free from sexual harassment, corporal punishment, mental or physical coercion or verbal abuse and be able to associate freely.
5. **Every employee must be entitled to working hours that adhere to local laws and industry standards**, and are provided with reasonable time off and overtime compensation.
6. **Every employee must be paid fairly for their work** with wages paid for a standard work week that meet legal and industry standards. Dell discourages the practice of deducting from wages for disciplinary purposes and in no cases should such deductions reduce pay below legal minimums.
7. **Every employee should be allowed to work in a safe and healthy work environment**, and where company housing is provided, have clean, safe living facilities. Suppliers are expected to comply with all appropriate laws regarding working conditions, provide protection from fire, ensure regular access to bathrooms and potable water, and ensure appropriate health and safety train-

ing for employees, consistent with the requirements of achieving
OHSAS 18001 certification."

Interestingly, Dell keeps more plants in the United States than its
competitors, but that's because of logistics, not due to any particular
avoidance of outsourcing—Dell wants its suppliers close by for quick-
er delivery and greater responsiveness. For example, Dell considered
moving a plant to Mexico from Austin but decided that it was simply
too far away. Here's a summary from the Austin *American-Statesman*
newspaper[36]: "The dramatic productivity improvements achieved at
Dell Computer Corp.'s Parmer North 2 plant, in part, helped keep the
production of corporate desktop computers in Austin instead of
Mexico.

"Just a year after Parmer was built, Dell dispatched a team to Mexico
to evaluate the idea of building a plant there. Ultimately, the company
decided that the added distance and costs of shipping computers from
Mexico outweighed the benefits of using Mexican labor, which could be
as much as 80 percent cheaper.

"'Mexico was a simple matter of economics,' President Kevin Rollins
said in a recent interview with the Austin *American-Statesman*. 'We can
manufacture closer here and transport to the customer because we don't
want to ship a lot by air. Unless you get a sizeable advantage in either
labor or incentives, you've got a sizeable transportation cost that you've
got to win back.'"

That doesn't mean that Dell is going to insist on U.S.-made components, however. From the same article: "Although Dell couldn't figure out
a way to make Mexico work out logistically for its own finished PCs,
components are another story. Many of the computers coming down the
conveyors at Parmer join up with monitors bearing the Dell logo that are
assembled in Mexico. Several Dell suppliers have moved to Mexico
because of the ever-shrinking profits in the computer-industry food chain.

"SMTC Corp., which makes motherboards for Dell, laid off 100 workers in Austin recently and moved production to Chihuahua, in central
northern Mexico. Flextronics Inc., which made metal computer housings
for Dell, closed its plants in New Braunfels, laying off the last of about
1,000 workers this month, and moved production offshore.

"Trend Technologies Inc., which also makes computer housings and
notebook-computer docking stations, has been shifting production from
a Round Rock facility to Guadalajara, Jalisco, to handle work for Dell.

"Trend will be closing its Round Rock plant at the end of November,
according to a letter sent to employees Aug. 13. The company declined

to comment. The plant employed about 1,600 workers at its peak in 2000."

It's a matter of economics, not principle. The article adds this: "Rollins didn't completely rule out moving some Dell production to Mexico.

"'I would never say we would never have a facility in Mexico,' he said. 'We're getting a lot bigger. We've got 25 percent of the world's market share (in large corporate accounts). There will come a time when we'll have 40 percent, so we'll have to have other factories and other (production) capability.

"'If we can figure out how to do that in our (Central Texas) factories by getting more efficiency, great. If we have to add additional capability to handle the Mexican market and handle the South American market, it may be in Mexico.'"

Choose Your Government Partners Carefully

When Dell makes a move and builds a new plant, it makes sure that it gets the best deal in incentives and tax breaks from local government. Dell is finding governments so eager in this regard that they not only give incentives to Dell, but also to the ever-present cloud of suppliers that follow Dell. Here's from *The Business Journal* of the Greensboro/Winston-Salem, North Carolina Triad area[37]: "While state Senate leader Marc Basnight, D-Dare, says North Carolina will do all it can to lure a $190 million Dell manufacturing plant to the Triad, local sources say suppliers of the computer manufacturing giant are currently 'kicking the tires' in the region and looking at sites.

"One supplier has already visited the region several times to look at sites, a source said.

"Those close to the deal said there are six to eight companies closely allied with Dell that tend to open facilities near Dell manufacturing plants. The suppliers range from the company that makes the plastic bags that Dell uses to ship its computers to logistics companies that work with the computer maker....

"Those close to the negotiations in North Carolina said they believe that part of the deal to lure Dell to the Triad would be incentives packages for the company's suppliers as well. Details on such incentives were unavailable."

Once again, it's easy to see Dell's financial clout at work. That's not to say that smaller companies shouldn't try to emulate Dell's care in choosing partners; it's to say that until you grow to Dell's size, you can't expect to influence those partners to the same degree.

Chapter 9

Know How to Grow

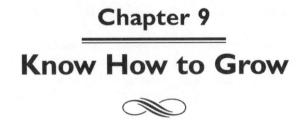

One out of three computers sold in the U.S. is a Dell. Hopefully soon, that will be one out of two.

—Michael Dell, 2004[1]

Since its beginnings, Dell Inc. has been in an almost permanent state of hypergrowth. Because of that, it's been crucial for Dell to understand how to handle fast growth, and it's developed strong strategies to do that. Because growth is such an issue at Dell, watching Dell offers clearer lessons on handling growth than you'll find elsewhere. Dell has not only had to handle hypergrowth, it has had to purify and hone its response to that kind of growth. Even if a corporation isn't growing at 80 percent a year, it can still learn from Dell. The story at Dell is drawn in strong lines and, if you're interested in learning how to deal with growth, Dell's is one of the purest examples you can find.

Going direct was Dell's original inspiration, and a great one. But one idea wasn't enough to sustain growth, and Dell—both the man and the corporation—have shown genius in being able to find new inspirations and make the business grow at astounding rates. Dell Direct was a good idea, but if that's all there was, Dell Computer would have been a one-trick pony. Few people outside the industry appreciate that Dell Inc. is not just about that one inspiration, but rather a consistently masterful set of steps that have let it grow to where it is now.

As Michael Dell has said,[2] "Some businesses are founded on the idea of the silver bullet—one almighty product or patent that sits in a safe, guarded place twenty-four hours a day. But that's not where growth is coming from in today's—or tomorrow's—economy. The key is not so much one great idea or patent as it is the execution and implementation of a great strategy." And that strategy changes too.

About Dell Inc., he says[3]: "How we navigate the inevitable changes in our industry will define whether Dell is a good company, or a truly great company."

The genius of Dell Inc. is evident in how it's been able to grow. Originally just an upstart among dozens of upstarts, it's made the right moves time and time again: It is primarily a business, not high-tech, success story. That kind of growth has gotten Dell to its present level—here's the global market share for PCs in the first quarter of 2005, according to *USA Today*[4]:

- Dell, 19 percent
- Hewlett-Packard, 15 percent
- IBM/Lenovo, 7 percent
- Fujitsu/Fujitsu Siemens, 5 percent
- Acer, 4 percent
- Toshiba, 4 percent
- NEC, 3 percent
- Apple, 2 percent
- Gateway, 2 percent

A July 2005 News.com article[5] says: "Worldwide shipments of PCs rose 16.6 percent from the same period a year ago, according to IDC, far above the research firm's May forecast of 12.3 percent...The surge in growth was due to the usual suspects. Dell, No. 1 worldwide and in the United States, saw its shipments grow by 23.7 percent, according to IDC."

These numbers say it all; the Dell Direct model was important to get started, but in the 21 years that the company has been around, it has had to make the right decisions—and handle growth in the right way—dozens of times.

Dell's Growth

And grow Dell has, all around the world. You can see its headquarters in Kawasaki, Japan in Figure 9.1, in Bracknell, UK in Figure 9.2, in Glasgow, UK in Figure 9.3. Dozens more such buildings exist nationally and internationally.

From *Money Magazine*[6]: "On Wednesday, the eve of its annual analyst meeting, Dell reaffirmed guidance for its fiscal first quarter, saying that it expects sales and earnings growth of 16 percent.

Figure 9.1 Kawasaki, Japan.

"That looks positively fantastic when compared to the expected sales and earnings increases of just 6 percent for top rival Hewlett-Packard. For IBM, the forecast is for 6 percent sales growth and 12 percent earnings growth."

From eWEEK[7]: "Officials with Dell Inc. expect the company's strong growth to continue for the foreseeable future.

"First-quarter revenues are on target to come in at about $13.4 billion, and the computer maker expects to reach its goal of $80 billion in annual sales within the next two or three years, officials said here at a meeting with analysts and reporters."

Figure 9.2 Bracknell, UK.

From *Industry Analyst Reporter*[8]: "Dell was the worldwide leader in the sale of desktop LCD monitors due to their ability to ship monitors with their desktop PCs. Dell shipped almost 4.2M desktop LCD monitors in Q4, a Q/Q growth of 51 percent in unit volume shipments with a 19.8 percent market share. This is almost twice as large as the #2 player in the market, Samsung, which had 10 percent of the worldwide unit volumes in Q4 '04. Dell's growth in North America was even more impressive, where they enjoyed a 39.5 percent market share for Q4 '04.

From *The Register*[9]: "Dell saw robust growth from its storage unit, which increased sales by 49 percent. The company's much larger server business only increased revenue 12 percent year-over-year.

"Mobile product sales driven by laptops also jumped 22 percent from last year's first quarter.

"'Customers worldwide are increasingly relying on us for their diversified information-technology requirements,' said Dell CEO Kevin Rollins.

"Dell has been on a mission to prove that it's much more than just a PC company that happens to sell other hardware. Improving sales of servers, storage systems, printers and consumer goods is key to Dell's goal of being an $80 billion firm by 2008 or 2009.

Figure 9.3 Glasgow, UK.

Dell's growth confounds its competitors. Usually, larger corporations don't grow quickly, but that's just not the case at Dell—this is a corporation that knows how to grow. This in itself is a powerful observation about Dell. It's common knowledge that, when corporations, mutual funds, or any other financial entities get large enough, they stop being nimble. You don't invest in huge mutual funds, because you know the return won't be there. When your corporation becomes a giant, growth becomes a dwarf; everyone knows that. But Dell bucks the trend. And industry watchers know it. From *Forbes Magazine*[10]: "The conventional wisdom in business is that big companies are like dinosaurs: They move slower than molasses in January.

"While that is sometimes true, it's not always the case. We found 25 U.S. companies, each with a minimum of $5 billion in annual sales, with five-year sales growth rates of at least 16 percent. Each day this week, we'll profile industries or companies on the list that, for one reason or another, stand out.

"It may be surprising that there are any tech companies on the list. There are only two, the result of slack demand for almost all things digital. Dell Computer was founded almost ten years after Microsoft, but the two grew up together as the PC industry exploded in the 1980s and throughout most of the 1990s.

"Microsoft's sales have grown 18.7 percent, annualized, since 1998 to $28.3 billion for fiscal 2002, ended June 30. Dell's growth has been even more impressive, 22.5 percent in the same period, to $35.4 billion for fiscal 2003, ended in January."

Grow or Die

Dell's growth has not been just about going for the gusto; in the high-tech field, you have to grow or you die, and it's crucial to understand that. *Fast Company* says[11]: "Michael Dell is fond of saying that in the high-tech business, you either grow or die. It all just happens much, much faster when you're living in Dell time."

All public companies must grow but, for Dell, this has always been a particularly pressing point. It's true that the technology has changed quickly, but that wasn't the main reason for their phenomenal growth.

The reason was that there were too many upstarts, and the larger corporations, who were beginning to buy PCs in great numbers, wanted to buy only from a few, reliable, PC vendors. And those vendors had to be *large* before larger corporations would feel comfortable with them.

In other words, Dell faced the process of *consolidation* in the PC industry, and it's a process that knocked out many of its competitors.

In Dell's own words[12]: "Our growth rate had risen from 50 percent to more than 100 percent per year, and we were earning a 5 percent profit on sales. The company was introducing new desktops and notebooks, and even took its first foray into servers. We had expanded all over western and central Europe and were planning to launch operations in Asia.

"Our potential seemed limitless.

"Boy, were we ill-prepared for what we had coming.

"In retrospect, it's easy to talk about managing rapid growth. But on a day-to-day basis, you hardly notice how fast—or how slowly—you're growing. You walk into the office, you talk to customers, you work to develop products, you expand into other countries. It's not like there are sirens going off or people running through the hallways saying, 'You're growing too fast! Stop!' In fact, while it's happening, it seems to happen in slow motion.

"There were, however, industry forces at work that were causing me some concern as far as our growth rate went. And that had to do with the problem of consolidation.

"In the U.S., corporate customers were looking to narrow their choices—they didn't want to buy from eight different PC vendors.... All over the world, there were PC companies that were strong enough to survive on their own....

"We believed that they would disappear in the consolidation of the PC industry. And because of our size, we were afraid the same thing might happen to us....

"At this critical juncture, I realized that we had to decide whether we should stay the size we were—and face the consequences—or go for big-time growth.

"Obviously, we went for growth...."

Consolidation has been a continuing threat. About the company's situation in 1995, Dell has said[13]: "But as unbelievable as it sounds, we again realized that we were facing the proposition of grow or die. The industry continued to consolidate, and we had to meet the challenge of extending the Dell brand beyond our strong desktop and notebook franchises.

"The next logical step was servers."

In other words, growth has always been important at Dell, which has come to live with a scalable culture, in which growth is sustainable and part of normal business operations. As *USA Today* comments[14]: "Kevin Rollins, who runs Dell side-by-side with Michael Dell, calls the quest The Soul of Dell. 'It's not just about how much bigger we can get and how much more money we can make,' says Rollins, 'but about how we can make it sustainable.'"

Not every company has the luxury of handling growth so large that it can become a problem. But every executive can learn a great many lessons from the way that Dell has handled growth. It's become a company that reacts organically to growth, growing in a very natural way as the situation requires, rather than being constricted by artificial internal structures. Dell has had to learn how to grow. As Dell has said[15]: "If we had stayed a small PC company, we would have been killed."

How Dell Has Been Able to Grow

As a company, Dell has been constantly revising its strategies, and it's worth examining the major steps on this ladder. Dell has been able to top the charts by making the right choice over and over at five or so crucial points. An overview of these strategic decisions follows—a sort of history of Dell growth.

Go Direct

Dell Direct was the original inspiration, and an excellent one, starting the Dell growth engine. Because it could market PCs with a far greater margin than its competitors, it could undercut them and gain market share.

Dell Inc. is still very proud of this inspiration, and you'll find it mentioned prominently in the About Dell pages on the Dell web site[16]: "Dell was founded in 1984 by Michael Dell, the computer industry's longest-tenured chief executive officer, on a simple concept: that by selling computer systems directly to customers, Dell could best understand their needs and efficiently provide the most effective computing solutions to meet those needs. This direct business model eliminates retailers that add unnecessary time and cost, or can diminish Dell's understanding of customer expectations. The direct model allows the company to build every system to order and offer customers powerful, richly configured systems at competitive prices. Dell also introduces the latest relevant technology much more quickly than companies with slow-moving, indirect distribution channels, turning over inventory every four days on average."[17]

Dell historically has gotten a better margin than its competitors using this model; *Enterprise Innovator*, in discussing the business model, says that "[Paul Bell, Dell's SVP for EMEA (Europe, Middle East and Africa)] added that he gets asked a lot about the Dell model, and noted that the 'most commonly understood' aspects of its model is that 'we took out the middle man' so there's 'no markup,' and that customers 'have the ability to order' products 'at a higher velocity' thanks to Dell's efficient distribution model, so they may purchase items today 'at a lower price than someone two months earlier' at the competition due to their distribution model. He added that 'we believe our cost advantage is that many points percent of revenue,' and the range of this advantage varies depending upon the competitor. 'If you look at the aggregate' Bell said that this cost advantage will be 'anywhere between 10 and 20 points.'"

That's a significant advantage, and it gives you the kind of room you need to grow, when compared with your competitors.

Bell adds: "'As you can see, we made 8.8 percent operating income last quarter,' when Dell's 'average competitor makes zero to one' percent. Bell said that 'part of that gap is our profit margin to their profit margin' but that the 'rest of it is we price it lower—that is why we are growing twice as fast as the marketplace.' He added Dell can be 'highly price-elastic,' and as a result we 'consistently have a lower cost position,' and this 'lower price point is why you see our faster growth than our competitors.'"

This combination of direct selling and lower prices started the great growth spurt at Dell, but it was just the beginning; as important as knowing *how* to grow, it's important to know *where* to grow.

Invade a Market When It's Ripe

The Dell Direct strategy has proved its worth for Dell, but Dell needed another growth engine. Next was the now-familiar strategy of invading market sectors when they became standardized. In other words, Dell carefully targeted where it wanted to grow: in those sectors where current players were making terrific profits with proprietary hardware, and Dell could start undercutting them with standardized components.

Michael Dell says as much[18]: "We looked at our market share...product by product, and examined its growth potential. We carefully analyzed our competitors' cost structures, and if they were winning against us, examined them closely in order to understand why. This intense review led us to conclude, for example, that to gain share in the home and small business market, we would have to change our cost structure over the next several years to price our products more aggressively. And at the same time, we needed to evolve our product design strategy for this segment to focus on much higher levels of power and performance.

"We figured out where we could afford to make new investments, identified where we might be more aggressive, and determined where caution was warranted."[19]

From *Enterprise Innovator*: "[Paul Bell] added that Dell aims to 'ride the wave of open standards technology to the most extreme degree,' and on top of getting the 'most share profitably we can in the client space' to also pursue growth in the enterprise, where the 'fastest growing part happens to be open standards.' In addition, Dell has 'added or expanded our capability around our portfolio of services,' and in particular to provide 'consulting to help people make transitions from proprietary high cost systems to open standards.' Bell concluded that Dell thus has a high 'confidence level that we can grow and reach our U.S. share level everywhere else in the world,' and he noted that Dell's growth in 'most of the countries are above that "blue line"' as depicted on a widely shown slide comparing Dell's relative growth in the world's many markets, noting that overseas, Dell is thus 'gaining share faster than in the US.'"

Identifying target sectors for profitable growth is still a huge part of the Dell story. As eWEEK noted recently[20]: "In a prepared statement released Wednesday, Rollins attributed Dell's growth to carefully selecting new product and service areas for the company and ramping up existing businesses.

"Dell officials said that during the meeting Thursday, Rollins will talk about four areas that the company expects will continue to grow quickly: servers, storage, mobile computing and printing.

"Growth in regions beyond the United States also will be a factor, they said.

"During the series of meetings with analysts and reporters, Dell officials focused on the printing and services businesses as examples of their company's deliberate strategy for moving into high-growth opportunities and adding revenue streams that aren't tied directly to selling boxes."

Never underestimate the strength of that strategy when it comes to driving growth. *Chief Executive* magazine interviewed Michael Dell and asked[21]:

"Q. Back to the technology, what really gets your juices flowing?

"A. The magic formula in our business is figuring out what stage of the evolution a given technology is at and when it's right for Dell to use its business model and customer relationships to make a product that is much higher in volume and lower in cost. Some would call it commoditization or standardization, but we constantly look at our business and say, "Well, where are these new technologies on the continuum? And when is it the right time for us to start a new activity? When is the right time to go after a new type of customer, a new geography? Should we be focusing more on large businesses vs. small businesses vs. consumers? What about services? What about professional services or financial services? We have many more choices than we could ever execute on. We're not constrained by capital. We're constrained by, "How many of these things can you actually achieve with a high degree of success and profit?" We've got that paradox.

"Q. You seem to be putting a particular emphasis on the corporate market these days.

"A. The business market is growing very nicely for us. The consumer market is growing very nicely for us. We're growing in Asia quite rapidly. We had 30 percent growth in Europe last quarter. If you look at our business, we're growing across all product segments, all geographies, all customer segments. And we have a growth premium to the market. If the market is growing zero percent, Dell has been growing at 20 percent. We've had that premium for about two and a half years, which is pretty remarkable. We've increased our market share by about 180 percent in five years, a more than 50 percent increase just in the past two years, a period of pretty tumultuous industry consolidation. We grew more share than anyone, not through acquisition but the old-fashioned way."

From an *Internet News* article[22] on Dell's move into servers and printers: "'The pricing environment has been the same. The key to our success was execution,' CEO Kevin Rollins said during a conference call to analysts and press. 'Our teams were keeping an eye on what was selling, and we went after the appropriate businesses. We have a good insight into the corporate business market and the purchase cycle.'"

As Rollins says, Dell's "teams" keep an eye on what is selling. When they locate a sector ripe for the Dell effect, Dell goes after it. When Rollins says that Dell has "a good insight into the corporate business market and the purchase cycle" as far as their competitors go, you can believe him.

What does Dell look for when it's pursuing growth? Imagine how this juicy report from *Network World*[23] must have looked to Dell in the days before it decided to enter the services market: "Big Blue shames Dell and HP in the profit column, exposing the brilliance of IBM's early focus on highly profitable services. IBM generated a 9 percent return on revenue last year—$7.6 billion—more than twice HP's number." How could Dell resist something like that? They've since entered that market and are pursuing the Dell effect there.

To grow, Dell continually enters new markets; it's a fundamental strategy for them. The PC market in the United States has been stagnant for years (although Dell's share of the market is increasing, which does provide growth), but Dell has been moving into other markets overseas to explicitly pursue growth, as highlighted in the *InfoWorld* article[24]: "Dell reported strong results from business units located outside of the U.S. in the first quarter, leading to solid increases in revenue and net income on the back of solid growth in storage and mobile products, the company said Thursday.

"First-quarter revenue was $13.4 billion, up 16 percent from $11.5 billion in revenue during last year's first quarter and meeting the expectations of analysts polled by Thomson First Call.

"The increase in revenue was driven largely by a 21 percent increase in sales to businesses and consumers outside the U.S., said Kevin Rollins, chief executive officer, on a conference call following Dell's earnings announcement. Customers outside the U.S. now account for 42 percent of Dell's total revenue, he said. Shipments in Europe, the Middle East, and Africa increased by 26 percent compared to last year, while shipments in Asia-Pacific, including Japan, increased 27 percent.

"Dell needs to stick to that 16 percent growth pace to reach its stated target of $80 billion in yearly revenue by the end of 2008 or 2009. Rollins pointed to the company's efficient operating model and expanding global reach as two factors that will help it achieve that goal."

In other words, the international market has become vital for Dell. That doesn't necessarily mean it'll be selling huge amounts of entry-level PCs in China; Dell will continue with its business model as usual and presumably target second-time or third-time PC purchasers as the market matures. In the mean time, it'll pursue markets with higher ROIC, such as the enterprise and server sectors. Dell's ROIC is consistently higher than that of other companies in the markets where Dell is operative. It's the key to Dell growth—smart growth, not simply growth for its own sake.

Beside the international component, Dell enters new product market sectors as they present themselves in order to pursue growth. From an article titled "Servers, Printers Drive Dell's Growth" in *Internet News*[25]: "Dell continues to take market share away from its rivals and is showing no sign of slowing down, the company said Thursday during its second-quarter earnings report.

"The Round Rock, Texas-based computer maker said its revenue was a record $11.7 billion for the quarter ending in July. Net income was $799 million, with earnings per share at 31 cents—also a Dell record....

"Rollins said he did not see a sales slowdown in June or at the end of July in the same way that HP warned investors of today. Much of Dell's sales came from its enterprise and small-to-medium business customers, although the company said its back-to-school sales should be good, as well....

"Dell said demand for its servers and printers were especially high during the quarter. The company saw a 31 percent increase in server shipments in Q2. The company said it is on tap to introduce a new, eighth generation of PowerEdge servers, which feature more powerful processors and enhanced systems-management software.

"Likewise, revenue from software and peripheral products increased 31 percent, due to a strong demand for Dell printers. Those products are being introduced in more countries, including Japan during the second quarter and China in Q3. The company said it expects to sell five million printers during fiscal 2005, up from an original target of four million. Dell's overall printing and imaging business is now at a $1 billion annual run rate."

The article also mentions international sales: "Dell's success also included a lot of overseas sales. The company said its Q2 shipment growth in Europe, the Middle East and Africa was 30 percent. Research firm IDC's numbers support Dell's claims that it shipped product 12 points higher than the average of rivals like IBM and HP in the region. Among its highlights, Dell saw a 44 percent rise in server shipments, and a 60 percent increase in total storage revenue.

"The Asia-Pacific markets, including Japan, showed a similar trend, with shipment growth of 28 percent and server volumes in the region up 33 percent."

Michael Dell gives his signature statement on growth in *CFO* magazine as he comments on expanding into the enterprise market sector[26]: "Michael Dell has said that his ambitious revenue target will co-exist with a further $2 billion in cost cuts. 'In this business, you grow or die,' says Dell. 'At the moment, enterprise computing offers us the best revenue growth and market-share opportunities.'"

Here's some commentary from *CFO* magazine[27] on how Dell seeks out new markets to grow: "How does Dell plan to grow so fast and become ever leaner? Primarily by moving 'up the stack,' extending its proven business model to a range of products and services essential to corporate computing. It's a path Dell has followed for several years, and if Merrill Lynch's projection of 27 percent annual growth in enterprise product sales through 2006 hits the mark, analysts believe $60 billion is possible—even with a modest 5 percent annual growth in Dell's core PC, notebook, and workstation business. 'I think it's doable,' says [former] Merrill Lynch analyst and first vice president Steven Milunovich. 'As various technologies commoditize over time, Dell's direct-to-the-customer strategy presents a highly attractive cost advantage that's tough to ignore.'"

After the original Dell Direct strategy, finding those markets ripe for invasion—tech markets where the products were between standardization and commoditization—was Dell's next major growth engine. But it still had to be able to handle its hypergrowth internally, and that meant segmenting.

Segment to Mirror the Market

As you know, Dell's major growth crisis came in 1993. Dell's ultimate solution was to segment the business and to watch metrics obsessively. I've discussed segmentation in terms of adapting to market conditions, but it's just as important in terms of handling growth. In fact, segmenting the company has been Dell's chief way of dealing with organizational growth.

Michael Dell has said,[28] "When you've got a huge market opportunity facing you, the only way to handle it is to divide and conquer. That's the basis behind our concept of segmentation. It ensures that as we grow, we are able to serve each individual customer more effectively, and it has become the organizing philosophy of our company."

A great part of Michael Dell's insight has to do with how to scale his company as it grew. With typical year-to-year growth rates of 80 percent or so, that became an essential skill. Dell knew that he could manage and control his company of ten employees, and the interesting thing is that as it grew massively, he made it scale so that it retained the small company feel.

As mentioned in passing in Chapter 6, here's what Michael Dell has said on that score[29]: "You can grow small companies quickly, but it becomes increasingly more difficult to sustain a high rate of growth in a large corporation. Segmentation allows us to scale our business very rapidly, because every time we determine that there is sufficient momentum to segment a unique customer group, we'll break it off, give it its own organization team, and let it act as a small company.

"Together, our segments enable us, as a large company, to post the growth rates of a small one."

And he describes the company as[30]: "We're a bunch of entrepreneurs who work as a team."

The insight here is to let Dell Inc. act like a small company. Or a set of small companies. Small companies can grow fast, while large ones can't, and small companies are far more manageable than large companies. Michael Dell knew how to work with a small company and, because he had control over the way Dell Inc. grew, he was able to make the corporation work much as a small company would.

When segmenting Dell Inc. into a collection of small companies, those segments were designed to follow the market—another important strategy as far as growth is concerned. In other corporations, where growth is not such an issue, the internal divisions can be made according to some plan. Even if those divisions are artificial ones, the organizational problems are not as acute as they'd be in a fast-growing corporation like Dell.

At Dell, however, setting up fundamentally artificial internal divisions would be a problem because of Dell's hypergrowth. No structure that did not make Dell competitive and able to handle fast growth could endure for long, and that was the lesson Dell learned in 1993. Other companies could tolerate a nonresponsive corporate structure, but not Dell. In that sense, Dell is the extreme that points the way for other organizations.

Dell needed a structure that was able to grow responsively and follow the markets. So, what better model to use than the markets themselves? As you know, segmenting at Dell was originally done to let the sales teams work better with customers. But, as time went on, the company itself was organized around those market-driven segments as well.

That lets Dell scale *automatically* as it grows. Each segment only has to handle the growth of Dell's share of its own market sector and, if that growth makes the unit too large, Dell segments it into smaller units. When a unit becomes too large, too ungainly and unresponsive, Dell segments it into smaller units. In this way, its internal segmentation mirrors the market. As the market grows—and as Dell's market share grows—Dell automatically makes the right moves to follow. Therefore, growth can be accommodated naturally.

Michael Dell says[31]: "We work hard to ensure that the direct relationships that characterize our business model also characterize our corporate structure."

And[32]: "Look at it this way: If you organize a company like ours around products, you have to assume that the people who are running the business know everything there is to know about the customers who buy those products—not just here, but everywhere in the world. That's a pretty big assumption. Believing that an organization that is focused on a particular type of customer in a particular region of the world knows everything about those customers is a lot easier to fathom."

John Ellett, CEO of nFusion Group and former marketing executive at Dell, also agrees. In a white paper on Results-Oriented Integrated Marketing, he says you should[33] "Align the entire organization to deliver your value proposition to distinct market segments profitably."

Ellet explains: "Why are some companies successful while others flounder? As CEO of an integrated marketing agency and a former marketing executive at Dell, I'm frequently asked for an insider's perspective on what has made Dell such a success...."While it's one thing to acknowledge that Fortune 500 companies and consumers are very different, it's another to align the entire organization around the differences. It's even harder to serve the distinct needs of the Department of Defense, local school districts and small businesses. Because Dell has organized its primary business units around these segments, there is financial accountability for building distinct capabilities to serve these segments. Product platforms are engineered to distinct segments. Manufacturing and logistics capabilities are built to meet the demands of each segment. Service and support programs are designed to meet the needs and cost parameters of distinct segments. Sales forces are a combination of inside and outside representatives based on the segment requirements and economics. Marketing programs are created to fulfill the acquisition and retention needs of each segment. This organizational alignment has proven a huge competitive advantage, and one that most product-focused companies have a difficult time replicating."

"Organizational alignment" is an excellent way of describing what Dell does, and a central strategy on how it's been able to handle growth in an organic way.

Does it work? In Michael Dell's words[34]: "By the mid-1990s, everything was coming together. Thanks to segmentation, we were scaling glocally. In 1995, sales in the United States, Canada, and Latin America grew nearly three times faster than the market rate. We had offices in fourteen countries in Europe, solidified our position as the second-largest computer company in the United Kingdom, and continued to extend the direct model in France and Germany, posting sales rates well above the average."

Chase Return on Invested Capital (ROIC)

To make growth happen in a controlled way, you need metrics to focus on. Dell goes after profitable growth, as measured most systematically using ROIC. As you grow, unless you have a systematic tracking mechanism, it's difficult to know what's going on and what parts of the organization need attention. Dell does. By watching ROIC, it's able to know what fields are working and which aren't.

Internet News interviewed Kevin Rollins[35] on this point: "Kevin Rollins, the company's president and chief operating officer, attributed to the success to the company's unique low-cost business model. He also differentiated Dell's growth from rest of the PC-making pack, including IBM, HP, and Gateway.

"'Much of the industry's quarterly growth was at the low ends of the desktop and notebook categories, which offer little if any profitability,' Rollin said in the statement. 'Dell met its operating targets by pursuing profitable growth.'

"The profitable growth Rollins referred to is rooted in the enterprise, with servers and storage. Dell sold 40 percent more PowerEdge servers from the year-ago quarter, as well as 47 percent greater total storage revenue for the same period."

Enterprise Innovator interviewed Paul Bell on the idea of managed growth[36]: "Bell added, 'We think we're well positioned for profitable growth' and by 'adding so many different products,' Dell's 'available, servable market is way bigger' than it once was, as Dell is a 'new entrant in many' product categories and emerging markets owing to its 'geo-

graphic expansion opportunities.' All this, he said, 'reinforces our commitment to manage this growth tightly and predictably,' as 'we care very
much about consistency—and reliability,' on both a quarter-to-quarter
basis and 'not just according to our 2 to 5 year vision.'"

Tracking ROIC not only lets Dell plunge into market sectors that offer
profitable growth, but also makes it watch its costs. Here's what Austin's
American-Statesman newspaper had to say on that[37]: "Dell Inc. ignored
the rumblings of sluggish demand heard at some tech companies recently, fueling its drive to a strong third quarter with double-digit growth
overseas.

"Dell also leaned on its low-inventory model, taking advantage of
declining costs for parts such as memory chips and flat-panel monitors to
ratchet up earnings faster than revenue. The company's shipments grew
22 percent, boosting revenue 18 percent and net income 25 percent.

"Profit was $846 million, or 33 cents per share, on $12.5 billion in revenue. A year ago, Dell earned $677 million, or 26 cents, on sales of $10.6
billion."

The moral is that, to manage large-scale growth, you have to know
what's going on; you have to have the information you need to proceed.
Dell manages that using its internal metrics; ROIC is the flagship metric
that got them out of the 1993 hypergrowth mess and allowed them to
manage their growth by jettisoning underperforming segments.

Rely on Your Partners

Dell has a history of relying on its partners to handle the tech innovation,
something that helps it grow faster and more nimbly. When it comes to
Dell and tech innovation, *InformationWeek* says[38]: "While many of the
largest technology companies budget 5 percent, 15 percent, and higher
portions of revenue for research and development, one computing industry star isn't even in the ballpark. Dell Computer spent a paltry 1.3 percent of revenue for its second quarter ended Aug. 2—about $111 mil-
lion—on R&D.

"The investment is typical for Dell, which has been profitable in the
tough PC and enterprise computing markets where others have faltered.
A year ago, Dell spent 1.5 percent of revenue on R&D.

"By contrast, Hewlett-Packard spent 6 percent of revenue, or $983
million, on R&D during its third quarter ended July 31. Sun Microsystems
spent 16 percent of revenue, or $437 million, during its first quarter,
ended Sept. 30. And IBM's R&D spending was $1.2 billion, or 6.1 percent
of revenue, for its third quarter ended Sept. 30.

"Kevin Rollins, Dell's president and chief operating officer, says the company relies on 'collaborative R&D,' leveraging the research and engineering investments of its suppliers—including Microsoft and Intel—to reduce costs as more business-computing products become standardized. 'There are myriad suppliers who have developed the components that go into our systems,' Rollins says. 'We think there's a lot of hoopla about big research budgets in companies.'"

"Dell is trying to pare $1 billion in costs this year from product design, manufacturing, and other areas, and slipstreaming innovation from other vendors into its products could help."

Lower investment in R&D is good to help keep margins down and growth up. The less you have invested in R&D, the more you have to invest in other areas.

Michael Dell notes the importance of keeping R&D costs down; explicitly, he's said, "Unlike many of our competitors, we actually had an option: to buy components from the specialists, leveraging the investments they had already made and allowing us to focus on what we did best—designing and delivering solutions and systems directly to customers.

"In forging these early alliances with suppliers, we created exactly the right strategy for a fast-growing company."

If you're a supplier and don't perform, Dell dumps you. It's famous for being direct—very direct—with its suppliers. But that's just another cost of doing business, according to Dell. As *Fast Company* says[40]: "Despite such tough talk, even Dell's alumni bristle at any suggestion that their alma mater beats up its suppliers. 'If you aren't performing, Dell won't hesitate to take some of your business and give it to a competitor, so boo-hoo,' says Jerry Gregoire, who was Dell's CIO from 1995 to 2000. 'That's bullying? It's called holding the supplier's feet to the fire. If you want my business, you're going to have to meet my expectations.'"

Dell grew up in an environment in which it took business away from its R&D-heavy competitors. That was central to Dell's growth pattern. It's worth bearing in mind that Dell grows *following* the market curve, not leading it. It invades markets, it doesn't pioneer them. That means it can't be as aggressive in new markets as it would like to be, and as people expect it to be.

The Register has this to say[41]: "But could a lack of imagination and research and development come back to haunt Dell?

"AMD will shortly announce a dual-core version of its 64-bit Opteron processor that will immediately slide into servers from Sun, HP and IBM. This will turn one-ways into two-ways and two-ways into four-ways and help customers save money on some software. Dell will have to wait until

2006 to offer its customers a comparable Intel chip. It won't go the AMD route because of the disruption a second-supplier would cause to its server production system. We'll see if being lean and mean equals customer satisfaction in this case.

"Elsewhere Dell admits that a lack of R&D can be a pain.

"Rollins told the analysts that getting into the laser printer business was no problem since intellectual property issues could be overcome. 'When you get to the inkjet side, things are a bit more restricted in terms of the IP,' he said. Dell has managed to find some 'disruptive technologies' from other 'sources' but Rollins wouldn't comment on exactly what such inkjet technology is or where it came from. With all its printer giveaways, Dell said its new printer business isn't producing any profit at all. Heavy R&D firm HP might have the better model on this one."

As it happens, Intel turned up the steam, moving up the delivery of its dual-core processor, so the gap was less than it could have been. (My personal opinion? I bet Dell was one of the big reasons for the faster delivery.)

You already know that Dell relies on its partners in other ways too, such as requiring them to hold inventory. That's a great growth trick if you can pull if off because, if you need to change directions, you're not left holding the bag. Even if you don't have to change directions quickly, you still have so little capital tied up in inventory that you can afford to move it to those areas that will provide growth.

Delegate

Dell has grown fast enough to make it clear that you can't expect to do everything yourself. In the end, you have to delegate responsibility. That lesson became clear early on at Dell, and it's another lesson in growth that Dell offers. Michael Dell says[42]: "For any company to succeed, it's critical for top management to share power successfully. You have to be focused on achieving goals for the organization, not on accumulating power for yourself. Hoarding power does not translate into success for shareholders and customers; pursuing the goals of the company does."

Dell is true to his word here, having made Kevin Rollins CEO while stepping down to become chairman. Here is the announcement on that from the Dell web site[43]: "Twenty years after founding Dell, Michael Dell will transfer the title of chief executive officer to Kevin Rollins, with whom he has led the world's fastest growing, most profitable computer systems company since 1997.

"Dell's board of directors, meeting today in New York City, appointed Mr. Rollins CEO effective at the company's July 16 annual meeting of shareholders. Mr. Rollins, currently president and chief operating officer, will become president and chief executive officer. He will also be nominated for election to the Dell board at the annual meeting.

"Mr. Dell will remain deeply involved in the company's day-to-day business as chairman of the board, leaving intact a unique, successful 'two-in-a-box' senior-management structure. The company said the pending title change is consistent with current primary roles: Mr. Dell emphasizing trends in technology and customer preference, including research and development, Mr. Rollins leading company strategy and operations."

Interestingly, the "two-in-a-box" senior-management strategy really seems to work at Dell. Kevin Rollins has the CEO title, which gives him the power. But Michael Dell has the name, which means he's nearly synonymous with the company. The balance, and the sense of shared goals between the two men, seems functional.

Delegating responsibility permeates the organization. *Chief Executive* magazine asked Dell his thoughts on this process[44]:

"Q. Is it possible that running a $40 billion-a-year company is just too complex for one person?

"A. It depends on whether you're trying to do everything yourself. I don't think it's possible. Kevin and I don't necessarily run the whole company. We have a series of businesses with general managers in them and those folks are CEOs unto themselves, running $5 billion, $8 billion, $10 billion businesses. They have the final accountability and responsibility and strategies. Yeah, the overall strategy of the company is pretty tightly held, for good reason. Kevin, I and our global executive management team spend a lot of time on that. But the guy who's running Asia doesn't call us back and ask, 'Now what do I do?' He knows what to do. He's got a strategy and he's executing to it. Same for our folks who run our businesses in the United States and Europe."

You can see why, in Dell's opinion, it's not enough to go simply for the best people; you also have to go for those people best aligned with your organization.

Stay Flexible

Reading this chapter may give you the feeling that Dell follows a set number of rules to handle growth, but it's important to realize that nothing could be further from the truth. Growth is a dynamic process and, fundamentally, Dell's response is to stay flexible and adaptable.

If you want to sum up Dell's strategy for handling growth in a nut-shell, it's this: Always adapt. Don't think you're all set and never have to examine structures or strategies again.

Chief Executive magazine asked Michael Dell what he had to say on this topic[45]:

"Q. So how will you keep evolving your structure? Will you have to become more like, say, an IBM? More corporate and bureaucratic?

"A. We don't want to do that. We don't want to act like a big compa-ny as we get bigger in terms of our structure. Our structure is still very fast, very flexible. It doesn't have a huge number of layers in it. Communication happens quickly. Our goal is to retain that as much as we possibly can.

"Q. But with size, you need more training programs, more mecha-nisms, more checks and balances, right?

"A. Sure, but if you did an audit of that today, at $40 billion I'd think you'd come away with the sense that it doesn't feel like a $40 billion com-pany. We make decisions very quickly. We communicate rapidly."

The message is: stay supple, stay hungry.

By remaining flexible, by keeping a clear overview and responding to issues as needed, Dell is able to manage growth. Behind all the growth strategies at Dell is that simple mantra: stay flexible; always adapt, always execute. It's another example of corporate will.

Plan

Another way that Dell handles growth is to look ahead. In its early days, Dell as a company didn't plan ahead much. But, even if you can't chart exactly where you're going to be going, it's important to chart your road as much as you can. Michael Dell says[46]: "Planning is one of those areas where experience counts as much as intellect. When you're trying to grow a new business, it's hard to anticipate the ups and downs of busi-ness cycles that you've actually never experienced before.

"It seems a little naïve in retrospect, but before [former Vice chairman] Mort [Topfer], we didn't do a heck of a lot of detailed long-range planning. We didn't have to when we were 'young,' and by the time we should have, we were already working hard to meet our short-term goals....

"Mort helped us identify the need to insert more discipline into our planning process. He helped us understand that planning was not a quar-terly event, but an ongoing process. And it was not just an internal initia-tive, but a system that involves every part of the supply chain, customer and employee base...."

"For the first time, we put together a robust three-year plan for the entire company. This planning process revealed a number of key issues about the organization, its facilities, infrastructure, and growth opportunities....

"There was no area of the company that wasn't affected by this new approach of integrated planning. We looked at our head count and realized that we'd need to hire a huge number of people over the next several years, and that we'd need to develop a large team of senior managers to run the new businesses that we could create. We looked at our supplier relationships and concluded that to meet our goals, we would need tremendous unit volumes of supply.... We looked at our sales process and knew that if we were to meet our goal of achieving 30 percent of our sales in notebooks, we would need a commensurate capacity in our manufacturing plants, as well as the sales force and the component supply to make this all happen.

"Strategically, at least, we were back on track—and it felt good."

Chief Executive magazine had this to say on Dell and planning[47]:

"Q. The notion that your business model wasn't scalable—that it could never expand beyond selling a few PCs—was one of the things that confronted you in the early days. What do you think about that now?

"A. If you think about the first 14 years of our company the math is pretty incredible. We grew 80 percent a year for eight years. Obviously, it was scalable. It sounds easier than it actually was. Then we grew 60 percent a year for six years after that. This is compounded year over year growth. It's the only way to get to $40 billion in 20 years.

"The fundamental business model had incredible legs, and still does. The question is how do you build a support structure around it to take advantage of the all the opportunity, things like talent and leadership and information technology. We need to plan enough ahead of time so that you don't totally outgrow things but not too far ahead of time. It's been a lot of fun.

"Q. After these 20 years, do you get tired? Do you have a sense of fatigue about having worked so hard for so long? Do you want to ease back?

"A. No, not really, no. I'm having a great time. It's a lot of fun. I love what I do and I see tremendous opportunity. We have the potential to grow and go into new markets."

Growing Pains

Dell's growth hasn't been accomplished without growing pains. The most notable problem was the 1993 growth fiasco, of course, but the growing pains are happening all the time. Right now, Dell still has major issues with customer support in its PC market, and it'll be a while before things are running smoothly. From a recent (July 2005) article in *The Register*[48]: "Want to complain on Dell's web site about its customer service? Too late—the Customer Support Forums, operational until last Friday, have been shut down, apparently to try to quell bad publicity there about Dell products and especially after-care service....

"Why? Could it be anything to do with the unbelievably corrosive effect on Dell's reputation that has followed its insistent refusal to deal with problems with the Dell Dimension 4600 power supply?

"Noted Windows expert Ed Bott, who has been tying together some of the threads of the tale, comments: 'Dell continues its race to the bottom with the new management strategy: If your customers continue to ask annoying questions, stop listening.'

"Dell didn't have a response to our query about why it had shut the forums, although in a chat with Christopher Carfi one Dell service bod said: 'We are closing the Customer Service boards on the Dell Community Forum for the time being as there are certain updates which need to be taken care of.'...

"Part of the problem seems to have stemmed from Jeff Jarvis, a columnist on the *San Francisco Examiner*, who summed up his anger in a letter to a Dell VP, saying: "This machine is a lemon. Your at-home and complete care service is a fraud. Your customer service is appalling. Your product is dreadful. Your brand is mud."

"That has snowballed into growing pressure on Dell to improve its customer service, at precisely the time it has been driving ever-harder to improve margins. Unfortunately, the two conflict: excellent customer service can't be measured by standard accounting metrics because it doesn't show up until people renew purchases or service contracts— which is a future, uncertain, event. However, you can cut costs in customer service today and it shows up in the bottom line.

"Jarvis's travails sparked a little civil war in Blogistan, where some thought he deserved special treatment from Dell as an 'A-lister' and 'influential,' while Bott pointed out that 'Google Dell customer service problems and you get 2,950,000 hits, which seems like a lot by any standards.'...

"In fact Dell's growth has clearly been putting increasing [pressure] on its customer service operations. In 2000 it won high marks in a *PC World* survey of subscribers. But fast forward to 2004 and it was slipping badly."

So, do you get 2,950,000 hits when you Google "Dell customer service problems?" No. You get about that many hits if you Google that phrase without the quotation marks, because any document that has one of those words matches. But if you Google it as a phrase, with quotation marks around it, you get just 61 hits. Nonetheless, there's an ongoing support issue here, and Dell is going to have to work on containing it.

Chapter 10

Look to the Future

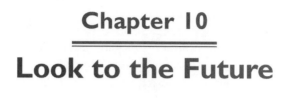

We've been migrating the last three or four years out of being a PC company. We've moved into servers and storage, mobility products, services, software peripheral categories, and printers, and become a diversified IT company.

—Kevin Rollins[1]

Dell is a company that looks ahead and plans for the future. It's a smart, fast-growing dynamo that stays true to its business model and moves forward inexorably. But, to keep going, Dell needs to grow, and it needs to keep growing fast.

So, what's next for Dell? What's coming up over the next few years? That's what this chapter is all about. It's hard to predict exactly where Dell is going, but it's easy to discuss Dell's plan of attack and the goals it wants to pursue. Dell's plan of attack is going to be to invade markets as it has done in the past and where it knows so well what it is doing. As for the goals it plans to pursue? That can be summed up in two words: "Profitable Growth."

Growing Profitably

If there's one thing that Dell is going to keep on doing, it's growing. It's going to keep searching out growth with new products and new international markets. According to an article in the 2005 *Forbes Investment Guide*[2]: "Deutsche Bank analyst Christopher Whitmore says Dell could approach $100 billion in sales by 2010. And although today IBM is twice

199

Dell's size, Whitmore believes Dell could one day be bigger than IBM. 'That would not surprise me, quite frankly. Toward the end of this decade, that is feasible,' he says."

From a recent *Forbes Magazine* piece[3]: "Prudential Equity Group maintained an 'outperform' rating on Dell after its second-quarter chief information officer survey yielded positive sentiment for the company. 'Dell continues to lap the competition with respect to future hardware spending intentions. Our survey confirms that the IBM/Lenovo transition should present an opportunity for future Dell share gains; especially in the U.S.' The survey indicated that approximately 12 percent of IBM's PC customers could be available—or what Prudential sees as roughly $1 billion in business. The research outfit also sees printers as a growth driver for Dell. '[We] were pleased to see that the company is increasingly being looked to as an enterprise printer supplier.' Prudential's survey also showed Dell was keeping up with competition in storage."

And that growth is going to come from more than just PCs.

More than PCs

As the U.S. PC market remains flat, Dell is going to move elsewhere. As an article in *InfoWorld* says,[4] "Dell took great pains to reassure financial analysts...that it can rise above a cooling PC market and continue to grow at rates that will enable it to record $80 billion in yearly revenue by 2009."

Dell downplays the PC in its future, although it's obviously still a huge section of the business. Another *InfoWorld* article states[5]: "Dell plans to increase its stakes in higher-margin markets such as printers, services, enterprise servers and mobile products such as notebook PCs and personal digital assistants, said Kevin Rollins, chief executive officer.... Executives sought to downplay any adverse effects of a gradual slowdown in the PC market over the next few years, as forecast by analysts such as IDC and Gartner.

"'We're not tied to PC growth rates,' Rollins said. After two solid years of double-digit percentage growth in PC shipments, the PC industry is expected to ship 9.7 percent more units in 2005 than in the previous year, IDC said in March.

"PCs as a share of Dell's revenue will decline in the upcoming years as businesses continue to adopt Dell servers, storage devices and networking products as the backbone of their IT infrastructures, Rollins said. Dell also believes it can increase revenue from services tied to the installation and support of that hardware, he said. The IT services market represents a huge amount of potential revenue, but Dell will tread carefully as it grows its services arm, preferring to work mostly with current customers running Dell hardware....

"But most of the focus at the meeting was on how Dell will improve its other businesses to reach its $80 billion target for yearly revenue, which the company hopes to achieve by the next three or four years, Rollins said. The clock started on that goal as of this quarter, the first quarter of the company's 2006 fiscal year.

"Dell is just beginning to make strides in markets such as printing, software and peripherals, and storage, Rollins said. And it also has room for growth in markets outside the U.S. where HP leads, such as Europe, he said."

All of which is to say that Dell is no one-trick pony. People who assume that it's all about PCs are going to be repeatedly surprised. Dell is about profitable growth, and pursuing that is going to take it into many new fields in the coming years. Look for more expansion in printing, servers, peripherals, and possibly consumer electronics. Dell has been expanding into providing services for corporate clients and is doing well there, often eclipsing more established providers like IBM. And you're going to see massive efforts overseas as Dell works to grow.

In fact, Dell shows every indication of staying true to its business model by going after not just growth, but profitable growth. From the same article: "The company made it clear, however, that profitable growth is more important in its eyes than just growth itself.

"'Our competitors are trying to gain share unprofitably or through acquisitions,' said founder and Chairman Michael Dell. The company does not plan to sacrifice profits in order to gain market share, and thinks it can have both profits and market share because its costs are much lower than the competition, he said."

Dell likes to challenge itself internally by setting high goals and, sometimes, those goals leak out and become expectations. That's been the case with its goal of becoming an $80 billion (in sales) company by the end of 2009. Now that that goal has become public and been accepted, Dell is trying to live up to it. *Enterprise Innovator* says[6]: "TBR also finds that Dell's 'well on the way to achieving its $80 billion revenue target by year-end 2009.'... Indeed, 'by year-end 2009,' TBR predicts Dell will enjoy revenues of '$41 billion in PCs; $9 billion in servers; $3.3 billion in storage; $10.2 billion in services; and $16.5 billion in software and peripheral sales.'" Will it? Time will tell.

Testing the Limits of the Model

Dell is primarily a market invader, not a pioneer, so it's interesting to consider the upper limits of its business model as it begins to thrust the pioneers out of those markets it competes in. Dell's business model is based on following the leaders with disruptive innovation—but what ultimately happens as the leaders are thrust aside?

As an article in *MacWorld* says[7]: "Dell is at the opposite extreme. It operates on a simpler model that requires more partners but fewer team players, focused more on costs and less on company cohesiveness at a product level. Basically, Dell is a sales and logistics engine that operates with minimal overhead. This is the model that became the ideal in the '90s, and Gateway is now emulating it. Easier to execute but containing risks associated with technology advancement, it depends heavily on IBM and HP's inability to execute, and Microsoft and Intel adequately make up the difference. Dell's exposure is one of control: It can dominate a segment but not an industry. Should the market move to AMD and/or Linux, Dell becomes increasingly exposed, because neither of these supplies the complete core platforms that Dell requires for its model to work."

Considering the upper limits of the Dell business model is by no means an academic question as its competitors consolidate, lose share, and fall by the wayside. From a July 19, 2005 article in TheStreet.com[8]: "Hewlett-Packard detailed a broad restructuring Tuesday that will result in the elimination of 14,500 jobs over the next six quarters.

"The company, struggling to rein in costs under new CEO Mark Hurd, hopes to save $1.9 billion annually from the actions, which also include aligning sales and marketing operations with their respective manufacturing units."

Add that to announcements like this, in *Forbes Magazine*[9]: "IBM recently announced it will slash 13,000 jobs in Europe." You get a picture of Dell's primary competitors falling by the side of the road. Dell's business model is the engine powering this success, and its competitors can't keep up. They're dropping jobs along the way and shrinking. Dell relies on the business side of the equation, to the detriment of those who still put all their faith in innovation. Dell knows what it's doing, and it's grabbing market share left and right.

What will happen if IBM and HP continue to weaken? There's no question that tech innovation would suffer. In fact, plenty of indications suggest it already is; industry watchers are decrying the outsourcing of innovation as never before.

Take a look at this from *CIO* magazine[10] (can you detect undertones of the Dell effect?): "Innovation is the route out of low-margin manufacturing. IBM, Xerox, AT&T, and HP built their R&D capabilities with cash from unique products that commanded high margins—or, in the case of AT&T, from an outright monopoly. But those companies have a harder time justifying investments in research today. 'It's difficult to make an ROI argument for creating fundamentally new scientific knowledge,' says Mark Bernstein, president and center director of PARC, the former Xerox think tank that was spun out into an independent subsidiary in 2002. 'Faster product cycles and the increased focus on efficiency and productivity have made it harder for companies to have a long-term vision.'

"The loss of manufacturing and design could make it difficult for the traditional R&D powerhouses to innovate in the future. 'Real breakthrough product development usually requires manufacturing and research to be located together," says NIST's Tassey. Supercomputers and high-tech weapons, for example, required close collaboration between engineers and manufacturers.

"But PARC's Bernstein says R&D must become more global by necessity. 'The breadth of research required to master a market these days is pretty significant,' he says. 'You're going to see a lot more partnering' around the globe to do research. Besides outsourcing manufacturing and design, many U.S. companies have opened their own dedicated R&D facilities in low-cost countries such as India and China. Innovation still occurs under the banner of a U.S. corporation, but it happens elsewhere, employing lower-cost engineers. Though U.S. corporations will continue to innovate under this model, the United States and its pool of engineers will become lesser engines of that innovation."

Market pioneers will suffer, but don't forget that Dell still has an entire world to go after. From an article in *Chief Executive* magazine,[11] interviewing Michael Dell:

"Q. Give me some hint about the technologies that might be at the right stage for Dell to come in and make them more widely available at a lower price.

"A. I think you can see some of the things we're already doing. First of all step back and ask, 'What is our market share today?' Well, in the whole IT services sector, it's about 5 percent of an $800 billion business. One strategy to grow is you just go from 5 percent to 10 percent or even 15 percent. That's tremendous growth, if you can achieve that.

"If you look inside the individual businesses, in PCs we have 17 percent share, in all servers it's less than 17 percent, but if you look at Intel-based servers, it's in the 20s. Storage is in the single digits. Software and peripherals are pretty small-share today. We have lots of opportunity to grow.

"If you take a geographic cut, in about 45 percent of the market, we have roughly 25 percent share, but in the other 55 percent of the market, we have less than 10 percent share. So there's a lot of opportunity to grow in new markets and new product areas."

Growing Overseas

Much of Dell's future is tied up with its overseas markets, and that's going to represent a growth area for the foreseeable future. The following is from an *InfoWorld* interview with Kevin Rollins[12]:

"*InfoWorld*: In terms of growing your desktop sales, do you think you have everything in place internationally?

"Rollins. Over the last several quarters we have been growing faster in Asia and Europe than any other place on the planet. We have 18 percent of the global PC share, about 12 percent in Europe, and 8 percent in Asia."

From the Austin *American-Statesman* newspaper, which likes to watch what Dell's doing now[13]: "Computer company reports double-digit gains overseas in third quarter and could reach $60 billion target early.... Dell Inc. ignored the rumblings of sluggish demand heard at some tech companies recently, fueling its drive to a strong third quarter with double-digit growth overseas."

And from a BBC article entitled "Dell Rises on Overseas PC Growth"[14]: "Dell has seen non-U.S. sales grow to make up 42 percent of total sales. Dell, the world's largest personal computer maker, shrugged off weakness in the PC market to increase profits in the three months to 29 April. Its profit rose 28 percent to $934m (£500.7m), compared with $731m a year earlier.

"Sales rose 16 percent to $13.39 billion from $11.54 billion a year ago, benefiting from overseas sales growth and from the sale of storage systems and mobile products.

"Non-U.S. sales grew 21 percent compared with a year ago, and now make up 42 percent of total revenues."

Dell may have publicly committed to that $80 billion goal by the end of 2009, but it's not going to rely on its U.S. PC market to get it there. From a July 15, 2005 news.com article[15]: "Dell CEO Kevin Rollins says the computer maker has the potential to be an $80 billion company in the next three to four years, but not through its U.S.-based bread-and-butter PC business.

"Though the company enjoys great success in the United States, with $49.2 billion in revenues reported for its fiscal 2005, Dell ranks second behind Hewlett-Packard in overseas sales. Dell said it currently averages $135.2 million in revenues per day, a number that would need to nearly double to reach Rollins' lofty goals....

"Rollins said he expects more than 80 percent of Dell's future growth to come from products other than desktop PCs, which the company started selling 10 years ago. The CEO also said he expects about 55 percent of Dell's growth in the next four years to come from outside the Americas."

Along with that overseas growth comes overseas hiring. The following is from a 2004 *MacNewsWorld* article[16] entitled Dell Sends Most New Jobs Overseas: "Of the nearly 7,000 jobs Dell added in 2003, about 1,000 were in the United States. The computer maker now employs 6,600 people in the Asia-Pacific-Japan region, 6,900 in the Americas outside of the United States, and 10,300 in the Europe-Middle East-Africa region."

Printers

Dell has invaded the printer market, and much of its expected growth is going to come from this sector. From news.com[17]: "For example, Rollins said, Dell shipped 10 million printers in just more than the two years since the company introduced the first of its own line of printers. Dell says it is No. 2 in the U.S. in both the inkjet and laser categories, behind HP."

From the 2005 *Dell Annual Report*[18]: "Our growth in printing and imaging represents the most successful new-product entry in Dell history, and is the latest example of how prices drop and customer value increases when we enter a product segment."

Dell probably will continue its low-price printer offerings, hoping to make profits in the long run using proprietary printing supplies such as ink cartridges. Dell computers interact with Dell printers and let the user know when to reorder ink, which users can do with a few clicks. The ink refills can cost as much as the discounted Dell printer did—an eye-opening experience for the millions of Dell printer users.

Enhancing the interface between printer and computer is a part of Dell's plans. The following is from an article in *InfoWorld*[19]:

"*InfoWorld*: How effectively do you think you can compete against HP in imaging and printing?

"Rollins: HP is much, much larger than we are and has a great business with a tremendous annuity stream, and that annuity steam is in ink. They also have this great installed base. Our goal is to establish an installed base of both inkjet and laser printers and then move to the next level of that annuity associated with cartridges and toner.

"It is not as mission critical as systems and storage management, but printing and imaging management is becoming a bigger issue for corporations and it is a big expense. How you manage a ton of copiers and laser printers throughout an entire organization is now becoming something they can do from a console. So that is all part of the future wave for us."

Services

Dell will also be looking to services more in the future. According to the 2005 *Forbes Investment Guide*,[20] Dell's services division grew 34 percent in fiscal 2004 to $3.7 billion, while IBM's grew 4 percent to $46.2 billion. Obviously, there's room for Dell growth here; the Investment Guide says: "Dell expects its services group to double in size within four years."

Forrester Research notes that[21]: "Desktop outsourcing prices are at the lowest levels in history, having fallen approximately 20 percent in the past 18 to 24 months. Dell has been the driving force behind this phenomenon. In 2004, Dell Services will increase market share in the midmarket (1,000 to 4,000 seats) with services based on its own product set, hardware price advantages, and a highly automated, flexible, partner-driven services strategy. At the same time, the midmarket is selectively outsourcing their desktop operations, aligning nicely with Dell's services portfolio."

The article goes on to make predictions about the future: "Dell may not have nearly as much success against IBM Global Services and HP Services in the Global 1,000 in the next 12 to 18 months. For Dell to improve its position in the changing Global 1,000 market, it must offer broader, more complete outsourcing services, improve its ability to manage multivendor platforms on a global scale, and move to a more relationship-based, high-touch services mindset."

Yet, it appears that Dell has different plans—it's not going after growth here at all costs. Dell is providing services mostly to its existing customers, as part of an overall contract, and that's proving to be more profitable, at least at the moment. The following is an *InfoWorld* interview with Kevin Rollins[22]:

"*InfoWorld*: Dell services business has been growing at a rapid pace. How aggressively do you want to match IBM's (Profile, Products, Articles) Global Services?

"Rollins: We are not trying to match them at all. Our services business and strategies are really very different [from IBM's]. Consequently, we do not bump into them very much on the services front. We are usually selling enhanced services that surround the hardware, versus out-sourcing or architecture design engagements.

"When we are selling a large installation of servers or storage, we will add a menu of services items in order to facilitate the installation and the management of them. It becomes Dell-centric at that point.

"*InfoWorld*: Well, can you give us a road map of what your ambitions are for your services and support business for both larger and smaller companies? It can be an expensive proposition, given it is a human-intensive business.

"Rollins: Our goal is to leverage what is already out in the field in terms of partners, but then hire in project management capability and a bit of technical capability. Just a little of that can go a long way in terms of leveraging field resources. It has been growing at about twice that of our hardware business and is now in the $4 to $5 billion range, so it is reasonably good-sized.

"We are going to continue to do that, but it will grow in tandem with the hardware and at a multiple, because we are penetrating more and more accounts and are adding more and more menu items to the list whether they are professional services or managed services. They are very much tied to hardware; they are not independent. We rarely go after a services-only deal.

"*InfoWorld*: In terms of pursuing opportunities among the larger end-user companies, are you willing to put Dell services and support people inside your customers' sites?

"Rollins: We don't put a lot of people in there on-site, although we will put some there. Most of the services staff is for the larger corporations, not so much for small and medium businesses because they cannot afford an extensive services army.

"But in the large corporations where most of our service and staff are, they are doing things like storage or server consolidation, or doing an Exchange migration, or migrating off of Unix to Linux or to Microsoft (Profile, Products, Articles). We also work with them on that to help port applications to help in the rollout of that globally. We have Dell people involved in managing these processes and partners who help do the arm and leg work. In those cases we might have 10 or 15 Dell folks who are focused inside those companies to help do it. But we don't just start putting revenues generating people on-site."

Providing services is going to become more and more popular for Dell. This is an expanding area for them, and you should see a great deal more coming up here in the future. Expect Dell to sign service contracts with some major clients in the upcoming years.

Servers and Storage

The servers and storage market also is increasing, and Dell will follow this market as it matures, following the tech curve. From a news.com article[23]: "Other high growth areas Dell has identified include its storage systems and services. The company's server and storage business accounted for about $35 billion in the last year, with more than 70,000 installations piggybacking on deals involving database-software from Oracle. Rollins said Dell is encouraged by the more than 750 high-performance computing clusters the company has contracted out to financial services and telecommunications companies."

More from the *InfoWorld* interview with Kevin Rollins[24]:

"*InfoWorld*: What do you see for Dell in the immediate future for storage?

"Rollins: One of the things we have always tried to do is make storage easier for customers to use. With the launch of a number of platforms through the partnership with EMC, we have been able to take storage to new price points and take capabilities up a notch.

"We will continue to push the envelope with easier-to-use systems. SATA drives are going to play a large part of that, and eventually iSCSI will too. We will be announcing an iSCSI product this coming quarter along with EMC. Storage is likely to be our key strategic initiative in the coming year."

Dell is not a tech pioneer here and, as of this writing, has not produced a four-processor blade server. Yet, they can compete on price. As blade servers become more ubiquitous, you can expect Dell to move to the forefront here.

Optical Disk Drives

Another area that Dell plans to expand into are optical disk drives, according to Dell's CTO, Kevin Kettler. From a computerworld.com interview with him[25]:

"[*ComputerWorld*]: What emerging technologies are you most excited about that are likely to appear in Dell products for enterprise users over the next 12 to 24 months?

"[Kettler]: One of those is the work we're doing around Blu-ray disk, [an] emerging standard for next-generation optical disk drives. We've been working with a number of partners in defining the fundamental technology, what it is, how it's going to operate.

"We're also excited about the delivery of technologies in the multi-core area around processors. Not just multicore processors but multicore coupled with some of the virtualization technologies and techniques.

"[*ComputerWorld*]: Why did you back Blu-ray and not the competing HD-DVD standard?

"[Kettler]: When you look at the capacity of the drives, Blu-ray provides significantly more headroom than what HD-DVD does. We consider Blu-ray a pretty major change, and we wanted to make sure we had a technology that was going to have some longevity around it, especially given the investment in transitioning customers to a new format for all of their content."

In addition to optical drives, it's a safe bet that Dell is looking into the possibility of large-scale, solid-state internal drives, an idea that has been percolating around the industry.

Music Players

In January 2005, Kevin Rollins went on record calling Apple's iPod a fad, in an article in *Ars Technica*[26]:

"[*Ars Technica*:] Do you resent the amount of publicity Apple gets given its market share?

"[Rollins:] Apple's created a niche. If you look at the grand scheme of things this quarter, we are supposed to achieve something like $13.5 billion in revenue. Apple's in the $2.4 billion [region] so the size and scale is not even in the same league. But what they do they do very well and they've had great success with the iPod. It's interesting the iPod has been out for three years and it's only this past year it's become a raging success.

"Well, those things that become fads rage and then they drop off. When I was growing up there was a product made by Sony called the Sony Walkman—a rage, everyone had to have one. Well, you don't hear about the Walkman anymore. I believe that 'one-product wonders' come and go. You have to have sustainable business models, sustainable strategy. But don't read that as any sort of disparagement of Apple. They've done a nice job."

But Dell's gotten more serious and has its own music player out there; here's from an article in the July 2005 *Forbes magazine*[27]: "Dell and Napster are teaming up in a bid to help colleges alleviate network bottlenecks caused by students stealing digital music. If successful, the project may help boost Dell's paltry market share in portable music players."

TVs

Dell is still active in its pursuit of flatscreen TVs. The market has not been particularly strong for Dell, but they continue to work with it. A July 2005 article in news.com[28] reports: "Likewise, Dell is holding its own in the flat-panel-display category as it continues to expand into digital and high-definition television.

"The company is expected to launch about a dozen new models of flat panels this fall as part of a holiday sales blitz. Executives have said they expect the 30-inch to 40-inch models to be the so-called sweet spot of their sales focus. Dell is also launching a premium brand series of desktop and laptop computers aimed at customers who are not afraid of high-ticket items."

Another news.com article[29] makes the point about the unexciting nature of this market: "Part of the reluctance to go whole hog on consumer electronics is that, taken all together, the business generates only about 15 percent of Dell's revenue, Kevin Rollins, the company's CEO, told News.com."

Michael Kanellos, CNET news.com editor-at-large, says, "This [2005] Christmas could be a testing point. They want to drive prices down. If they can gain market share, TVs will rise in profile at the company. It also doesn't take much effort on their part to sell TVs. The HD upgrade gives a potential for future sales. But if sales aren't great in the holidays, you may start to see less emphasis on this."

On the other hand, the article notes that Dell consumer electronics customers are more likely to become Dell PC buyers, a big plus for Dell: "'We recently measured a few of our newer categories, such as music players and TVs. For those products, 52 percent are going to new customers,' Mike George, general manager of Dell's consumer business, said in an interview with CNET News.com. 'It would appear that those customers have a disproportionally high likelihood of then coming back to us and buying a PC. It's given us more confidence to be bolder in how we talk (in advertising) about our electronics.'"

Dell is not about to get out of consumer electronics anytime soon. It's even taking a look at new areas, such as phones and digital cameras (see the section Dell Looks to New Technologies later in this chapter).

Digitizing the Home

Michael Dell has said,[30] "As homes become more digital, with wireless networking and broadband, that's a huge opportunity for Dell as the leader in the consumer market in the United States, as microprocessors continue to scale up into clusters and grids that can replace minicomputers and mainframes, that's an enormous opportunity for us."

Enterprise Innovator also brought up this topic[31]: "Another new frontier Dell is eyeing, in addition to grid computing, is the digital home. Michael Dell noted that in the home, 'the PC is becoming more and more the center of the entertainment experience,' and whether 'it's music, it's videos, it's televisions,' most of the devices 'are proprietary as well,' and still 'don't connect so easily to each other.' But Dell said that 'if you have an IP network at home,' it can serve as the backbone for 'digital media streams' throughout the home environment, and 'the PC is right at the center of that.' Dell said that this is a 'more compelling vision.' With the PC at the center of a home entertainment environment, Dell said, 'I think you'll have more and more of these devices' connected to home networks, distributing digital content like 'movies, music throughout the household.'...

"Dell observed that in Japan, 50 percent of consumers 'use their PCs as televisions,' though he acknowledged things 'might be different in the U.S. where the homes are bigger, and the screens are bigger.' But nonetheless, Dell said that it still 'makes sense to take this information and distribute it throughout the home.' Dell noted that while 'consumer devices' such as TVs are 'easier to understand,' they're 'not nearly at the volume of the business devices.' He said 'about 85 percent'" of Dell's volume is 'business and institutional-related customers,' and just 15 percent consumer."

Dell Might Do More Business with AMD

What about AMD? Is Dell married to Intel? Not necessarily, according to Kevin Rollins in an *InfoWorld* article[32]:

"*InfoWorld*: It seems a lot of your competitors have supported AMD. What is your stance on that?

"Rollins: Two things. I am sure there will come a time when we are going to use AMD. The products have been getting better. The acceptance is getting better. But we have not been suffering as a company for either growth or profitability because we haven't had AMD. In fact, frankly, I think just the opposite. The companies that have been using AMD have been doing the worst.

"*InfoWorld*: Interesting. So, do you see AMD being a viable competitor in the long run?

"Rollins. Yes, we do. The technology is better, and in some areas now they are in the lead on Intel. That is what interests us more than anything. But we have not been losing a ton of business because we haven't had AMD. At the end of the day we have to be profitable and grow, and so that is going to be the main indicator of what we might do. But my guess is that we are going to want to add that to our product line in the future....

"*InfoWorld*: Are you looking more at the server side of things or the desktop side?

"Rollins: Well, they [AMD] are too small, frankly, to do a whole lot of damage in the desktop arena. If we basically sucked up all of AMD's capacity it still would not be enough. They do not have enough capacity as we speak today. They really would be more interesting for us in the server and workstation and gaming arenas. But that is a fairly small unit volume category of the CPU business."

Here's more on that topic, in a piece entitled "Dell Gives AMD Another Look," in late 2004 at arstechnica.com[33]: "Since its release in early 2003, AMD's Opteron server CPU has made great inroads almost everywhere... except with Dell. The CEO of Dell, Kevin Rollins, says that may very well be about to change, as the company is considering selling Opteron servers sooner rather than later...

"This isn't the first time Dell has made noises about selling machines with AMD processors. In the past, such statements have been aimed primarily at extracting concessions from Intel, which currently supplies the CPUs for all of Dell's products. What leads many to believe that Dell isn't just blowing smoke this time is that the Opteron rules the commodity 64-bit server space, a fact not lost on Dell, which is the lone holdout among the major computer manufacturers when it comes to AMD.

"While there could very well be Opteron servers in Dell's future, Athlon desktops probably are not. However, Rollins did leave open the possibility that the PC maker could sell gaming boxes powered by Athlon 64s, as the AMD platform has become more popular with gamers due to its solid price-to-performance ratio.

"If Dell does begin offering AMD systems, even if they are confined to servers and high-end gaming boxes, it would still be major accomplishment for AMD. It looks as though four straight profitable quarters plus some sound architectural decisions (especially when compared to Intel) have finally caught Dell's eye."

Don't Be Surprised to See Mac OS on a Dell

Here's a somewhat unexpected one from Dell, as reported on The Motley Fool's web site[34]: "That's when Fortune columnist David Kirkpatrick got Michael Dell on the record saying he would offer Mac OS-powered PCs to his customers if Apple were to allow it.

"The interest taken by Michael Dell in Mac OS X and the fact that he said he's ready to sell computers having Apple's operating system preinstalled on them might be considered a personal opinion, but it can also be a masked offer to Apple.

"But if Apple decides to port Max OS X on the PC, then it will have to solve many problems, some of them even too tough to crack."

It's interesting conjecture, but it would take massive hardware and software modifications to get that off the ground. From *Softpedia*[35] on Mac OS X: "Mac OS X doesn't possess Windows's flexibility to run on any platform: from brand name systems to clones. As a result, Apple would be forced to demand very strict configurations from PC producers, a request not many would agree with."

Dell Might Become a Linux Booster

So, how about Linux? The media had a field day when Michael Dell invested big money in Red Hat, as in this May 2005 *ZDNet* article[36]: "Michael Dell, the founder and chairman of Dell, has invested a significant sum of money into Linux vendor Red Hat.

"Nearly $100m (£53.1m) of Red Hat debentures were bought by MSD Capital on behalf of the Dell founder, according to business news site *Triangle Business Journal* this week. Debentures are loans that are usually secured and have associated fixed or floating charges. Financial filings indicate that Dell's debentures are being converted into Red Hat equity.

"RedMonk analyst James Governor said the investment shows that the Dell founder approves of Red Hat's business model. The Linux vendor makes money from selling subscriptions for its version of the open source operating system.

"'From Red Hat's perspective, it's a wonderful endorsement,' said Governor. 'Michael Dell's a cautious guy—he's not in the business of taking risks.'

"Michael Dell's belief in Red Hat is not shared by everyone at Dell. Last year Judy Chavis, the Dell executive who oversees the strategic partnership with Red Hat, said the Linux vendor needs to lower its prices, or it will risk losing customers to free versions of the open source operating system.

"Dell's personal investment has led to speculation that the company may acquire Red Hat, but Governor disagrees. 'It wouldn't make sense for Dell to buy Red Hat,' said Governor. 'Dell is in the business of flogging kit, Red Hat makes its money from subscriptions. We haven't seen any indications that Dell is planning to extend its business model in this direction.'"

Despite the tizzy, this is not about PCs. From a *Chief Executive* interview[37] with Michael Dell: "We're actually No. 1 today in the high-performance clustered server market in the U.S.

"Q. Using Linux?

"A. Most of them use Linux. I recently visited CGG, a French company, in Houston. They've installed 3,000 Dell servers doing seismic analysis and for exploration data in the Gulf of Mexico. They just added another 1,100 servers, some in France, some in the United Kingdom, Canada, Kuala Lumpur, more in Houston. The range of opportunities we have is pretty diverse, from supercomputing all the way down to your buying a second PC for your home or your child."

So, will Dell pump Linux on the desktop? Kevin Rollins says no, in an *InfoWorld* article[38] in late 2004:

"*InfoWorld*: How do you plan to push desktop Linux, and how much do you expect that to gain in the next year or two?

"Rollins: We don't expect to push it, to be frank. And the reason is we do not make money on it, whether it is Microsoft or Linux. So if a customer wants it and they believe that Linux on the desktop for office productivity is a good thing, we are thrilled to help them do that. But we are agnostic about [operating systems]. We do not make any more money whether it is Linux or Microsoft."

A check of Dell's Linux Community Web at http://linux.dell.com/desktops.shtml also makes it clear that Dell does not officially support running Linux on Dell laptops or Dell desktops. The truth is that what Dell does here depends on market conditions. If Linux rises, you can expect Dell to take more interest in it; it's as simple as that. Dell isn't married to a particular operating system; it's married to profitable growth.

Dell Looks to New Technologies

What kinds of new technology is Dell looking in to? The field is open, but you can glean some hints. News.com says[39]: "Smart phones, which combine the attributes of a cellular phone and a PDA like Dell's Axim, represent a potential opportunity for Dell, executives say. But the company will carefully examine what it can do to differentiate its products from those of incumbents such as Nokia. Similarly, Dell executives note that digital camera sales are growing, but they say they're still examining whether a Dell-brand camera would meet the company's requirements for sales and profitability."

And, from a recent post on the Dell web site entitled "Dell to Lead in Offering Dual-Core Technology"[40]: "Dell, the world's leading supplier of desktop and workstation computers, today announced its intention to offer Intel's dual-core processor technology on its high-performance personal computers for consumers and businesses.

"Dell has worked closely with Intel on the new technology for several years and has successfully tested dual-core processor-based systems in its engineering labs over the past few months.

"'Dell is the world's preferred technology provider because we have the ability to bring the benefits of the latest technology to the everyday computer user,' said John Medica, senior vice president, Dell Product Group. 'Our leadership in the desktop and workstation markets demonstrates Dell's ability to deliver innovative technologies that customers value and appreciate.'

"Dell plans to offer Dimension XPS gaming systems and Dell Precision workstations with Intel dual-core processor technology later this year."

Internal solid-state drives are another possibility, according to manufacturers like Samsung, in this June 2004 article in *AppleInsider*[41]: "Samsung hopes that falling prices for flash-memory chips will mean solid-state memory can eventually replace hard-disk drives in Apple PowerBooks and iBooks as well as other devices, *Macworld UK* is reporting." These days, you can pick up 16GB solid-state internal drives easily.

You also can get some indications from Dell itself, as in this *InfoWorld* article[42] with Kevin Rollins:

"*InfoWorld*: What are the top five technologies that you plan to focus on in the next five years?

"Rollins: One is the whole area of software management. But we need the software capability to integrate our [management software] with those of others in a common platform. That will take a little while, obviously, to get the standards established. We think Microsoft is a great partner to work on that. Altiris (Profile, Products, Articles) is another partner we have worked closely with. [They have] done a very nice job for systems management.

"We believe there is a lot of hope in VMware (Profile, Products, Articles) virtualization, which seems to be one of the hotter platforms we are working with and helping drive. In terms of technologies, systems management is going to enable most of the standards-based technologies. So we are looking to set up standards rather than proprietary ones. And we have also new thrust in the whole imaging and printing area, which is a new and huge financial opportunity for us."

Solid-state drives, dual core processors, software management—nothing really stands out in the breakthrough category. Dell's not going to find many breakthrough products in consumer electronics, either. But Dell's not really known for its tech innovation, of course. You look to Dell for business insights; in general, Dell watches other companies for its tech insights.

Dell Must Address the Support Issue

Support continues to be a big issue at Dell, and it's not clear how it's going to play out. Will Dell be able to "educate" its customers to expect less support? Will Dell's customers keep demanding more support, even as PC prices drop? Who's going to win this tug of war?

At this point, Dell sees the need for some concessions in this area, at least for the moment. From a recent article in news.com[43]: "Earlier this year, Dell added a second building to its customer contact center in Oklahoma City and opened new centers in El Salvador and Chandigarh, India."

In the long run, though, you can most likely expect to see less support, and more built-in diagnostics, from Dell.

Summing Up

To sum up the outlook for Dell's future—at this point, Dell gives every indication of staying true to its consistent business model, even when that confuses Dell watchers. The ultimate focus is on bottom-line ROIC, and that doesn't seem likely to change. Dell is going to pursue growth where it finds it, following the markets and entering them when the time is ripe for the Dell Effect. Can it keep growing at double-digit rates? Yes. Will it reach $80 billion in sales by 2009? Stay tuned.

Notes

Notes for Introduction

1. http://www.businessweek.com/1997/14/b3521131.htm.
2. Direct from Dell, p. xiii.
3. http://en.wikipedia.org/wiki/Dell%2C_Inc.
4. Ibid.
5. http://www.forbes.com/lists/forbes400/2004/09/22/rl04land.html?chan=
   b1usrichest05.
6. http://en.wikipedia.org/wiki/Dell%2C_Inc.
7. http://www.infoworld.com/article/05/04/08/HNdelldownplayspc_1.html
   ?NOTEBOOKS.

Notes for Chapter 1

1. *Direct from Dell*, p. 23.
2. http://www.dell.com/downloads/global/corporate/annual/2005_dell_
   annual.pdf.
3. *Fortune,* March 7, 2005.
4. *Direct from Dell*, p.175.
5. *Direct from Dell*, p.13.
6. *Direct from Dell,* p. 202.
7. http://www1.us.dell.com/content/topics/global.aspx/corp/background/en/
   facts?c=us&l=en&s=corp&~section=000.
8. http://www1.us.dell.com/content/topics/global.aspx/corp/background/en/
   facts?c=us&l=en&s=corp&~section=000.
9. *Direct from Dell*, p. 220.
10. *Direct from Dell*, p. 24.
11. *Direct from Dell*, p. 206.
12. http://www.usatoday.com/money/industries/technology/2003-01-19-dell-
    cover_x.htm.

13. http://news.com.com/2100-1001-222646.html?legacy=cnet.
14. http://www.usatoday.com/educate/college/careers/profile16.htm.
15. http://www1.us.dell.com/content/topics/global.aspx/corp/analystrel/en/home?c
=us&l=en&s=corp.
16. http://www.fastcompany.com/magazine/88/dell-rollins.html.

Notes for Chapter 2

1. *Fortune* magazine, March 7, 2005.
2. http://www1.us.dell.com/content/topics/global.aspx/corp/analystrel/en/home?c
=us&l=en&s=corp.
3. *Direct from Dell*, p. 142.
4. http://pcworld.about.com/magazine/2207p086id116015.htm.
5. http://www.pcmag.com/article2/0,1759,924266,00.asp.
6. *Fortune* magazine, June 6, 2005.
7. http://www.infoworld.com/article/05/04/08/HNdelldownplayspc_1.html.
8. http://www.usatoday.com/money/industries/technology/2003-01-19-dell-cover_x.htm.
9. http://www.fastcompany.com/magazine/88/dell-rollins.html.
10. http://www.infoworld.com/Dell_5100cn/product_50841.html?view=1&cur
NodeId=0.
11. http://www.pcworld.com/reviews/article/0,aid,119290,00.asp.
12. http://www.businessweek.com/1997/14/b3521131.htm.
13. http://www.fool.com/news/commentary/2005/commentary05061005.htm.
14. Dynamic Computing Industry Report Card: Systems Vendors—Summit Strategies
March 2005. http://www1.us.dell.com/content/topics/global.aspx/corp/analystrel/
en/home?c=us&l=en&s=corp.
15. http://news.zdnet.co.uk/business/0,39020645,2125642,00.htm.
16. http://news.zdnet.co.uk/business/0,39020645,2125642,00.htm.
17. http://www1.euro.dell.com/content/topics/topic.aspx/emea/products/awards/
en/uk/Enterprise_PE2850?c=ae&l=en&s=bsd.
18. http://www.pcworld.com/reviews/article/0,aid,120201,00.asp.
19. http://www.pcmag.com/article2/0,1759,87189,00.asp.
20. http://www.pcworld.com/reviews/article/0,aid,112915,pg,8,00.asp.
21. http://www.pcworld.com/reviews/article/0,aid,118514,pg,2,00.asp.
22. http://www.pcmag.com/article2/0,1759,1186134,00.asp.
23. http://en.wikipedia.org/wiki/Dell percent2C_Inc.#Criticism.
24. http://www1.ap.dell.com/content/topics/topic.aspx/ap/corporate/en/
pressoffice/2005/ap/2005_04_27_cn_000?c=ap&l=en&s=corp.
25. http://www1.us.dell.com/content/topics/global.aspx/services/en/awards?c=
us&cs=04&l=en&s=bsd.
26. http://www1.us.dell.com/content/topics/global.aspx/services/en/awards?c=
us&cs=04&l=en&s=bsd.
27. http://www1.us.dell.com/content/topics/global.aspx/services/en/awards?c=
us&cs=04&l=en&s=bsd.
28. http://www.networkworld.com/weblogs/outsourcing/008768.html.
29. http://www.pcworld.com/reviews/article/0,aid,118514,pg,2,00.asp.
30. http://computergripes.blogspot.com/2004/09/dell-gripes.html#commentsanon
comment.
31. http://www.pcworld.com/news/article/0,aid,115648,tk,cx041304a,00.asp.

32. http://news.com.com/Growing+pains+hit+Dells+customer+service/2100-1042_3-5162141.html.
33. http://www.enterpriseinnovator.com/index.php?articleID=3837&section ID=98.
34. http://www1.us.dell.com/content/topics/global.aspx/services/en/service_contracts ?c=us&cs=555&l=en&s=biz.

Notes for Chapter 3

1. *Direct from Dell*, p. 143.
2. http://www1.us.dell.com/content/topics/global.aspx/corp/analystrel/en/home?c =us&l=en&s=corp.
3. *Direct from Dell*, p. 167.
4. http://www.enterpriseinnovator.com/index.php?articleID=3837&sectionID=98.
5. http://www.Internetnews.com/bus-news/article.php/3446721.
6. http://www.usatoday.com/educate/college/careers/profile16.htm.
7. *Direct from Dell*, p. 43.
8. *Direct from Dell*, p. 145.
9. http://www1.us.dell.com/content/topics/global.aspx/innovation/en/index?c= us&l=en&s=corp.
10. *Direct from Dell*, p. 71.
11. http://news.com.com/2100-1001-222646.html?legacy=cnet.
12. http://www.enterpriseinnovator.com/index.php?articleID=3837&sectionID=98.
13. http://www.eweek.com/article2/0,1759,1827515,00.asp.

Notes for Chapter 4

1. *Fortune* magazine, March 7, 2005.
2. http://news.zdnet.co.uk/business/0,39020645,2125642,00.htm.
3. *Direct from Dell*, p. 172.
4. http://www.cfo.com/article.cfm/3010363/2/c_3046599?f=related.
5. *Direct from Dell*, p. 38.
6. Ibid.
7. http://www.forbes.com/2003/09/04/cx_ld_0904data.html.
8. http://www1.us.dell.com/content/topics/global.aspx/corp/analystrel/en/home?c =us&l=en&s=corp.
9. http://www.techweb.com/wire/26803723#_ Bolaji Ojo, EE Times.
10. http://www.businessweekasia.com/magazine/content/05_14/b3927003.htm.
11. http://www.usatoday.com/educate/college/careers/profile16.htm.
12. http://www.businessweekasia.com/magazine/content/05_22/b3935108_mz063 .htm.
13. http://www.usatoday.com/educate/college/careers/profile16.htm.
14. http://www.chiefexecutive.net/dell.htm.
15. *Direct from Dell*, p. 176.
16. http://www.enterpriseinnovator.com/index.php?articleID=2057&sectionID=98.
17. *Fortune* magazine, March 7, 2005.
18. http://www.computerworld.com/printthis/2005/0,4814,101541,00.html.
19. http://www1.us.dell.com/content/topics/global.aspx/corp/analystrel/en/ home?c=us&l=en&s=corp.
20. http://www.techweb.com/wire/26803723#_ By Bolaji Ojo, EE Times.
21. http://www.enterpriseinnovator.com/index.php?articleID=2057&sectionID=98.

22. *Fortune* magazine, March 7, 2005.
23. http://www.cfo.com/article.cfm/3010363/2/c_3046599?f=related.
24. http://msnbc.msn.com/id/6959937/site/newsweek/.
25. http://msnbc.msn.com/id/6959937/site/newsweek/.
26. http://www.enterpriseinnovator.com/index.php?articleID=2057&section ID=98.
27. *Fortune* magazine, March 7, 2005.
28. http://www.techweb.com/wire/26803723#_ By Bolaji Ojo, EE Times.
29. *Fortune* magazine, March 7, 2005.
30. http://www.pcmag.com/article2/0,4149,1429808,00.asp.
31. *Direct from Dell*, p. 193.
32. *Direct from Dell*, p. 192.
33. http://www.computerworld.com/printthis/2005/0,4814,101541,00.html.
34. http://www.computerworld.com/printthis/2005/0,4814,101541,00.html.
35. *Direct from Dell*, p. 130.
36. http://www.businessweek.com/@@TE@iroUQN3X4eQAA/magazine/content/
03_25/b3838611.htm.
37. http://www.sharewatch.com/story.php?storynumber=72402.
38. http://www.enterpriseinnovator.com/index.php?articleID=3750&sectionID=5.
39. http://www.yeald.com/Yeald/a/29711/bruised_dell_in_need_of_chinese_medicine
_2.html.
40. http://enterpriseinnovator.com/index.php?articleID=3837&sectionID=98.

Notes for Chapter 5

1. http://www.fastcompany.com/magazine/88/dell.html.
2. http://news.com.com/2009-1069_3-1014102.html.
3. *Direct from Dell*, p. 78.
4. *Direct from Dell*, p. 43.
5. http://news.com.com/2009-1069_3-1014102.html.
6. http://www.fool.com/school/returnonequity/ReturnOnEquity03.htm.
7. *Fortune* magazine March 7, 2005.
8. http://www.fastcompany.com/magazine/88/dell.html.
9. *Direct from Dell*, p. 36.
10. Ibid.
11. *Direct from Dell*, p. 179.
12. http://www.fastcompany.com/magazine/88/dell.html.
13. *Direct from Dell*, p. 177.
14. *Direct from Dell*, p. 81.
15. *Direct from Dell*, p. 187.
16. http://www.fastcompany.com/magazine/88/dell.html.
17. http://news.com.com/2009-1069_3-1014102.html.
18. http://www.accenture.com/xd/xd.asp?it=enweb&xd=industries%t5
Ccommunications%5Chigh-tech %5Ccase%5Chigh_dell.xml#top.
19. *Direct from Dell*, p. 190.
20. *Direct from Dell*, p. 188.
21. *Direct from Dell*, p. 191.
22. http://www.fastcompany.com/magazine/88/dell.html.
23. http://www.integratedsolutionsmag.com/Articles/2002_06/020601.htm.
24. *Direct from Dell*, p. 178.
25. Ibid.

26. *Fortune* magazine, March 7, 2005 p. 82.
27. http://www.fastcompany.com/magazine/88/dell.html.
28. http://www.businessweek.com/ap/financialnews/D8B0MH9G0.htm?campaign_id=apn_home_down.
29. http://www.economist.com/displaystory.cfm?story_id=2610485.
30. *Direct from Dell*, p. 188.
31. http://www.fastcompany.com/magazine/88/dell.html.
32. http://news.com.com/2009-1069_3-1014102.html.
33. http://www.fastcompany.com/magazine/88/dell-rollins.html.
34. http://news.com.com/2009-1069_3-1014102.html.
35. http://www.fool.com/news/foth/2002/foth020715.htm.
36. http://minneapolisfed.org/pubs/region/00-06/runkle.cfm.

Notes for Chapter 6

1. http://business.timesonline.co.uk/article/0,,9075-1610970,00.html.
2. http://knowledge.wharton.upenn.edu/index.cfm?fa=viewfeature&id=728.
3. http://www.fool.com/CashKing/1998/CashKingPort981112.htm.
4. http://www.randomhouse.com/crown/catalog/display.pperl?isbn=9780609610572&view=desc.
5. http://www.Internetnews.com/bus-news/article.php/3446721.
6. *Direct from Dell*, p. 206.
7. http://www.thinkingmanagers.com/management/change-continuity.php.
8. http://news.com.com/Reshaping+Dell/2008-1001_3-5102330.html.
9. http://www.usatoday.com/educate/college/careers/profile16.htm.
10. http://harvardbusinessonline.hbsp.harvard.edu/b01/en/common/item_detail.jhtml?id=R0503G.
11. *Direct from Dell*, p. 134.
12. *Direct from Dell*, p. 214.
13. http://www.themanufacturer.com/us/detail.html?contents_id=1227.
14. *Direct from Dell*, p. 214.
15. *Direct from Dell*, p. 215.
16. *Direct from Dell*, p. 127.
17. *Direct from Dell*, p. 127.
18. http://www.fool.com/portfolios/rulemaker/2000/rulemaker000629.htm.
19. http://www.cio.com/archive/091597/dell.html.
20. *Direct from Dell*, p. 173.
21. http://www.centerdigitaled.com/converge/?pg=magstory&id=3790.
22. http://www.journalnow.com/servlet/Satellite?pagename=WSJpercent2FMGArticlepercent2FWSJ_BasicArticle&c=MGArticle&cid=1031783146643.
23. http://www.latimes.com/business/taxes/la-fi-dell24jun24,1,6290405.story?coll=la-headlines-business-taxes.
24. *Direct from Dell*, p.133.
25. *Direct from Dell*, p. 62.
26. *Direct from Dell*, p. 133.
27. *Direct from Dell*, p. 71.
28. *Direct from Dell*, p. 76.
29. *Direct from Dell*, p. 74.
30. *Direct from Dell*, p. 70.
31. http://logistics.about.com/library/bllogisticsatdellcomputerschat2.htm.

32. http://www.dell.com/downloads/global/corporate/iar/20030312_bloor.pdf.
33. *Fortune* magazine, March 7, 2005, p. 82.
34. http://www.fastcompany.com/magazine/88/dell-rollins.html.
35. http://knowledge.wharton.upenn.edu/index.cfm?fa=viewfeature&id=728.
36. http://www.dell.com/downloads/global/corporate/iar/20030312_bloor.pdf.
37. http://www.fastcompany.com/magazine/88/dell.html.
38. http://www.memagazine.org/backissues/sept02/features/dfortime/dfortime .html.
39. *Direct from Dell*, p. 63.
40. *Direct from Dell*, p. 60.
41. http://www.careerjournal.com/myc/climbing/20030506-mcwilliams.html (Part of the *Wall Street Journal*).
42. http://www.businessweek.com/magazine/content/04_16/b3879114_ mz063.htm.
43. http://www.enterpriseinnovator.com/index.php?articleID=4874&sectionID=86.
44. http://www.cio.com/archive/011505/outsourcing.html?printversion=yes.

Notes for Chapter 7

1. *Direct from Dell*, p. 117.
2. *Fortune*, March 7, 2005.
3. *Direct from Dell*, p. 94.
4. *Direct from Dell*, p. 132.
5. *Direct from Dell*, p. 59.
6. http://www.cfo.com/article.cfm/3010363/.
7. http://www.cfo.com/article.cfm/2990099.
8. *Direct from Dell*, p. 59.
9. *Direct from Dell*, p. 60.
10. *Direct from Dell*, p. 99.
11. *Direct from Dell*, p. 124.
12. *Direct from Dell*, p. 74.
13. *Direct from Dell*, p. 149.
14. *Direct from Dell*, p. 91.
15. *Direct from Dell*, p. 174.
16. *Direct from Dell*, p. 100.
17. *Direct from Dell*, p. 190.
18. *Direct from Dell*, p. 188.
19. http://www.enterpriseinnovator.com/index.php?articleID=2057&sectionID=98.
20. *Direct from Dell*, p. 117.
21. *Direct from Dell*, p. 131.
22. *Direct from Dell*, p. 84.
23. *Direct from Dell*, p. 131.
24. http://www.industryweek.com/research/bestplants/bp_profiles.asp?Input=94.
25. *Direct from Dell*, p. 115.
26. *Direct from Dell*, p. 100.
27. *Direct from Dell*, p. 115.
28. *Fortune*, March 7, 2005, p. 76.
29. *Direct from Dell*, p. 128.
30. *Direct from Dell*, p. 116.
31. *Direct from Dell*, p. 82.
32. http://www.forbes.com/markets/2005/04/07/0407automarketscan01.html.

33. http://www1.us.dell.com/content/topics/global.aspx/corp/pressoffice/en/2002/2002_10_01_aus_000?c=us&l=en&s=corp.
34. *Direct from Dell*, p. 48.
35. http://www1.us.dell.com/content/topics/global.aspx/corp/background/en/facts?c=us&l=en&s=corp&~section=000.
36. http://news.com.com/2100-1001-252781.html?legacy=cnet.
37. http://www.businessweek.com/1997/14/b3521131.htm.
38. http://www.cfo.com/article.cfm/2990099.
39. *Direct from Dell*, p. 135.
40. http://slate.msn.com/id/1001931/.
41. Book quotation from http://www.microsoft.com/billgates/speedofthought/additional/gurleypp.asp.
42. http://www.businessweek.com/magazine/content/04_16/b3879114_mz063.htm.
43. mba.tuck.dartmouth.edu/pdf/2002-2-0014.pdf.
44. http://www.fool.com/news/foth/2001/foth010612.htm.
45. http://slate.msn.com/id/1001933/.
46. http://www.businessweek.com/bwdaily/dnflash/may2000/sw00523.htm.
47. www.dell.com/downloads/global/corporate/speeches/msd/2000_11_03_msd_growing.pdf.
48. http://www.knowledgeadvisors.com/Docs/Dell_Case_Study.pdf.

Notes from Chapter 8

1. *Direct from Dell*, p.173.
2. http://www1.us.dell.com/content/topics/global.aspx/innovation/en/index?c=us&l=en&s=corp.
3. http://www.industryweek.com/research/bestplants/bp_profiles.asp?Input=119.
4. http://www.enterpriseinnovator.com/index.php?articleID=4275&sectionID=98.
5. http://www.usatoday.com/educate/college/careers/profile16.htm.
6. http://www.cfo.com/article.cfm/3010363/4/c_3046599?f=magazine_featured.
7. http://www.business2000.ie/cases/cases_8th/case1.htm.
8. http://harvardbusinessonline.hbsp.harvard.edu/b01/en/common/view FileNavBean.jhtml;jsessionid=KNMBEVB45KGTKAKRGWCB5VQBKE0YIIPS?_requestid=21540.
9. http://www.businessweek.com/magazine/content/05_22/b3935108_mz063.htm.
10. http://www.enterpriseinnovator.com/index.php?articleID=3837&sectionID=98.
11. http://www.businessweek.com/technology/content/apr2005/tc2005046_6483_tc119.htm.
12. http://www.enterpriseinnovator.com/index.php?articleID=4579&sectionID=98.
13. *Direct from Dell*, p. 107.
14. *Direct from Dell*, p. 119.
15. *Direct from Dell*, p. 111.
16. http://www1.us.dell.com/content/topics/global.aspx/corp/soulofdell/en/index?c=us&l=en&s=corp.
17. http://www.enterpriseinnovator.com/index.php?articleID=3032&sectionID=98.
18. *Direct from Dell*, p. 111.
19. *Direct from Dell*, p. 108.
20. http://www.findarticles.com/p/articles/mi_m3495/is_4_44/ai_54545827.
21. *Direct from Dell*, p. 109.
22. http://www.1000ventures.com/business_guide/cs_im_dell.html.

23. *Direct from Dell*, p. 119.
24. *Direct from Dell*, p. 112.
25. http://www.eiro.eurofound.eu.int/2005/06/feature/ie0506202f.html.
26. Direct from Dell, p. 171.
27. http://www.eweek.com/article2/0,1759,1589226,00.asp.
28. http://www.businessweek.com/magazine/content/05_22/b3935108_mz063.htm.
29. http://www.careerjournal.com/myc/management/19991201-mcwilliams.html.
30. *Direct from Dell*, p. 173.
31. *Direct from Dell*, p. 174.
32. *Direct from Dell*, p. 179.
33. Ibid.
34. *Direct from Dell*, p. 180.
35. http://www.dell.com/downloads/global/corporate/vision_national/Globalization _Principles.pdf.
36. http://www.statesman.com/news/content/business/stories/archive/082602_02 _dell.html.
37. http://www.bizjournals.com/triad/stories/2004/10/04/story1.html.

Notes for Chapter 9

1. http://www.chiefexecutive.net/dell.htm.
2. *Direct from Dell*, p. 206.
3. *Direct from Dell*, p. 87.
4. http://www.usatoday.com/tech/news/2005-05-11-pcs-usat_x.htm.
5. http://www.businesswire.com/webbox/bw.051998/698880.htm.
6. http://money.cnn.com/2005/04/07/technology/techinvestor/lamonica/.
7. http://www.eweek.com/article2/0,1759,1783463,00.asp.
8. http://www.industryanalystreporter.com/T2/Analyst_Research/Research AnnouncementsDetails.asp?Newsid=4733.
9. http://www.theregister.co.uk/2005/05/12/dell_q1_06/.
10. http://www.forbes.com/2003/05/19/cx_ld_0519biggrowth.html.
11. http://www.fastcompany.com/magazine/88/dell.html.
12. *Direct from Dell*, p. 41.
13. *Direct from Dell*, p. 82.
14. http://www.usatoday.com/educate/college/careers/profile16.htm.
15. *Direct from Dell*, p. 47.
16. http://www1.us.dell.com/content/topics/global.aspx/corp/background/en/facts?c =us&l=en&s=corp&~section=000&~ck=mn.
17. http://theshoestring.com/index.php?articleID=4202&sectionID=98.
18. *Direct from Dell*, p. 67.
19. http://theshoestring.com/index.php?articleID=4202&sectionID=98.
20. http://www.eweek.com/article2/0,1759,1783463,00.asp.
21. http://www.chiefexecutive.net/dell.htm.
22. http://www.internetnews.com/ent-news/article.php/3394411.
23. http://www.networkworld.com/nw200/2004/0426main.html.
24. http://www.infoworld.com/article/05/05/12/HNdellgrowth_1.html.
25. http://www.internetnews.com/ent-news/article.php/3394411.
26. http://www.cfo.com/article.cfm/3010363/c_3046599?f=magazine_featured.
27. Ibid.
28. *Direct from Dell*, p. 71.

29. *Direct from Dell,* p. 76.
30. *Direct from Dell,* p. 132.
31. Ibid.
32. *Direct from Dell,* p. 72.
33. http://www.nfusion.com/about/best_practices/Results-Oriented_Integrated_ Marketing.html.
34. *Direct from Dell,* p. 82.
35. http://www.internetnews.com/bus-news/article.php/3312711.
36. http://www.enterpriseinnovator.com/index.php?articleID=4202&sectionID=98.
37. http://www.statesman.com/business/content/business/stories/archive/111204 dell.html.
38. http://informationweek.com/story/IWK20021025S0004.
39. *Direct from Dell,* p. 173.
40. http://www.fastcompany.com/magazine/88/dell.html.
41. http://www.theregister.co.uk/2005/04/08/dell_critics_circle/page2.html.
42. *Direct from Dell,* p. 65.
43. http://www1.us.dell.com/content/topics/global.aspx/corp/pressoffice/en/2004/ 2004_03_04_rr_000?c=us&cs=555&l=en&s=biz.
44. http://www.chiefexecutive.net/dell.htm.
45. Ibid.
46. *Direct from Dell,* p. 46.
47. http://www.chiefexecutive.net/dell.htm.
48. http://www.theregister.com/2005/07/11/dell_customer_support/.

Notes for Chapter 10

1. *Fortune* magazine, March 7, 2005.
2. *Forbes Investment Guide,* June 2005, p. 48.
3. http://www.forbes.com/technology/enterprisetech/2005/06/22/0622auto marketscan14.html?partner=moreover.
4. http://www.infoworld.com/article/05/04/08/HNdelldownplayspc_1.html? NOTEBOOKS.
5. http://www.infoworld.com/article/05/04/08/HNdelldownplayspc_1.html.
6. http://www.enterpriseinnovator.com/index.php?articleID=4874&sectionID=86.
7. http://www.macnewsworld.com/story/39082.html.
8. http://www.thestreet.com/_googlen/tech/hardware/10233050.html?cm_ven= GOOGLEN&cm_cat=FREE&cm_ite=NA.
9. *Forbes* magazine, June 6, 2005, p. 48.
10. http://www.cio.com/archive/011505/outsourcing.html.
11. http://www.chiefexecutive.net/dell.htm.
12. http://www.infoworld.com/article/04/11/12/HNrollinsq&a_2.html.
13. http://www.statesman.com/business/content/business/stories/archive/111204 dell.html.
14. http://news.bbc.co.uk/2/hi/business/4542563.stm.
15. http://news.com.com/Dells+Rollins+shoots+for+80+billion+by+2009/2100-1041_ 3-5790288.html?part=rss&tag=5790288&subj=news.
16. http://www.macnewsworld.com/story/33421.html.
17. http://news.com.com/Dells+Rollins+shoots+for+80+billion+by+2009/2100-1041_ 3-5790288.html?part=rss&tag=5790288&subj=news.
18. Dell 2005 annual report.

19. http://www.infoworld.com/article/04/11/12/HNrollinsq&a_3.html.
20. *Forbes Investment Guide*, June 2005, p. 48.
21. http://www.forrester.com/Research/Document/Excerpt/0,7211,34094,00.html.
22. http://www.infoworld.com/article/04/11/12/HNrollinsq&a_1.html.
23. http://news.com.com/Dells+Rollins+shoots+for+80+billion+by+2009/2100-1041_3-5790288.html?part=rss&tag=5790288&subj=news.
24. http://www.infoworld.com/article/04/11/12/HNrollinsq&a_3.html.
25. http://www.computerworld.com/printthis/2005/0,4814,101541,00.html.
26. http://arstechnica.com/news.ars/post/20050118-4533.html.
27. http://www.forbes.com/business/services/2005/07/06/dell-napster-partnership-cx_ld_0706music.html.
28. http://news.com.com/Dells+Rollins+shoots+for+80+billion+by+2009/2100-1041_3-5790288.html?part=rss&tag=5790288&subj=news.
29. http://news.com.com/Dell+angles+for+the+best+seat+in+the+living+room/2100-1041_3-5427993.html.
30. http://www.chiefexecutive.net/dell.htm.
31. http://www.enterpriseinnovator.com/index.php?articleID=2057&sectionID=98.
32. http://www.infoworld.com/article/04/11/12/HNrollinsq&a_2.html.
33. http://arstechnica.com/news.ars/post/20041111-4395.html?43007.
34. http://www.fool.com/news/commentary/2005/commentary05061706.htm.
35. http://news.softpedia.com/news/Dell-fancies-Mac-OS-X-3343.shtml.
36. http://news.zdnet.co.uk/software/linuxunix/0,39020390,39197819,00.htm.
37. http://www.chiefexecutive.net/dell.htm.
38. http://www.infoworld.com/article/04/11/12/HNrollinsq&a_2.html.
39. http://news.com.com/Dell+angles+for+the+best+seat+in+the+living+room/2100-1041_3-5427993.html.
40. http://www1.us.dell.com/content/topics/global.aspx/corp/pressoffice/en/2004/2005_02_08_rr_003?c=us&l=en&s=corp.
41. http://www.appleinsider.com/article.php?id=1147.
42. http://www.infoworld.com/article/04/11/12/HNrollinsq&a_3.html.
43. http://news.com.com/Dells+Rollins+shoots+for+80+billion+by+2009/2100-1041_3-5790288.html?part=rss&tag=5790288&subj=news.

Index

Note: Boldface numbers indicate illustrations.